COMPULSORY MENTAL HEALTH INTERVENTIONS AND THE CRPD

This book delineates the scope of permissible compulsory mental health interventions under the Convention on the Rights of Persons with Disabilities (CRPD).

The initial impetus for this study was provided by a conflict between two competing positions within the current debate over the future of coercive psychiatry. According to one position, defended by the CRPD Committee, among others, compulsory mental health care necessarily violates the prohibition of discrimination. According to the competing position, supported by the vast majority of states, compulsion is sometimes necessary to protect health and life and, if coupled with appropriate legal safeguards, it is lawful under such circumstances. This book disputes both positions and argues that the scope of permissible compulsory care can be identified using proportionality reasoning.

Drawing on the work of Robert Alexy, it develops a framework for proportionality assessments within the context of non-discrimination. The framework can assist decision-makers to design principled and evidence-based mental health care regimes. This book thus provides a new way forward for states parties looking to reform their mental health care regimes and to improve compliance with the CRPD. It will appeal to academics and practitioners engaged in mental health reform in the post-CRPD era.

Hart Studies in Law and Health

Hart Studies in Law and Health aims to publish the best existing and upcoming voices in scholarship on law and health. Viewing law as a broad church, the series welcomes a range of methodologies from the doctrinal to the critical and including regulation and governance, and law and ethics approaches.

Compulsory Mental Health Interventions and the CRPD

Minding Equality

Anna Nilsson

•HART•

OXFORD • LONDON • NEW YORK • NEW DELHI • SYDNEY

HART PUBLISHING
Bloomsbury Publishing Plc
Kemp House, Chawley Park, Cumnor Hill, Oxford, OX2 9PH, UK
1385 Broadway, New York, NY 10018, USA
29 Earlsfort Terrace, Dublin 2, Ireland

HART PUBLISHING, the Hart/Stag logo, BLOOMSBURY and the Diana logo are trademarks of Bloomsbury Publishing Plc

First published in Great Britain 2021

A catalogue record for this book is available from the British Library.

Library of Congress Cataloging-in-Publication data

Names: Nilsson, Anna, 1977– author.

Title: Compulsory mental health interventions and the CRPD : minding equality / Anna Nilsson.

Description: Oxford, UK ; New York, NY : Hart Publishing, an imprint of Bloomsbury Publishing, 2021. | Series: Hart studies in law and health | Includes bibliographical references and index.

Identifiers: LCCN 2020038479 (print) | LCCN 2020038480 (ebook) | ISBN 9781509931576 (hardcover) | ISBN 9781509944576 (paperback) | ISBN 9781509931583 (Epub) | ISBN 9781509931590 (pdf)

Subjects: LCSH: Mental health laws. | Mental health services. | Mentally ill—Care. | Convention on the Rights of Persons with Disabilities and Optional Protocol (2007 March 30)

Classification: LCC K3608 .N55 2021 (print) | LCC K3608 (ebook) | DDC 344.04/4—dc23

LC record available at https://lccn.loc.gov/2020038479

LC ebook record available at https://lccn.loc.gov/2020038480

ISBN: HB: 978-1-50993-157-6
ePDF: 978-1-50993-159-0
ePub: 978-1-50993-158-3

Typeset by Compuscript Ltd, Shannon

To find out more about our authors and books visit www.hartpublishing.co.uk. Here you will find extracts, author information, details of forthcoming events and the option to sign up for our newsletters.

In memory of my father Bengt

Acknowledgements

MANY PEOPLE HAVE in different ways contributed to this book, and for this I wish to express my heartfelt gratitude. *Thank you*. Among all of you, I want to mention a few. First, I want to thank my excellent supervisors, Gregor Noll, Anna Bruce and Lena Wahlberg for their invaluable support and guidance throughout the research project that forms the basis of this book. Gregor, thank you for thoughtful comments on my work, for your intellectual generosity, and for believing in me as a legal scholar. Anna and Lena, your careful readings, intelligent suggestions and moral support were instrumental to the completion of my doctoral thesis. Second, I want to express my sincere gratitude to Peter Bartlett and Julian Rivers for your astute comments on earlier versions of this manuscript and for your encouragement to take my analysis one step further.

Among my colleagues and friends at the Faculty of Law in Lund, I am indebted in particular to Ulf Linderfalk, Britta Sjöstedt and Martina Axmin. Thank you for being such great colleagues! I also wish to thank Moa Kindström-Dahlin, my dear colleague at Uppsala University with whom I share, among many things, a strong interest in mental health law. Our discussions made this journey so much more enjoyable. I would also like to acknowledge Tim Carter, who helped me to improve the language of this book.

My final words of gratitude go to my much-loved family; to my partner Rickard, my daughter Siri, my son Vilhelm, and to my mother, Carina.

Anna Nilsson,
July 2020

Table of Contents

Introduction

I. TO INTERVENE OR NOT TO INTERVENE?

IMAGINE THAT YOU are a clinician working within mental health care. A 54-year-old woman, Nancy, is brought to your hospital by her son after she accidently started a small fire at home because she was smoking in bed. The son tells you that Nancy has been diagnosed with bipolar disorder, that she has trouble sleeping at night, and that she has unpredictable mood swings. He is worried about his mother, who is recently divorced and lives alone. You examine Nancy, who tells you that she is not feeling well. She is tired and struggles with feelings of hopelessness. When you try to discuss treatment options with her, she is pessimistic. She does not think any of the treatments you propose will help her. She has tried medication before and dreads the side effects. She just wants to go home again. You believe medication is absolutely necessary to prevent her condition from worsening. You explain your assessment to her, and she nods at the information but insists on leaving the hospital. If she leaves, the chances of her sticking to any course of treatment you prescribe would be very slim. As a result, there is a risk that Nancy's condition will deteriorate further, and that her basic needs, such as food and hygiene, will not be met. The facts of her case also indicate that she is at an increased risk of suicide. The decision is up to you: should you respect her wish to leave, or intervene against her will?

In making such a decision, several interests are at stake: the protection of health and life, and respect for personal liberty, integrity and autonomy. On the one hand, Nancy's medical condition is serious. She has lost weight, has no interest in taking care of herself, and does not sleep at night. Without treatment and support, her health and life are at risk. Her behaviour also indicates that she is not taking into account the safety of others. Smoking in bed jeopardises not only her own safety but also the safety of her neighbours. She lives alone in a two-room apartment, and if the son had not come by, the fire might have spread to other apartments. This speaks in favour of intervention. On the other hand, Nancy insists on leaving the hospital. She tells you that she has been hospitalised before. It helped a little, but not for long, and she dreads having to go through it again. The idea of being locked up causes her a great deal of stress; it makes her feel anxious and helpless. She is equally negative about the prospect of taking medication. She had, in the past, been on medication for long periods of time, but she stopped taking it because of its unpleasant side effects (severe weight gain, drowsiness, blurred vision and tremors). She does not want to start again; the side effects are too painful. You consider her response to your treatment proposals to be misguided. You are not denying that the treatment in question has unpleasant side effects, but you believe that the prospect of it curing Nancy, or relieving her symptoms, more than makes up for these drawbacks. Nancy, however, disagrees, and she appears to take in and understand the information provided to her about the potential benefits of hospitalisation and medication. In fact, her rejection of these is understandable in light of her appraisal of the pros and cons of inpatient treatment. The disagreement between you and the woman before you can be said to hinge on the different values the two of you attach to the potential benefits and costs of psychiatric care.

The question of whether to intervene against an individual's expressed wishes has been at the heart of debates in recent decades concerning the design of mental health care regimes, and it was central to the negotiation process of the UN Convention on the Rights of Persons with Disabilities (CRPD).[1] This treaty's answer to the question is new and refreshing, but it requires interpretation. Previous human rights instruments explicitly authorised compulsion within the context of mental health. The European Convention for the Protection of Human Rights and Fundamental Freedoms (ECHR) is the most obvious example here. It explicitly provides for the civil detention of people of 'unsound mind'.[2] The Human Rights Committee has interpreted the International Covenant on Civil and Political Rights as permitting the detention of people with 'serious mental disorders' at risk of harming themselves or others.[3] Soft-law instruments like the UN Principles for the Protection of Persons with Mental Illness[4] and its European equivalents set out rather detailed provisions on the acceptable use of restraints and the administration of medication without consent within psychiatric care.[5] On the face of it, the CRPD is radically different. It contains no provisions explicitly legitimising civil detention or the compulsory administration of medication. Instead, its reference to equal treatment sets limits to what

[1] Convention on the Rights of Persons with Disabilities (adopted 13 December 2006, entered into force 3 May 2008) 2515 UNTS 3 (CRPD).

[2] Convention for the Protection of Human Rights and Fundamental Freedoms (as amended) ETS 5. Art 5(1)(e) reads: 'Everyone has the right to liberty and security of person. No one shall be deprived of his liberty save in the following cases and in accordance with a procedure prescribed by law: […] (e) the lawful detention of persons for the prevention of the spreading of infectious diseases, of persons of unsound mind, alcoholics or drug addicts, or vagrants.' For a discussion of the interrelation between the CRPD and the ECHR, see P Fennell and U Khaliq, 'Conflicting or Complementary Obligations? The UN Disability Rights Convention, the European Convention on Human Rights and English Law' (2011) 6 *European Human Rights Law Review* 662; E Flynn, 'Disability, Deprivation of Liberty, and Human Rights Norms: Reconciling European and International Approaches' (2016) 22 *International Journal of Mental Health and Capacity Law* 75.

[3] Human Rights Committee, 'Communication No 754/1997' *A v New Zealand* (1999) UN Doc CCPR/C/66/D/754/1997 paras 7.2–7.3.

[4] Principles for the Protection of Persons with Mental Illness and the Improvement of Mental Health Care, UNGA Res 46/119 (17 December 1991) principles 11 and 16.

[5] Council of Europe, 'Recommendation No R(99)4 of the Committee of Ministers to Member States' (23 February 1999) principles 22–26; Council of Europe, 'Recommendation No Rec(2004)10 of the Committee of Ministers to Member States' (22 September 2004) principles 10, 12 and 17–18.

is acceptable in the context of mental health care. This book explores this new vision for mental health law, which has equality and non-discrimination as its core standards. It analyses the normative content of the prohibition of discrimination in the CRPD and discusses the implications of the obligation, laid down in the treaty, for signatories to ensure that their domestic mental health legislation allows people with psychosocial disabilities to enjoy liberty, integrity and legal capacity on an equal basis with others.

The initial impetus for this study was provided by a conflict between two competing positions within the current debate over the future of coercive psychiatry, which is still ubiquitous around the world. According to one position, defended by the Committee on the Rights of Persons with Disabilities (the CRPD Committee), among others, compulsory mental health care necessarily violates the prohibition of discrimination. In its first general comment, the Committee asserts that compulsory mental health interventions constitute 'an ongoing violation [of the CRPD] found in mental health laws across the globe, despite empirical evidence indicating its lack of effectiveness' and notwithstanding the fact that people subjected to such practices 'have experienced deep pain and trauma as a result'.[6] The Committee argues that targeting people with psychosocial disabilities for such interventions is arbitrary and constitutes disability-based discrimination, which is why the Committee believes states parties must abolish legislative provisions that allow for such interventions.[7] According to the competing position, supported by the vast majority of states, compulsion is sometimes necessary to protect the health and lives of patients or to prevent violence against others, and, if coupled with appropriate legal safeguards, it is lawful under such circumstances. This position is expressed, for instance, in states parties' interpretative declarations and in their communications with the CRPD Committee; it was also articulated by negotiating parties during the drafting process of the Convention.[8] This debate over the implications of human rights law for the lawfulness or otherwise of compulsory care is not only present in the dialogue between the CRPD Committee and the states parties to this treaty. During the last decade, a new treaty, with the working title 'Additional Protocol Concerning the Protection of Human Rights and Dignity

[6] Committee on the Rights of Persons with Disabilities (CRPD Committee), 'General Comment No 1 on Article 12: Equal Recognition before the Law' (19 May 2014) UN Doc CRPD/C/GC/1 para 42.

[7] *Ibid* paras 40–42. For other critical voices, see T Minkowitz, 'Abolishing Mental Health Laws to Comply with the CRPD' in B McSherry and P Weller (eds), *Rethinking Rights-based Mental Health Laws* (Oxford, Hart Publishing, 2010); E Flynn and A Arstein-Kerslake, 'Legislating Personhood: Realising the Right to Support in Exercising Legal Capacity' (2014) 10 *International Journal of Law in Context* 81.

[8] See, eg, interpretative declarations from Australia, Norway, the Netherlands and Poland, cited below in chapter 1, section II, and responses from states parties to the CRPD Committee's draft version of General Comment No 1, in particular responses from Germany, Denmark, Norway and New Zealand, available at www.ohchr.org/EN/HRBodies/CRPD/Pages/DGCArticles12And9.aspx.

of Persons with Mental Disorder with Regard to Involuntary Placement and Involuntary Treatment', is under negotiation within the Council of Europe. The protocol would permit the use of compulsion within mental health care. Its stated aim, however, is to prevent abuses of this power and to minimise the use of compulsion by promoting the use of alternatives to compulsory care. This would provide safeguards to ensure that involuntary measures are only used as a last resort, and ensuring that the people concerned have access to appropriate support and procedural safeguards so that they can exercise their rights effectively.[9] Draft versions of the protocol have been subjected to a great deal of criticism by civil society and human rights bodies, and a recurring theme of this criticism is that the draft protocol fails to comply with the state-of-the-art human rights standards set out in the CRPD.[10]

In this book, I argue that the line between lawful and unlawful uses of compulsion within mental health care can be identified using proportionality reasoning. Drawing on the work of Robert Alexy, I develop a framework for proportionality assessments within the context of non-discrimination.[11] This framework provides a tool that will allow both academics and practitioners to interpret the CRPD's vision for mental health care and to assess whether domestic mental health regimes comply with the treaty. Domestic laws and policies authorising compulsory psychiatric care are based on (often unstated) value judgements and assumptions about the effectiveness of such care and the necessity of using compulsory interventions to protect patients. The framework set out in this book makes explicit these underlying value judgements, and by doing so provides a means for decision-makers to design principled and evidence-based mental health care regimes. This book thus provides a new way forward for states parties that do not wish to abolish coercive care altogether (as recommended by the CRPD Committee) but do want to reform their mental health care regimes to make them comply with the Convention. It resolves a major conflict in the interpretation of the law relevant to coercive psychiatry. It will appeal to policy-makers, disability rights advocates, practitioners of

[9] Council of Europe, 'Draft Additional Protocol Concerning the Protection of Human Rights and Dignity of Persons with Mental Disorder with Regard to Involuntary Placement and Involuntary Treatment: Frequently Asked Questions' (9 January 2019) CoE Doc DH-BIO/INF(2018)10.

[10] Council of Europe Committee on Bioethics, 'Additional Protocol on the Protection of the Human Rights and Dignity of Persons with Mental Disorders with Regard to Involuntary Placement and Involuntary Treatment: Compilation of Comments Received during the Public Consultation' (9 December 2015) DH-BIO/INF(2015)20. See also Parliamentary Assembly of the Council of Europe, 'Recommendation No Rec 2158(2019)' (26 June 2019); Council of Europe, 'Comments by Dunja Mijatović, Council of Europe Commissioner for Human Rights on the Draft Additional Protocol to the Convention on Human Rights and Biomedicine Concerning the Protection of Human Rights and Dignity of Persons with Mental Disorder with Regard to Involuntary Placement and Involuntary Treatment' (8 November 2018) paras 7–10.

[11] Alexy's model is originally described and explained in *Theorie der Grundrechte* (Frankfurt am Main, Suhrkamp, 1986). I make use of the English translation of the book, *A Theory of Constitutional Rights* (translated by J Rivers) (New York, Oxford University Press, 2010).

human rights and other stakeholders engaged in mental health reform relevant to the CRPD.

The framework is also a contribution to proportionality and non-discrimination scholarship. Proportionality argumentation is an established form of legal argumentation under international human rights law, employed by the UN human rights treaty bodies and regional and domestic courts.[12] Still, relatively little has been written on its precise role and content in relation to equality norms. Proportionality scholars such as Alexy tend to draw on other examples to demonstrate how proportionality reasoning works in practice. Furthermore, legal scholarship on equality and non-discrimination has not explored in detail whether, and if so how, proportionality argumentation can help us distinguish lawful state practices from unlawful ones. This book picks up this loose end and develops a proportionality assessment framework tailored to the non-discrimination context. The formal elements of the model presented here are drawn from Robert Alexy's model of proportionality assessment, and the model's substantive norms from (an interpretation of) the CRPD and from scholarly work on equality.

II. METHODOLOGICAL REMARKS

The main arguments put forward in this book are anchored in legal sources: the CRPD treaty text, states parties' reservations and interpretative declarations, the *travaux préparatoires* and communications between states and the UN human rights treaty bodies.[13] In addition to such (conventional) legal material, I draw on empirical material from the fields of medicine and risk prevention. I make use of this material because the application of the norms analysed in this book to domestic mental health laws gives rise to empirical questions that cannot be answered on the basis of legal material alone. These include, for example, questions about the therapeutic benefits and negative effects of involuntary hospitalisation in closed psychiatric wards and of the administration of medication against the individual's expressed wishes. A key question when assessing the

[12] Proportionality reasoning is omnipresent in the jurisprudence of the European Court of Human Rights. For a description of the spread of proportionality reasoning from Germany to international and national legal systems in different parts of the world, see A Barak, *Proportionality: Constitutional Rights and Their Limitations* (translated by D Kalir) (Cambridge, Cambridge University Press, 2012) 181–201; A Stone Sweet and J Mathews, 'Proportionality Balancing and Global Constitutionalism' (2008) 47 *Columbia Journal of Transnational Law* 72, 111ff.

[13] Records from the negotiations and the adoption of the CRPD have been published on the UN website. The electronic negotiation archives have been relocated several times and are currently available via the website of the UN Division for Social Policy and Development: www.un.org/development/desa/disabilities/resources/ad-hoc-committee-on-a-comprehensive-and-integral-international-convention-on-the-protection-and-promotion-of-the-rights-and-dignity-of-persons-with-disabilities.html.

lawfulness of compulsory psychiatric care in light of the prohibition of discrimination concerns the effectiveness of such care in achieving its aims – protecting health and life and promoting public safety – *as compared with* the effectiveness of voluntary care in achieving the same aims. Within the field of medicine, there has been relatively little work comparing the outcomes of treatment imposed against the individual's expressed preferences with the outcomes of treatment provided on a voluntary basis. However, there have been some positive developments in this area. In 2018, Piers Gooding and colleagues conducted a review of research into voluntary mental health practices that may serve as alternatives to compulsory care.[14] In addition, within the Council of Europe, the Committee on Bioethics has been instructed to conduct a study on 'good practices in mental healthcare – how to promote voluntary measures', to be concluded by the end of 2021.[15]

A related problem arises in relation to another set of questions important to this enquiry – namely questions concerning how, if at all, people with psychosocial disabilities differ from other social groups in ways that could potentially explain the diverging rules governing somatic and psychiatric care, which restrict the use of compulsion to the latter. There are, for example, a number of studies that discuss the impact that certain psychosocial conditions have on our decision-making ability, but there is relatively little material that discusses the potential impact on our decision-making of somatic conditions that cause, for example, severe pain or paralysis. Likewise, the correlation between suicide and depression is well documented, but no studies compare the risk associated with such psychiatric diagnoses with the risk associated with other factors, such as certain somatic conditions and non-clinical factors (for example old age and recent traumatic events). These knowledge gaps complicate discrimination analysis, which necessarily involves comparisons of members of one group (in this study, people with psychosocial disabilities) with 'others' (in this study, people without psychosocial disabilities) in relevantly similar situations.

Moreover, it must be acknowledged that the vast majority of empirical studies on the outcomes of coercive psychiatric care have been conducted in high-income Western countries with rather similar cultures.[16] The findings of such studies are not generalisable to countries with different levels of mental health care provision and/or different cultures. For example, research into the

[14] P Gooding et al, *Alternatives to Coercion in Mental Health Settings: A Literature Review* (Melbourne, Melbourne Social Equity Institute, 2018). See also R Diseth and P Høglend, 'Compulsory Mental Health Care in Norway: The Treatment Criterion' (2014) 37 *International Journal of Law and Psychiatry* 168, 170f.

[15] Council of Europe Committee on Bioethics, 'Terms of Reference of the DH-BIO for 2020–2021' (26 November 2019) DH-BIO/INF(2019)12 2.

[16] Many of the studies were conducted in Australia, Canada, western Europe and the United States.

correlations between suicide and psychosocial conditions has taken the form of case–control studies of people who have committed suicide (often referred to as psychological autopsy studies).[17] This technique commonly involves a combination of interviews with those closest to the deceased and an examination of data from other sources, such as medical records, social work reports and criminal records. Based on such information, an assessment is produced of the suicide victim's mental and physical health, personality and social situation. The aim is to produce as full and accurate a picture as possible with a view to understanding why the person ended his or her life. The vast majority of such studies have been carried out in societies that tend to view suicide as an expression of 'mental illness'. Thus, there is a risk of overestimating the significance of the link between suicide and psychosocial conditions.[18]

A word of caution is also in order regarding the reliability of the sorts of empirical data relevant to this book. Studies of the outcomes of compulsory mental health care commonly take the form of prospective and retrospective observational studies.[19] In prospective studies, or so-called cohort studies, a group of individuals who have been committed to a psychiatric hospital are followed after discharge in order to assess the therapeutic benefits of a particular form of treatment. Common methodological problems with such studies include selection bias and high drop-out rates, which make the results less reliable. Retrospective studies, or case–control studies, look at people who have committed violent crimes or seriously harmed themselves, with the aim of understanding the reasons behind such acts and thereby finding ways to prevent them. The risk of confounding factors is a common problem with such studies. Take studies of violence, for example. Studies of people convicted of violent crimes have identified a number of general risk factors for such violence: for example, being male, having substance abuse problems, having anti-social personality traits, and being in certain socioeconomic groups. However, people with certain psychosocial diagnoses are over-represented among people with substance abuse problems and among those with anti-social personality traits; and these three groups of people are, in turn, over-represented among the homeless and unemployed, factors that are also positively correlated with conviction for violent crime. Together, these factors form a complex web of correlations within which causal factors, if they exist, are difficult to distinguish from confounding factors.[20] I will draw the reader's attention to these problems as we proceed through this book.

[17] See, eg, JTO Cavanagh et al, 'Psychological Autopsy Studies of Suicide: A Systematic Review' (2003) 33 *Psychological Medicine* 395.

[18] *Ibid* 401.

[19] For a general description of prospective cohort studies and retrospective case–control studies, see C Hennekens and J Buring, *Epidemiology in Medicine* (Philadelphia, Lippincot Williams and Wilkins, 1987) 132ff, 153ff.

[20] See chapter 2, section IV.C.

Moreover, it should be noted that there is disagreement about the effects, positive and negative, of compulsory care. The same is true of the nature of the link between psychiatric conditions, on the one hand, and decision-making ability and harmful behaviour, on the other hand. For these reasons, I rely mainly on systematic review studies and meta-studies. Systematic reviews cover all the research available on a certain topic and present the findings of previous studies along with discussions of their quality and reliability. Roughly speaking, meta-studies are less comprehensive but more detailed, analysing the results of a large number of studies and reporting them as though they were one large study. When presenting the findings of these studies, I will alert the reader to any conflicting conclusions.

Finally, it should be noted that most of the studies on these topics have been carried out by psychiatrists. As Gooding and his colleagues highlight, a small but significant amount of work has been produced by people who have themselves experienced compulsory psychiatric care.[21] Much of this work, however, has taken place outside the academic literature. Formal research typically does not involve people with psychosocial disabilities as active research participants or co-researchers.[22] In view of the fact that the CRPD states that people with disabilities should have the opportunity to be actively involved in processes that directly concern them, I make use of personal accounts of experiences of mental health care and research reports on similar matters in order to provide a more comprehensive picture of the positive and negative effects of compulsory mental health care.[23]

III. VOCABULARY AND KEY CONCEPTS

In order to avoid certain misunderstandings, some remarks about terminology are in order. This book focuses on two types of compulsory intervention and their compatibility with the CRPD: civil detention and compulsory clinical treatment. Civil detention refers to the practice of committing an individual to a closed ward in a psychiatric hospital and keeping him or her there to facilitate clinical treatment, support and supervision. Compulsory clinical treatment includes the administration of psychiatric medication and treatment with the aim of curing a condition or mitigating symptoms.

Moreover, I use the term 'psychosocial' instead of 'mental' (the CRPD's term) when talking about social categories of people and clinical conditions.[24] 'People with psychosocial disabilities' is the term preferred by many people

[21] Gooding et al, *Alternatives to Coercion* 11.
[22] Gooding et al (n 14) 11.
[23] CRPD preamble para (o) and Art 33(3).
[24] I still use 'mental' in relation to the care provided – that is, 'mental health care'.

belonging to this group, and it is now used by UN bodies, human rights practitioners and scholars alike.[25] People with psychosocial disabilities include people experiencing long-term mental health problems whose participation in society is limited because of environmental barriers, including discrimination and stigma. This accords with the description of people with disabilities provided in the CRPD (Article 1). Similarly, I also speak of 'psychosocial impairments' and 'psychosocial conditions' when referring to clinical or functional conditions that individuals experience or with which they have been diagnosed. 'Disability' is the *disadvantage* that arises when people with impairments are confronted with an inaccessible or excluding environment.[26] 'Impairment' is not defined in the treaty, but it is commonly understood to mean limitations of physical and mental functioning.[27] Such limitations should be long-term and, arguably, meet a certain threshold level of severity in order to count as impairments.[28] I use 'condition' when I wish to refer to a clinical state without taking a position on whether it qualifies as an impairment. Psychosocial conditions thus include phenomena referred to within the clinical context as 'mental illnesses' and 'mental disorders'; that is, patterns of thinking and behaviour that constitute diagnosable medical conditions.

My last remark concerns the terms 'capacity' and 'ability'. In many contexts, these terms are used as synonyms, referring to the powers needed to perform a certain act. However, I distinguish between these terms when speaking about individuals' abilities and capacities. I reserve the term 'capacity' for matters relating to *legal* capacity; that is, matters relating to legal recognition and protection of a person's choices and actions.[29] This is to be distinguished from what is sometimes referred to as 'mental capacity', which includes the ability to make free and informed treatment decisions and to communicate these with others. When discussing such matters, I use terms like 'decision-making ability'.

[25] The term was introduced by the World Network of Users and Survivors of Psychiatry during the drafting of the CRPD, and its use has subsequently been advocated on the basis that it is the group's preferred terminology.

[26] CRPD, preamble para (e).

[27] See, eg, World Health Organisation, *Towards a Common Language for Functioning, Disability and Health* (Geneva, World Health Organisation, 2002).

[28] Not all variations in levels of physical and mental functioning are considered to be impairments in the sense at issue in the human rights literature. Whether people with very mild anxiety or sleep problems should be categorised as people with impairments is a matter for debate, but for the purposes of this study such questions are peripheral, as there can be little doubt that the conditions that warrant compulsory intervention under domestic law are severe enough to be considered impairments. For a legal analysis of the concept of impairment under the CRPD, see A Bruce, *Which Entitlements and for Whom? The Convention on the Rights of Persons with Disabilities and Its Ideological Antecedents* (Lund, Mediatryck, 2014) 305ff.

[29] The phrase 'legal capacity' appears in the CRPD, but it is not defined in the treaty and its precise meaning is a contested matter. For an in-depth analysis, see O Lewis, 'Legal Capacity in International Human Rights Law' (PhD thesis, Leiden University, 2015).

IV. A ROADMAP FOR THIS BOOK

This book is divided into five chapters. The first chapter introduces the CRPD's vision for mental health care, in particular its emphasis on equal treatment and individual self-determination. It provides an overview of the state obligations laid down in Articles 12 (equal recognition before the law), 14 (liberty and security of the person), 17 (protecting the integrity of the person) and 25 (health), which are of particular relevance for compulsory mental health care, and highlights the particular constraints these obligations place on domestic mental health policy and legislation. An important finding of this chapter is that much of the originality of the CRPD's approach to mental health care lies in its emphasis on the principle of equal treatment. This means that the lawfulness under the Convention of a particular domestic system of civil detention and compulsory clinical care will, in many cases, hinge on discrimination analysis. Section VI lays the groundwork for this type of analysis by explaining the prohibition of disability-based discrimination set out in the CRPD and discussing the standard developed in legal practice for distinguishing legitimate restrictions of rights from unlawful discrimination (the 'objective and reasonable' standard). The chapter ends with a summary account of the Convention's approach to mental health care (section VII).

Chapter two puts domestic mental health laws to the test. This chapter applies the prohibition of discrimination, including the objective and reasonable standard, to domestic law, with the aim of providing a more concrete account of the legal implications of the Convention for domestic policies and practices. The chapter concludes with a summary of the main findings and an overview of the questions that discrimination analysis leaves open to argumentation (section VI). Chapter three explores whether a type of proportionality reasoning based on Robert Alexy's model can help us to better understand the scope and content of the non-discrimination provisions of the CRPD. It situates Alexy's model within his theory of constitutional rights and explains its basic elements and rules. It closes with a discussion of the advantages and disadvantages of drawing on Alexy's model to interpret the CRPD.

Chapter four outlines a proportionality assessment framework for domestic mental health laws. It applies this framework to domestic authorisations of civil detention and compulsory clinical treatment and argues that compulsory mental health care interventions that aim to prevent violence against others cannot be justified. By contrast, domestic regimes of compulsory care that cover *any person* who puts his or her own health and life at risk under circumstances in which free and informed consent cannot be obtained can be justified if a number of criteria are met. First of all, states must ensure that people with psychosocial disabilities have access to adequate support that facilitates free and informed treatment decisions. Second, compulsory care must be imposed only as a last resort. Third, the personal and social harms such a regime creates must not be excessive. This means that compulsory mental health care can only be justified in a domestic context where the care provided is of high quality and where people with psychosocial disabilities enjoy a relatively high level of social inclusion. The chapter ends with a discussion of the advantages of using proportionality reasoning to assess discrimination cases and the costs of adopting this approach. I argue that proportionality reasoning can help us to clarify the arguments that are relevant to discrimination analysis and that it sheds light on some characteristic aspects of equality norms. Application of the prohibition of disability-based discrimination to domestic systems of compulsory mental health care involves judgements about the reasonableness of such systems. Reasoning about reasonableness presupposes that we are able to weigh arguments for and against the system under review. Precisely how this weighing of arguments is to be carried out is a question that has received little attention from the UN treaty bodies and equality scholars. My framework can guide such reasoning. It illustrates how different (legally relevant) arguments affect the outcome of the analysis, and, further, it requires those applying it to be explicit about their arguments. This increases transparency and generates more predictable conclusions about the lawfulness of compulsory mental health interventions.

In the concluding chapter, I summarise the main findings of this book. I outline the constraints on compulsory care that can be inferred from discrimination analysis including proportionality argumentation in accordance with the model set out in chapter four (section II.B.), and provide a succinct account of the scope of lawful compulsory mental health interventions under the CRPD (section II.C.). The concluding chapter ends with some reflections on the future of mental health care. Transforming domestic mental health legislation to make it comply with the CRPD will be no easy task. It is a project beset with both legal and political difficulties. It is clear that governments are still committed to keeping compulsory elements within their health care systems, and human rights bodies and civil society organisations continue to call for a compete abolition of compulsory care. The debate among human rights lawyers over what constitutes best practice in the field of mental health law will continue. This book is my contribution to this important debate.

1

The Convention's Approach to Mental Health Care

I. A NEW APPROACH TO MENTAL HEALTH CARE

The UN Convention on the Rights of Persons with Disabilities (CRPD) sets out a new vision for mental health care that has equal treatment and non-discrimination as core standards. The principles of equality and non-discrimination are not only enshrined in the provisions that are most relevant to the mental health context; they run like golden threads through almost all of the Convention's substantive Articles. The purpose of the Convention is to 'promote, protect and ensure the full and *equal* enjoyment of all human rights and fundamental freedoms by all persons with disabilities',[1] and equality and non-discrimination are among the general principles set out in Article 3 to guide the interpretation and application of the treaty.[2] Another important principle that guides the CRPD's approach to mental health care is respect for inherent dignity and individual autonomy, which includes the freedom to make one's own choices.[3] None of these principles are new to the human rights context. On the contrary, equality is one of the most important principles underpinning the very concept of human rights. As Anne Bayefsky argued as early as 1990, achieving equality and effective protection against discrimination is 'the dominant and recurring theme of international human rights law'.[4] Likewise, respect for dignity and autonomy are deep-rooted principles in international human rights law. Since the Universal Declaration of Human Rights,[5] the concept of 'dignity', or 'human dignity', has been a key

[1] Convention on the Rights of Persons with Disabilities (adopted 13 December 2006, entered into force 3 May 2008) 2515 UNTS 3 (CRPD) Art 1.

[2] Most notably in Art 3(b), (e), (g). The principles of equality and non-discrimination are, however, closely linked to other general principles in that Article, such as the principles of full and effective participation and inclusion in society in paragraph (c), respect for difference and acceptance of persons with disabilities as part of human diversity and humanity in paragraph (d), and accessibility in paragraph (f).

[3] CRPD Art 3(a).

[4] A Bayefsky, 'The Principle of Equality or Non-Discrimination in International Law' (1990) 11 *Human Rights Law Journal* 1, 2.

[5] Universal Declaration of Human Rights (adopted 10 December 1948) UNGA Res 217 A(III). The opening words of the preamble to the Declaration are: 'Whereas recognition of the inherent

principle of human rights theory.[6] References to dignity are commonplace in UN human rights treaties.[7] The CRPD's reference to individual autonomy as a general principle is more innovative. None of the other core UN human rights conventions refer directly to individual autonomy. Its inclusion in the CRPD treaty text is probably best explained by the fact that this principle is crucial to protecting the human rights of people with disabilities. Denial of the right to make decisions and to pursue one's life projects has been, and still is, one of the most pressing human rights concerns for people with disabilities, and it is a concern that the CRPD seeks to address.

The general principles of equality, dignity and autonomy are given a more precise content in the substantive provisions that have a direct impact on the organisation and regulation of mental health care. The most important rules can be found in Articles 12 (equal recognition before the law), 14 (liberty and security of the person), 17 (protecting the integrity of the person) and 25 (health). Article 12 states that people with disabilities enjoy legal capacity 'on an equal basis with others' in all spheres of life.[8] In other words, people with disabilities have the same right to make legal decisions – such as whether to accept or reject health care treatment – as people without disabilities. In addition, states must ensure that people with disabilities who need decision-making support have access to such support.[9] Article 14 grants people with disabilities equal protection from arbitrary deprivation of liberty. The text further clarifies that the existence of a disability cannot justify a person being deprived of liberty.[10] Article 17 asserts that all people with disabilities have the right to respect for their physical and mental integrity on an equal basis with others. Last but not least, Article 25 affirms that people with disabilities have the right to enjoy the highest attainable standard of health without discrimination on the basis of disability and requires health care professionals to provide care on the basis of free and informed consent.[11]

The novelty of the CRPD lies in its emphasis on equal treatment and individual self-determination in the mental health context, and in the fact that it does not explicitly permit the civil detention of people with psychosocial disabilities

dignity and of the equal and inalienable rights of all members of the human family is the foundation of freedom, justice and peace in the world'.

[6] See, eg, J Waldron, 'Is Dignity the Foundation of Human Rights?' in R Cruft, SM Liao and M Renzo (eds), *Philosophical Foundations of Human Rights* (Oxford, Oxford University Press, 2015); M Rosen, *Dignity: Its History and Meaning* (Cambridge, Massachusetts, Harvard University Press, 2012).

[7] See, eg, the preambles to the Convention on the Elimination of All Forms of Discrimination against Women (adopted 18 December 1979, entered into force 3 September 1981) 1249 UNTS 13 (CEDAW) and the International Convention on the Elimination of All Forms of Racial Discrimination (adopted 21 December 1965, entered into force 4 January 1969) 660 UNTS 195 (CERD).

[8] CRPD Art 12(2).

[9] CRPD Art 12(3).

[10] CRPD Art 14(1)(b).

[11] CRPD Art 25(d).

for the purposes of psychiatric treatment. These innovations signal a break from previous human rights law and provide a much-needed means to challenge the inequalities inherent in much domestic mental health legislation.[12] This chapter discusses how we should understand this break from previous human rights standards and the constraints it places on states seeking to maintain systems of compulsory mental health care. In particular, this chapter discusses the implications of Articles 12, 14, 17 and 25 in order to establish precisely how these provisions constrain domestic mental health legislation. It ends with a summary account of the Convention's approach to mental health care (section VII).

II. ARTICLE 12 AND THE RIGHT TO ENJOY LEGAL CAPACITY

Article 12(1) of the CRPD reaffirms that people with disabilities have the right to recognition everywhere as persons before the law and 12(2) obliges states parties to recognise that 'persons with disabilities enjoy legal capacity on an equal basis with others in all areas of life'.[13] As noted above, this provision grants people with psychosocial disabilities the same right as people without such disabilities to accept or reject clinical treatment and to have these decisions respected. Moreover, Article 12 asserts that the primary response to situations in which someone has difficulty exercising his or her legal capacity should be to provide support, and it states that any measures relating to the exercise of legal capacity must respect the rights, will and preferences of the person concerned (Art 12(3)–(4)). The essential question for this book is whether, within the context of mental health, Article 12 circumscribes states parties' power to use compulsory interventions to override a person's expressed preferences. As is evident from the above, the treaty text does not provide a clear-cut answer to this question. It neither prohibits nor explicitly permits compulsory care.[14] This is not because the question was not in the minds of the negotiating parties. It most certainly was. In fact, the legitimacy of domestic systems that transfer decision-making powers from people with disabilities to third parties such as guardians, relatives and doctors (often referred to as 'substitute decision-making') was by far the most controversial and fiercely debated issue during the negotiations.[15] The controversy concerned whether the fact that *some* people may benefit from systems of substitute decision-making was a sufficient reason to justify

[12] See above, section I.

[13] The full Article is available in the Appendix to this book.

[14] A Dhanda, 'Legal Capacity in the Disability Rights Convention: Stranglehold of the Past or Lodestar for the Future?' (2007) 34 *Syracuse Journal of International Law and Commerce* 429, 460–61.

[15] A Bruce, *Which Entitlements and for Whom? The Convention on the Rights of Persons with Disabilities and Its Ideological Antecedents* (Lund, Mediatryck, 2014) 175. For an account of the different positions expressed during the Ad Hoc Committee sessions, see Dhanda, 'Legal Capacity' 438ff.

such systems, given that they potentially undermine the right of *all* people with disabilities to make choices for themselves. Put differently, do benefits enjoyed by a presumably small group of people justify disadvantages experienced by a much larger group? Those arguing against coercive regimes maintained that the (in their view questionable) benefits of such systems could not justify the negative effects they bring about. This position was held by representatives from the disability movement and a few state representatives.[16] In their view, in situations in which an individual's difficulty in exercising her legal capacity puts herself or others at risk, she should be provided with support. Non-disabled people take for granted their right to make bad decisions, and people with disabilities ought to have the same right. Those in favour of endorsing substitute decision-making regimes pointed to cases in which individuals were unable to communicate their preferences and/or engaged in severely self-destructive or violent behaviour. They further argued that the 'collateral damage' of systems of coercive psychiatry could be mitigated with legal safeguards.[17] Indeed, early drafts of Article 12 explicitly recognised the existence of procedures that allow decisions to be made by third parties on behalf of people with disabilities. Where states parties permit such regimes (referred to as procedures for 'personal representation'), these early drafts stated that they must be a matter of last resort, established by law, and coupled with adequate safeguards.[18] During the final session, these phrases were removed. The final text's silence on these controversial points was what allowed negotiators to reach a consensus on Article 12, which establishes a right to enjoy legal capacity on an equal basis with others and an obligation for states parties to make available the support that people with disabilities may require when making legal decisions.[19]

[16] Dhanda (n 14); See also Ad Hoc Committee on a Comprehensive and Integral International Convention on Protection and Promotion of the Rights and Dignity of Persons with Disabilities (Ad Hoc Committee), 'Daily Summary of Discussion at the Fifth Session' (3 February 2005) www.un.org/esa/socdev/enable/rights/ahc5sum3feb.htm; see statements by the World Network of Users and Survivors of Psychiatry and Support Coalition International.

[17] Ad Hoc Committee, 'Daily Summary of Discussion at the Seventh Session' (18 January 2006) www.un.org/esa/socdev/enable/rights/ahc7sum18jan.htm (statements by Australia, Yemen, New Zealand and the Russian Federation); Ad Hoc Committee, 'Daily Summary of Discussion at the Seventh Session' (3 February 2006) www.un.org/esa/socdev/enable/rights/ahc7sum03feb.htm (statements by Syrian Arab Republic, Kenya (on behalf of Africa Group), Austria (on behalf of the European Union) and Costa Rica).

[18] Report of the Coordinator to the Ad Hoc Committee at Its Fifth Session, Annex II to the Fifth Session Report of the Ad Hoc Committee on a Comprehensive and Integral International Convention to Promote and Protect the Rights and Dignity of Persons with Disabilities (23 February 2005) UN Doc A/AC.265/2005/2 Art 9(b); International Convention on the Rights of Persons with Disabilities Working Text, Annex II to the Seventh Session Report of the Ad Hoc Committee (13 February 2006) UN Doc A/AC.265/2006/2 Art 12(b).

[19] For a more detailed discussion of the discussions before the Ad Hoc Committee prior to the agreement on the final text, see L Series, 'Article 12 CRPD: Equal Recognition Before the Law' in I Bantekas, MA Stein and D Anastasiou (eds), *The UN Convention on the Rights of Persons with Disabilities: A Commentary* (Oxford, Oxford University Press, 2018) 342–48.

Subsequent state practice, including statements made in interpretative declarations, reservations, state reports and other communications between states parties and the CRPD Committee, has demonstrated states parties' unwillingness to do away with capacity-restricting regimes altogether.[20] Several states parties have declared their interpretation of the Convention to allow for compulsory health interventions under certain circumstances. Just which circumstances these are varies between declarations. The Australian, Dutch, and Norwegian declarations use generic language, limiting the use of compulsion to situations in which it is considered to be 'necessary' and a matter of 'last resort', and insisting that the use of compulsion must be 'subject to safeguards'.[21] The Polish and Estonian declarations state that a lack of certain abilities, such as the ability to understand and control one's actions, is a legitimate reason for restricting legal capacity.[22] A fair number of states parties have introduced reforms of their mental health systems in order, among other things, to comply with the CRPD.[23] Few if any, however, are considering the wholesale abandonment of all legal mechanisms that remove the right to decide from an individual and vest this authority in a third party.

As we know, the CRPD Committee adopts a different approach. The Committee interprets the CRPD as prohibiting any restrictions on legal capacity that are based on a lack of decision-making ability or that have a disproportionate impact on people with disabilities for other reasons.[24] The Committee makes

[20] See Vienna Convention on the Law of Treaties (adopted 23 May 1969, entered into force 27 January 1980) 1155 UNTS 331 Art 31(3)(b). There are currently 12 declarations or reservations that concern the lawfulness of compulsory care under the CRPD, from Australia, Canada, Egypt, Estonia, France, Georgia, Kuwait, Netherlands, Norway, Poland, the Syrian Arab Republic and Venezuela. For a general discussion about the merits and relevance of these statements, see O Lewis, 'Legal Capacity in International Human Rights Law' (PhD thesis, Leiden University, 2015) 57–62.

[21] The Australian declaration reads: 'Australia recognizes that every person with disability has a right to respect for his or her physical and mental integrity on an equal basis with others. Australia further declares its understanding that the Convention allows for compulsory assistance or treatment of persons, including measures taken for the treatment of mental disability, where such treatment is necessary, as a last resort and subject to safeguards.' The Dutch and Norwegian declarations are very similar.

[22] The Estonian declaration reads: 'The Republic of Estonia interprets Article 12 of the Convention as it does not forbid to restrict a person's active legal capacity, when such need arises from the person's ability to understand and direct his or her actions. In restricting the rights of the persons with restricted active legal capacity the Republic of Estonia acts according to its domestic laws.' The Republic of Poland has declared that 'it will interpret Article 12 of the Convention in a way allowing the application of the incapacitation, in the circumstances and in the manner set forth in the domestic law, as a measure indicated in Article 12.4, when a person suffering from a mental illness, mental disability or other mental disorder is unable to control his or her conduct'.

[23] United Nations General Assembly (UNGA), 'Report of the Special Rapporteur on the Rights of Persons with Disabilities' 37th Session (2018) UN Doc A/HRC/37/56 10f.

[24] In its General Comment No 1, the CRPD Committee states that 'a person's status as a person with a disability or the existence of an impairment (including a physical or sensory impairment) must never be grounds for denying legal capacity' and that the Convention does not permit 'perceived or actual deficits in mental capacity' to be used as justifications for denying legal capacity. CRPD Committee, 'General Comment No 1 on Article 12: Equal Recognition before the Law' (19 May 2014) UN Doc CRPD/C/GC/1 paras 9 and 13.

a point of distinguishing between decision-making ability (referred to as 'mental capacity') and legal capacity, and it asserts that the latter does not depend on the presence of the former. According to the Committee, systems that permit restrictions of legal capacity on the grounds of diminished decision-making ability are flawed for two key reasons: (1) they are discriminatorily applied to people with disabilities; and (2) they operate on the false presumption that we can accurately assess the inner workings of the human mind.[25] The first argument may be interpreted in two ways. Either the Committee is claiming that systems that permit restrictions of legal capacity are discriminatory per se, or the Committee opposes such systems because they can be and are misapplied in practice in a discriminatory fashion. Both interpretations are problematic, but for different reasons. The first interpretation is not fully argued for in the Committee's first general comment, which undercuts the value of this interpretation as an aid to understanding the CRPD. It is certainly correct that most, if not all, domestic systems of adult guardianship and compulsory health care have a disparate impact on people with disabilities. Regardless of whether they hinge on the presence of a disability/impairment as such or on the absence of decision-making ability, such systems mainly affect people with psychosocial, intellectual or cognitive disabilities. For this reason, such systems *may* be discriminatory, and they warrant scrutiny. But, as I will demonstrate below (in section VI), not all domestic systems that have a disparate impact on people with disabilities are thereby unlawfully discriminatory. Systems that serve legitimate aims and are based on objective and reasonable criteria are permissible under the CRPD.[26] Therefore, one needs to engage with the aims and justifications behind these systems before one can draw conclusions about their lawfulness under the Convention.

The alternative interpretation (which turns on the risk of malpractice) expresses an important observation. Any system that restricts an individual's capacity to make personal choices entails a risk of abuse, and there is compelling evidence of past and present abuses within coercive psychiatry.[27] Whether this constitutes a sufficient reason to outlaw such systems altogether is, however, debatable. The Committee's second argument against substitute decision-making regimes (see (2), above) stresses the difficulties involved in determining what ought to count as appropriate decision-making ability and in assessing whether such ability is present in individual cases. As the Committee puts it, decision-making ability is not a 'naturally occurring phenomenon' but a controversial concept that is contingent on social and political context.[28] The Committee is not alone in raising such concerns; similar points have been made

[25] *Ibid* para 15.

[26] See below, section VI.B.

[27] N Drew et al, 'Human Rights Violations of People with Mental and Psychosocial Disabilities: An Unresolved Global Crisis' (2011) 378 *The Lancet* 1664.

[28] CRPD Committee, 'General Comment No 1' (n 24) para 14.

by others.[29] Indeed, the difficulties involved in gaining knowledge of another person's will and ability to grasp a situation, make informed choices, and act in accordance with his or her intentions are well-known and the subjects of extensive discussion in the legal (and political, philosophical and bioethical) literature.[30] Even so, concepts like intent (*mens rea*), decision-making ability, and control over one's actions permeate much civil and criminal law, and it is difficult to imagine a legal system without them.[31]

All in all, the treaty text of Article 12 neither explicitly permits nor explicitly prohibits compulsory mental health care. Furthermore, treaty interpretation, drawing on historic and recent documentation, does not conclusively settle the question of its lawfulness. The reference to equal enjoyment of legal capacity means that answering this question will require discrimination analysis.[32] Nevertheless, Article 12 not only explicitly extends the idea of self-determination and legal capacity to cover people with disabilities but also places an obligation on states parties to support such people in exercising this capacity. Article 12(3) obliges states parties to make available the support that people with disabilities 'may require' when making legal decisions. The insertion of the word 'may' serves as a reminder that not all people with disabilities will need support. As Eilionóir Flynn and Anna Arstein-Kerslake point out, citing the Australian CRPD Committee member Professor Ron McCallum, some people with disabilities neither need nor want support. Their main problem is simply that they are denied their legal capacity.[33] The use of the term 'support' further indicates that assistance ought to be provided on a voluntary basis and not imposed against a person's expressed will.[34] That said, the CRPD does not prescribe a certain type or form of support that must be provided in order to comply with the Convention. Given the variety of situations in which a need for support may arise, this lack of specificity in the treaty text seems reasonable. This way, states parties are permitted to design support to meet the needs of people within their respective jurisdictions. In some situations, 'technical accommodations' such as

[29] See, eg, T Minkowitz, 'Abolishing Mental Health Laws to Comply with the CRPD' in B McSherry and P Weller (eds), *Rethinking Rights-based Mental Health Laws* (Oxford, Hart Publishing, 2010) 159; G Quinn and A Arstein-Kerslake, 'Restoring the "Human" in "Human Rights": Personhood and Doctrinal Innovation in the UN Disability Convention' in C Gearty and C Douzinas (eds), *The Cambridge Companion to Human Rights Law* (Cambridge, Cambridge University Press, 2012) 41ff; Lewis, 'Legal Capacity' 34ff; E Flynn and A Arstein-Kerslake, 'Legislating Personhood: Realising the Right to Support in Exercising Legal Capacity' (2014) 10 *International Journal of Law in Context* 81.

[30] J Dawson, 'A Realistic Approach to Assessing Mental Health Laws' Compliance with the UNCRPD' (2015) 40 *International Journal of Law and Psychiatry* 71, 73.

[31] *Ibid.*

[32] I begin such an analysis below, in section VI.

[33] A Arstein-Kerslake and E Flynn, 'The General Comment on Article 12 of the Convention on the Rights of Persons with Disabilities: A Roadmap For Equality before the Law' (2016) 20 *The International Journal of Human Rights* 471.

[34] Lewis (n 20) 42.

the provision of information in accessible formats, extra time to think, and/or assistive devices to facilitate communication, will be sufficient to enable (self-sufficient) decision-making. In other situations, personal support to assist the individual in making choices will be more appropriate. Such assistance may take the form of peer support or consist of assistance from family, friends or other formal or informal networks. Some decisions are more complex or urgent than others, and personal circumstances may affect the type of assistance required. Acute somatic conditions (such as high fever, severe pain, fatigue or dizziness) tend to impact on our reasoning abilities.[35] Psychotic episodes impact our perception of 'the world', and severe depression can affect our ability to appreciate the significance of the different treatment alternatives on offer.[36] Thus, different circumstances require different approaches to facilitate free and informed decision-making.

A few examples of domestic support systems are commonly put forward as models for other states parties. The Swedish personal ombudsman system is one such example. An ombudsman is a publicly employed professional whose only task is to support her clients in various matters, including in their interactions with health care authorities. The ombudsman has no special legal powers, and can neither consent to nor reject clinical treatment on her clients' behalf. Instead, the advantages of this system lie in the ombudsman's ability to develop trusting relationships with clients and to assist and encourage them to make their own decisions.[37] So-called advance directives are another way of allowing people with fluctuating decision-making ability to express their preferences about what care they wish to receive in the future.[38] These have mostly been used in relation to people with degenerative ailments (eg Alzheimer's or Parkinson's disease). Penelope Weller, however, illustrates their potential for mental health care. A critical question here is whether various support mechanisms could effectively cater for *all* the situations that currently fall within the ambit of compulsory psychiatric care and thus whether they might replace all uses of compulsion. Michael Bach and Lana Kerzner did not think so when they developed their model for decision-making support in Canada in 2010. In their view, in situations in which decision-making ability is lacking and the person is threatening or

[35] Raymont et al, 'Prevalence of Mental Incapacity in Medical Inpatients and Associated Risk Factors: Cross-Sectional Study' (2004) 364 *The Lancet* 1421. The authors studied a mixed sample of 302 adults admitted to acute general medical wards in London and showed that as many as a third of them lacked adequate decision-making abilities when assessed with the MacArthur competence assessment tool for treatment (the tool is described in the article).

[36] T Hindmarch, M Hotopf and G Owen, 'Depression and Decision-making Capacity for Treatment or Research: A Systematic Review' (2013) 14 *BMC Medical Ethics* 54.

[37] M Jespersson, 'Personal Ombudsman in Skåne: A User-controlled Service with Personal Agents' in P Stastny and P Lehmann (eds), *Alternatives Beyond Psychiatry* (Berlin, Peter Lehmann Publishing, 2007) 299ff.

[38] P Weller, *New Law and Ethics in Mental Health Advance Directives: The Convention on the Rights of Persons with Disabilities and the Right to Choose* (Hove, Routledge, 2015) 2–3, 9–11 and 159–61.

attempting to cause physical or psychological harm to him- or herself, compulsory hospitalisation is justified.[39] Compulsory administration of medication and treatment is appropriate if the person concerned would otherwise experience 'serious illness or injury'.[40] Other scholars have envisaged a narrower scope for compulsion and suggested that compulsion must be limited to situations of 'imminent and grave harm'.[41] While acknowledging that any determination of what constitutes such harm is inherently subjective and value-laden, Flynn and Arstein-Kerslake provide some examples. A person standing on the top floor of a building threatening to jump, for instance, is a case in which intervening, holding him or her back from the edge, would be justified. The preventive detention of people experiencing a mental health crisis, however, would not be justified.[42] Flynn and Arstein-Kerslake base this position on first-person descriptions of the trauma caused by coercive psychiatric care and on research that disputes the effectiveness of forced psychiatric medication.[43]

Representatives from the medical profession have raised serious concerns about this call for the abolition of coercive care. Paul Gosney, for example, recently argued that if the CRPD is to be interpreted as outlawing all forms of compulsory care, then the UK Government should withdraw from the Convention.[44] In the end, the effectiveness of different forms of intervention (voluntary and coercive) in preventing harmful behaviour is an empirical matter that cannot be settled by abstract argument. The process of developing support mechanisms to aid people with psychosocial disabilities has only recently begun, and there are good reasons to be optimistic about the future. There is a growing body of literature dealing with the prospects of voluntary alternatives to compulsory care that involve some form of support component, whether personal or technical.[45] Relatively little empirical research has been conducted,

[39] M Bach and L Kerzner, *A New Paradigm for Protecting Autonomy and the Right to Legal Capacity* (Law Commission of Ontario, 2010) 133ff.

[40] *Ibid* 133 and 140.

[41] E Flynn and A Arstein-Kerslake, 'State Intervention in the Lives of People with Disabilities: The Case for a Disability-neutral Framework' (2017) 13 *International Journal of Law in Context* 39, 49. See also P Gooding and E Flynn, 'Querying the Call to Introduce Mental Capacity Testing to Mental Health Law: Does the Doctrine of Necessity Provide an Alternative?' (2015) 4 *Laws* 245.

[42] Flynn and Arstein-Kerslake, 'State Intervention' 50–51. This accords with the authors' position in earlier writings. See for instance Flynn and Arstein-Kerslake, 'Legislating Personhood' 98–100.

[43] Flynn and Arstein-Kerslake (n 41).

[44] P Gosney and P Bartlett, 'The UK Government Should Withdraw from the Convention on the Rights of Persons with Disabilities' (2019) 14 *The British Journal of Psychiatry* 1. Bartlett contests Gosney's argument. See also MC Freeman et al, 'Reversing Hard Won Victories in the Name of Human Rights: A Critique of the General Comment on Article 12 of the UN Convention on the Rights of Persons with Disabilities' (2015) 2 *Lancet Psychiatry* 844. M Zinkler and S von Peter constitute an exception in this regard. In their paper 'End Coercion in Mental Health Services: Toward a System Based on Support Only' (2019) 8 *Laws* 19, they outline a mental health system based on support only.

[45] P Gooding et al, *Alternatives to Coercion in Mental Health Settings: A Literature Review* (Melbourne, Melbourne Social Equity Institute, 2018). See also P Gooding, *A New Era for Mental*

however, and it remains unclear whether the various forms of support being considered will meet the needs of *the entire group* of people who are currently subject to the compulsory care system.

III. ARTICLE 14 AND THE RIGHT TO LIBERTY

Article 14(1)(a) obliges states parties to ensure that people with disabilities enjoy the right to liberty and security of person 'on an equal basis with others'. Article 14(1)(b) states that disability 'shall in no case justify' detention.[46] The latter point is noteworthy given that domestic health laws often provide for the compulsory hospitalisation of people with psychosocial disabilities only.[47] Psychosocial disability, or rather psychosocial impairment or diagnosis, is a necessary, though not sufficient, condition of such detention. The central question here is whether Article 14(1)(b) should be interpreted to mean that the presence of a psychosocial impairment or clinical condition cannot be part of the justification *at all* or that detention cannot be justified on the basis of the existence of an impairment/clinical condition *alone*. Conventional language does not seem to rule out either option. The statement that X provides no justification for a certain act could mean either that X can never serve as a legitimate reason for that act or that X does not provide sufficient justification on its own. This ambiguity is mirrored in the debate that took place during the drafting process.[48] Draft proposals stating that disability/impairment could never serve as a legitimate basis for detention, whether alone or in combination with other factors, were rejected as too restrictive. The majority of state delegates argued for a draft text that reaffirmed what was undisputed – that is, that disability (understood as impairment), by itself, should never be sufficient reason for detention – but that still provided for the detention of those with disabilities in situations in which 'the effects of disability/impairment' warranted such intervention. A number of these delegates wished to insert the words 'solely' or 'exclusively', so that the Article would read 'deprivation of liberty shall in no case be based solely/exclusively on disability'. However, these proposals were opposed and ultimately not accepted.[49]

Health Law and Policy: Supported Decision-making and the UN Convention on the Rights of Persons with Disabilities (Cambridge, Cambridge University Press, 2017) Ch 6.

[46] The full article is available in the Appendix to this book.

[47] See ch 2, section II.

[48] M Perlin and A Szeli, 'Article 14 Liberty and Security of the Person' in I Bantekas, MA Stein, and D Anastasiou (eds), *The UN Convention on the Rights of Persons with Disabilities: A Commentary* (Oxford, Oxford University Press, 2018) 404–406.

[49] Report of the Coordinator (n 18) paras 27–28; Ad Hoc Committee, 'Daily Summary of Discussion at the Fifth Session' (26 January 2005) www.un.org/esa/socdev/enable/rights/ahc5sum26jan.htm (recorded statements by Jordan, Costa Rica, Mexico, Thailand, Kenya, Australia, Colombia and the Coordinator); International Disability Caucus, 'Chairman's Text as Amended by the International Disability Caucus' (Seventh Session, 2006) www.un.org/esa/socdev/enable/rights/ahc7contngos.htm,

Other treaty provisions relevant to this question do not take us much further. As I have mentioned, Article 12 reaffirms that people with disabilities have the same right as people without disabilities to make health care decisions and to have these decisions respected, without detailing what this right implies for the lawfulness of civil detention. Hence, this provision requires its own equality analysis before it can be used to inform an interpretation of Article 14. Similarly, Article 25(d) obliges states parties to ensure that health care is provided on the basis of free and informed consent, but remains silent about whether exceptions to this main rule may be justified. Indeed, a number of exceptions are uncontested within human rights discourse. Public health measures to control communicable diseases may involve people being hospitalised against their will, as may the clinical treatment of children.[50] In addition, few would argue that the urgent clinical care of people who are unconscious because of an accident constitutes a human rights violation.

As I noted in the previous section, some states parties have made interpretative declarations in connection with the ratification of the CRPD. Australia, the Netherlands and Norway take the Convention to allow for 'compulsory care and treatment', including the treatment of mental illness/disability.[51] Canada, Poland and Estonia have declared that they believe the treaty allows for substitute decision-making (that is, decisions taken by a third party on behalf of the individual concerned), though without detailing what that means for decision-making in the context of health care.[52] The Canadian declaration adds that, if it turns out that the CRPD outlaws substitute decision-making, then the state reserves the right to continue with such practices.[53] None of the other state parties have objected to these declarations, but neither have they expressly supported them. Implicit support may be inferred from states' reports to the CRPD Committee on measures undertaken to give effect to their treaty obligations. Most, though not all, interpret

comments to Art 14; Ad Hoc Committee, 'Daily Summary of Discussion at the Seventh Session' (19 January 2006) www.un.org/esa/socdev/enable/rights/ahc7sum19jan.htm, concluding words by the Chair.

[50] On the former, see Human Rights Committee, 'General Comment No 35 on Article 9 (Liberty and Security of Person)' (16 December 2014) UN Doc CCPR/C/GC/35 para 5; Committee on Social, Economic, and Cultural Rights, 'General Comment No 14: The Right to the Highest Attainable Standard of Health (Article 12 of the International Covenant on Economic, Social and Cultural Rights)' (11 August 2000) UN Doc E/C.12/2000/4 para 35; Convention for the Protection of Human Rights and Fundamental Freedoms (as amended) ETS 5 Art 5(1)(e). On the latter, see Convention on the Rights of the Child (adopted 20 November 1989, entered into force 2 September 1990) 1577 UNTS 3 art 12; Committee on the Rights of the Child, 'General Comment No 12 on The Right of the Child to be Heard' (20 July 2009) UN Doc CRC/C/GC/12 paras 98–104, concerning the health context.

[51] See n 21.

[52] See n 22.

[53] The Canadian reservation reads: 'To the extent Article 12 may be interpreted as requiring the elimination of all substitute decision-making arrangements, Canada reserves the right to continue their use in appropriate circumstances and subject to appropriate and effective safeguards.'

Article 14 as permitting civil detention where psychosocial impairment is one factor among others.[54]

The CRPD Committee adopts the opposite position. In its concluding observations, prepared in response to states parties' reports on their implementation of the Convention at the domestic level, the Committee frequently expresses its concern over legislation that authorises civil detention based on disability alone *or* in combination with other factors. 'Concern' is a common term used by the UN treaty bodies to signal that state practice conflicts with treaty provisions. The Committee has also recommended that states parties repeal such legislation in order to comply with their obligations under the CRPD.[55] In its first general comment, the Committee reiterates this position and states that the civil detention of people with disabilities against their will violates Article 14 of the Convention. The Committee does not, however, elaborate on the reasons behind its conclusion that civil detention is unlawful. The Committee declares that respect for legal capacity includes respect for liberty and that detention in medical facilities constitutes arbitrary detention in violation of the CRPD.[56] This conclusion builds on the Committee's position that *all* substitute decision-making regimes violate the CRPD.[57] Some UN human rights bodies, including the Office of the United Nations High Commissioner for Human Rights and the UN Special Rapporteur on the rights of persons with disabilities, have followed the Committee's lead and stated that Article 14 outlaws compulsory hospitalisation in a closed ward.[58] Other bodies, such as the Human Rights Committee and the Subcommittee on Prevention of Torture and Other Cruel, Inhuman

[54] See, eg, Initial Reports of States Parties under Article 35 of the Convention: Germany (submitted 19 September 2011, published 7 May 2013) UN Doc CRPD/C/DEU/1 paras 113–15; New Zealand (submitted 31 March 2011, published 1 October 2013, UN Doc CRPD/C/NZL/1 paras 83–86; United Kingdom of Great Britain and Northern Ireland (submitted 24 November 2011, published 3 July 2013) UN Doc CRPD/C/BGR/1 paras 133–34.

[55] See, eg, Concluding Observations of the CRPD Committee on the Initial Report of Spain (adopted 23 September 2011) UN Doc CRPD/C/ESP/CO/1 paras 35–36; Peru (adopted 20 April 2012) UN Doc CRPD/C/PER/CO/1 paras 28–29; Austria (adopted 11 September 2013) UN Doc CRPD/C/AUT/CO/1 paras 29–31; Sweden (adopted 11 April 2014) UN Doc CRPD/C/SWE/CO/1 paras 35–36; Denmark (adopted 2 October 2014) UN Doc CRPD/C/DNK/CO/1 paras 36–37; Thailand (adopted 11 April 2016) UN Doc CRPD/C/THA/CO/1 paras 29–30; Colombia (adopted 31 August 2016) UN Doc CRPD/C/COL/CO/1 paras 33–36); Italy (adopted 1 September 2016) UN Doc CRPD/C/ITA/CO/1 paras 33–34.

[56] CRPD Committee (n 24) para 40.

[57] CRPD Committee (n 24) paras 13–15. See also CRPD Committee, 'Guidelines on Article 14 of the Convention on the Rights of Persons with Disabilities: The Right to Liberty and Security of Persons with Disabilities Adopted during the Committee's Fourteenth Session' (17 August to 4 September 2015) paras 6–8.

[58] UNGA, 'Mental Health and Human Rights: Report of the United Nations High Commissioner for Human Rights' 39th Session (2018) UN Doc A/HRC/39/36 para 46; UNGA, 'Mental Health and Human Rights: Report of the United Nations High Commissioner for Human Rights' 34th Session (2017) UN Doc A/HRC/34/32 paras 29, 31; UNGA, 'Rights of Persons with Disabilities: Report of the Special Rapporteur on the Rights of Persons with Disabilities' 40th Session (2019) UN Doc A/HRC/40/54 paras 46–47, 61.

or Degrading Treatment or Punishment, have expressed dissenting views.[59] As I explained in the previous section, I am not convinced by the CRPD Committee's justification of its position. My conclusion is that paragraph 14(1)(b) clearly prohibits civil detention based on a psychiatric diagnosis alone. A psychosocial condition cannot *in itself* be a sufficient reason for detention. To the question of whether the existence of a psychosocial condition in combination with other factors may justify civil detention, Article 14(1)(b) provides no clear-cut answer. To determine all the implications of Article 14 for civil detention, it is necessary to engage in discrimination analysis. Section VI sets out the framework for such an analysis, and in chapter two I use this framework to assess domestic mental health laws.

IV. ARTICLE 17 AND THE RIGHT TO RESPECT FOR PHYSICAL AND MENTAL INTEGRITY

Article 17 states that 'every person with disabilities has a right to respect for his or her physical and mental integrity on an equal basis with others'. It thus locates compulsory clinical treatment within the equality framework. Being the shortest provision in an otherwise elaborately detailed human rights treaty, it does not provide any further information about how integrity is to be understood or what states parties must do to ensure respect for integrity on an equal basis with others. Within the human rights discourse, the term 'integrity' is connected to autonomy and the right *to decide* over one's body and mind, as well as to dignity and the entitlement to be *free from inhuman and degrading treatment*.[60] The negotiations over Article 17 were dominated by questions concerning the lawfulness of compulsory clinical interventions and their possible categorisation as inhuman or degrading treatment.[61] Some state delegates and representatives from civil society organisations argued that all compulsory medical treatment is tantamount to torture – either because of its intrusive nature, or because it is imposed against a person's expressed preferences – and should therefore be

[59] Human Rights Committee, 'General Comment No 35' para 19; Subcommittee on Prevention of Torture and Other Cruel, Inhuman or Degrading Treatment or Punishment, 'Approach of the Subcommittee on Prevention of Torture and Other Cruel, Inhuman or Degrading Treatment or Punishment regarding the Rights of Persons Institutionalized and Treated Medically without Informed Consent' (26 January 2016) UN Doc CAT/OP/27/2 paras 8, 11.

[60] Whilst the two aspects are intimately connected (the fact that a given treatment is administered against a person's will is a reason to label the treatment in question degrading), the overlap is not complete. Not all compulsory treatment is degrading, and there may be instances in which medical treatment may be considered degrading despite its initial acceptance by the individual concerned.

[61] B McSherry, 'Protecting the Integrity of the Person: Developing Limitations on Involuntary Treatment' in B McSherry (ed), *International Trends in Mental Health Laws* (Leichhardt, The Federation Press, 2008) 111–15; F Seatzu, 'Article 17 Protecting the Integrity of the Person' in I Bantekas, MA Stein, and D Anastasiou (eds), *The UN Convention on the Rights of Persons with Disabilities: A Commentary* (Oxford, Oxford University Press, 2018) 495–97.

dealt with under the provision prohibiting torture and inhuman or degrading treatment. The majority of the negotiating parties, however, argued that whilst certain medical interventions may count as inhuman and degrading treatment, such as, for example, the use of outdated or very painful treatment methods, this is not true of compulsory medical interventions per se.[62]

The question remains whether Article 17 establishes any further restrictions on the permissibility of compulsory clinical intervention. The right to refuse medical treatment is an important aspect of the protection of integrity within the human rights discourse. This fact suggests that we should interpret Article 17 in conjunction with Articles 12 and 25(d). Article 25(d) states that health care professionals are obliged to provide care to people with disabilities on the basis of free and informed consent.[63] The important point, however, is that neither Article 12 nor Article 25 provides clear answers to the central questions of this study: whether states parties may override an expressed rejection of treatment and, if they may, under what circumstances they may do so. On this point, both provisions state that people with disabilities are entitled to be treated on an equal basis with others, and thus these provisions require their own equality analysis before they can be taken to inform the meaning of equal respect for integrity in Article 17. The CRPD Committee argues that mental health laws permitting forced treatment discriminate because they deny people with psychosocial disabilities the right to exercise legal capacity within the context of health care.[64] The Committee cites as an additional reason for abolishing compulsory clinical treatment the fact that such treatment has been proven to be ineffective and to cause deep pain and trauma among those subjected to it.[65] The Office of the High Commissioner for Human Rights and the Special Rapporteur on the rights of persons with disabilities have also used the CRPD to call on states to end non-consensual care, without, however, elaborating on why compulsory mental health care constitutes unlawful discrimination.[66] I fully agree that the dearth of empirical evidence on the effectiveness of compulsory psychiatric treatment and the abundance of evidence on the harm caused by such practices speak against their lawfulness under the CRPD. But there are other reasons that speak in favour of permitting compulsion, and these need to be taken into account. Few seem to dispute that there are situations where there is a significant risk of serious harm to health and life if a person does not receive medical treatment

[62] Report of the Coordinator (n 18) paras 38–41 and 58–67; Ad Hoc Committee, 'Daily Summary of Discussion at the Fifth Session' (28 January 2005) www.un.org/esa/socdev/enable/rights/ahc5sum28jan.htm; Ad Hoc Committee, 'Daily Summary of Discussion at the Seventh Session' (19 January 2006).

[63] The full paragraph is available in the Appendix to this book.

[64] CRPD Committee (n 24) para 7. See also CRPD Committee, 'General Comment No 6 on Equality and Non-discrimination' (26 April 2018) UN Doc CRPD/C/GC/6 para 30.

[65] CRPD Committee (n 24) para 42.

[66] UNGA, 'Mental Health and Human Rights' (2017) para 33; UNGA, 'Report of the Special Rapporteur' paras 23, 63–64.

and where the provision of medical treatment would at least mitigate this risk. The contentious point is whether permitting compulsory care in these situations is compatible with the purpose behind Article 17, which is to constrain the use of compulsion, and with the general principles of respect for individual autonomy and self-determination, including the freedom to make one's own choices, undergirding the Convention as a whole. Most states parties to the Convention think that it is. To them, it is the call for the complete abolition of compulsory care that is unreasonable. Consequently, they interpret the CRPD as permitting the compulsory clinical treatment of people with psychosocial disabilities if such treatment is carried out in accordance with medical science, used as a measure of last resort and coupled with legal safeguards.[67] Some legal scholars and medical professionals have adopted a similar position.[68]

V. ARTICLE 25 AND THE RIGHT TO CONSENT

Article 25 of the CRPD starts by declaring that people with disabilities are entitled to the 'enjoyment of the highest attainable standard of health without discrimination on the basis of disability' and that states parties are to 'take all appropriate measures to ensure access for persons with disabilities to health services'. It goes on to detail a range of measures that states parties are obliged to implement, including the duty to ensure that health care staff provide treatment on the basis of free and informed consent. The treaty provides no definition of the terms 'free and informed consent'. The negotiation records tell us that various suggestions about terminology were discussed during the drafting procedure and that the phrase 'free and informed consent' was chosen because of its accepted meaning within human rights law. Under human rights law, approval for clinical intervention should be obtained without threats or improper inducements, and after the disclosure of relevant facts in a format and language understood by the patient.[69] All health care interventions must, as a general rule, proceed on the basis of such informed consent from the individual concerned. Clinical treatment without such approval interferes with, and

[67] States issued interpretative declarations on this matter upon ratifying the treaty (see n 21). They have also reacted to the CRPD Committee's position in commentaries to a draft version of General Comment No 1, which was posted on the Committee's website together with an invitation to all interested stakeholders to submit comments on the draft to the Committee. See, eg, submissions from Denmark, France, Germany, Norway and New Zealand, available at www.ohchr.org/EN/HRBodies/CRPD/Pages/DGCArticles12And9.aspx.

[68] Dawson, 'A Realistic Approach' 71; Freeman et al, 'Reversing Hard Won Victories'; J Dute, 'Should Substituted Decision-making Be Abolished?' (2015) 22 *European Journal of Health Law* 315.

[69] Report of the Coordinator (n 18) para 39; Ad Hoc Committee, 'Daily Summary of Discussion at the Fifth Session' (28 January 2005) (recorded statements by the Republic of Korea, Russian Federation, New Zealand, Jordan, Australia, Trinidad and Tobago, Luxembourg (on behalf of the EU), the Coordinator and the Office of the High Commissioner for Human Rights).

in many cases violates, the individual's entitlement to respect for her mental and physical integrity.

Before the CRPD, the right to refuse medical care was codified in documents relating to medical and scientific experimentation, practices that amount to torture or similar ill treatment if conducted without consent. A more general right to respect for health care choices had only been confirmed in international soft law and in regional human rights treaties and jurisprudence.[70] Nonetheless, the right to refuse medical care, save under exceptional circumstances, was taken to be a fundamental principle in bioethics and was widely accepted in jurisdictions worldwide. As noted above, a person may be hospitalised against her will in order to control the spread of a communicable disease. The same is true of the clinical treatment of children and the emergency treatment of people who are unconscious.[71] The rationale behind these exceptions turns on the following two factors: (1) the risk of adverse effects to the person concerned or to others; and (2) the difficulty in obtaining free and informed consent from the person concerned. Both of these factors appear in states' justifications of compulsory psychiatric care. Starting with the difficulties of obtaining free and informed consent, such problems typically involve situations in which persons are indeed able to communicate a preference but in which there are reasons to doubt whether a rejection of medical treatment truly reflects a personal choice. Typical examples would be people resisting treatment whilst experiencing an episode of psychosis or mania, people with anorexia refusing artificial feeding, and people with severe depression underestimating the benefits of clinical treatment. Must physicians refrain from treatment in such situations, or may treatment refusals be overridden? As noted earlier, the CRPD treaty text does not provide any details on this matter, and international human rights law has paid little attention to the question of which abilities (if any) need to be present when 'free and informed' treatment choices are made. It is clear that physicians have a duty to provide information about future medical procedures and to refrain from exerting any pressure on their patients, but pre-CRPD law had little to say about whether the individual concerned ought to be able to understand and reflect on the information provided. Although human rights law assumed that certain clinical conditions could affect our decision-making

[70] See, eg, Principles for the Protection of Persons with Mental Illness and the Improvement of Mental Health Care, UNGA Res 46/119 (17 December 1991) principle 11. The first paragraph confirms that the cardinal rule that no medical treatment shall be administered without the informed consent of the person concerned also applies in the mental health context. For regional treaties, see, eg, African Charter on Human and Peoples' Rights (adopted 27 June 1981, entered into force 21 October 1986) 1520 UNTS 217 Art 4; American Convention on Human Rights (adopted 22 November 1969, entered into force 18 July 1978) 1144 UNTS 123; Convention for the Protection of the Human Rights and Dignity of the Human Being with regard to the Application of Biology and Medicine (adopted 4 April 1997, entered into force 1 December 1999) ETS 164 Arts 5–7 and 26.

[71] See section III above.

abilities, by and large it deferred to states when it came to determining the details.[72]

Domestic health laws commonly endorse some version of the idea that, in situations in which an individual is able to understand her situation, process information about treatment alternatives, and make decisions in line with personal values, such decisions should be respected. To facilitate the day-to-day work of medical staff, it is generally assumed that patients possess such abilities, which is why a simple 'yes' or 'no' normally suffices to accept or decline an offer of medical treatment. When in doubt, medical staff must engage with the reasons behind an individual's refusal of treatment, and they may override refusals that are based on a misinterpretation of the relevant facts.[73] It is clear from interpretative declarations and other expressions of subsequent practice that most states parties intend to continue to use certain criteria to distinguish between refusals of treatment that must be respected and those that may be overridden, and reserve the right to refuse treatment to people who, with or without support, meet the relevant criteria for free and informed treatment decisions. It is equally clear that many states parties interpret the CRPD as accepting such practices.[74]

We also know that the CRPD Committee interprets the Convention differently. According to the Committee, compulsory care regimes violate several of the provisions of the CRPD, including Articles 12, 17 and 25.[75] The Committee recognises that, in situations where communication difficulties mean that an individual's wishes cannot be determined, doctors are allowed to proceed on the basis of the *best interpretation* of the individual's will and preferences. The Committee distinguishes the best-interpretation standard from the 'best-interest standard'. The best-interpretation standard, the Committee explains, focuses on the person's own views, whereas the best-interest standard relies on general assumptions about what ought 'objectively' to be in the best interests of that person.[76] Importantly, then, the Committee believes that personal views take precedence over generic accounts of best interests. Treatment decisions are value sensitive, meaning that the 'right' choice depends on the values and disvalues the person concerned attaches to the consequences of different possible decisions. How does the person concerned value the potential benefits of a certain treatment? Does he or she think that they outweigh the risk of negative effects

[72] This deference is most explicit in the jurisprudence of the European Court of Human Rights. See, eg, *Winterwerp v the Netherlands* Series A no 33 (1979) 2 EHRR 387 para 40; *Herczegfalvy v Austria* Series A no 244 (1992) 15 EHRR 437 para 82.

[73] A presumption of ability to make free and informed decisions is, for example, firmly established in common law. M Donnelly, *Healthcare Decision-making and the Law: Autonomy, Capacity, and the Limits of Liberalism* (Cambridge, Cambridge University Press, 2010) 93.

[74] See nn 21 and 22.

[75] CRPD Committee (n 24) paras 41–42.

[76] CRPD Committee (n 24) para 21.

associated with the treatment in question? The results of such balancing naturally differ between individuals, and between doctors and their patients. Therefore, any protocol used to decide on clinical treatment ought, arguably, to try to reconstruct the subjective point of view of the person concerned. Difficulties arise in cases of ambivalence towards treatment, which is fairly common. An individual may, for example, express a wish for relief from certain unpleasant symptoms but, at the same time, refuse any treatment; a refusal of a certain therapy or medication may conflict with treatment preferences expressed in previous advance directives.[77] In addition, although treatment refusals may be based on a personal evaluation of the pros and cons of the treatment in question, they may also be influenced by paranoid ideations about the doctor's intentions or misunderstandings about the effects of the treatment. The Committee seems to hold that the CRPD requires that such situations be treated in the same way, with unconditional respect for any expression of resistance. The Committee's position is reconcilable with the treaty text, and it gains support from the general principles of autonomy and individual self-determination.[78] However, other positions, including those held by many states parties, are also reconcilable with an interpretation of the text when viewed in conjunction with jurisprudence concerning exceptions to the right to refuse treatment. Further, it is not obvious that a domestic system that grants unconditional respect for any refusal of treatment is better at protecting personal autonomy than a system that differentiates between expressions of resistance in terms of the patient's decision-making ability and attaches more importance to treatment rejections that (appear to) reflect reasoned choices based on personal values. Any position on this matter implies a particular conceptualisation of the 'true will' and particular views on how and when such a will ought to be respected. These are questions to which the Convention offers no easy answers. However, as I will demonstrate in this book, the prohibition of discrimination has certain implications for this issue. If domestic law respects the irrational or misinformed treatment decisions of people without disabilities, it must, in principle, treat the irrational or misinformed treatment decisions of people with psychosocial disabilities in the same way (see, further, chapter four, section II.B).

I turn now to the other reason for allowing exceptions to the rule that medical treatment must be based on consent from the person concerned, namely the fact that treatment rejections often imply a risk of harm to the health or life of the individual concerned. As a general rule, under human rights law, the presence

[77] How to handle conflicts across time has been extensively discussed within biomedical ethics in relation to cognitive decline linked to the ageing process. See, eg, A Buchanan and D Brock, *Deciding for Others: The Ethics of Surrogate Decision-making* (Cambridge, Cambridge University Press, 1990) Ch 3; and A Jaworska, 'Respecting the Margins of Agency: Alzheimer's Patients and the Capacity to Value' (1999) 28 *Philosophy and Public Affairs* 105.

[78] CRPD Art 3.

of such a risk does not constitute a sufficient reason to override a treatment refusal. This applies to situations in which declining treatment might be fatal, as well as to instances in which the health implications of refusal are minor. Respect for personal choice is considered to be more important, and facilitating such respect implies that there must be room for disagreement and risk-taking.[79] The European Court of Human Rights expressed this point eloquently in a case regarding the right of Jehovah's Witnesses to refuse blood transfusions:

> The freedom to accept or refuse specific medical treatment, or to select an alternative form of treatment, is vital [...] For this freedom to be meaningful, patients must have the right to make choices that accord with their own views and values, regardless of how irrational, unwise or imprudent such choices may appear to others.[80]

The outputs of the CRPD Committee aside, within the human rights discourse this strong protection of risk-taking has been accorded only to adults with their decision-making abilities intact. Children and adults who are considered to be unable to understand and appreciate the consequences of their treatment refusals may still be compelled to undergo treatment.[81] Other factors also influence the weight attached to the risk of harm that would result if treatment were refused.

According to the European Court of Human Rights, individuals who are deprived of their liberty in state-run facilities, such as prisons and, indeed, psychiatric hospitals, may be treated against their will if the treatment is considered to be necessary to protect them from life-threatening or irreversible harm.[82] Being deprived of one's liberty, according to this jurisprudence, makes one vulnerable and undercuts one's freedom to make decisions that may seriously harm oneself. Moreover, the protection against non-consensual treatment interventions has been held to be weaker in the case of people who wish to end their own lives. Although it is recognised that people may have a genuine wish to end their lives, states appear to enjoy a margin of discretion about whether treatment may be imposed on people expressing such a wish.[83]

[79] Several authors speak about the 'dignity of risk'. See, eg, Quinn and Arstein-Kerslake, 'Restoring the "Human"' 41; P Gooding, 'Supported Decision-making: A Rights-based Disability Concept and Its Implications for Mental Health Law' (2013) 20 *Psychiatry, Psychology, and Law* 431, 432.

[80] *Jehovah's Witnesses of Moscow v Russia* (2011) 53 EHRR 4, para 136.

[81] With regard to children, see the Convention on the Rights of the Child Art 12; Committee on the Rights of the Child 'General Comment No 12' paras 98–104, concerning the health context. With regard to adults, see L Waddington and B McSherry, 'Exceptions and Exclusions: The Right to Informed Consent for Medical Treatment of People with Psychosocial Disabilities in Europe' (2016) 23 *European Journal of Health Law* 279, 297.

[82] According to the Court's case law on hunger strikes. *Nevmerzhitsky v Ukraine* (2005) 43 EHRR 32 paras 93–94; *Rappaz v Switzerland* (dec) (2013) ECHR 508 paras 66–72.

[83] See Human Rights Committee, 'General Comment No 36: Article 6 Right to Life' (3 September 2019) UN Doc CCPR/C/GC/36 para 9. To date, the European Court of Human Rights has not taken a position on so-called 'balance-sheet suicides'.

VI. THE ENJOYMENT OF LEGAL CAPACITY, LIBERTY AND INTEGRITY 'ON AN EQUAL BASIS WITH OTHERS'

The previous sections have demonstrated that the lawfulness of compulsory mental health interventions under the Convention hinges on equality or discrimination analysis. Indeed, defining 'on an equal basis with others' will be essential if we are to specify the precise state obligations that follow not only from the rights discussed in this book, but from almost all of the substantive Articles in the Convention.[84] This section takes on this task. It starts with a brief discussion of the concept(s) of equality undergirding the CRPD and goes on to discuss the normative content of the prohibition of discrimination. The Convention's numerous declarations that states must ensure equal enjoyment of the rights set out in the CRPD must be interpreted in light of the purpose of the treaty as a whole, its *raison d'être*. The idea of an international treaty protecting the human rights of people with disabilities grew out of an emerging consensus that the existing human rights framework had failed in this respect.[85] Although existing human rights instruments included people with disabilities within their scope and provided a structure that could serve to promote and protect their rights, this potential was not being tapped.[86] To remedy this state of affairs, a new treaty was needed in order to make people with disabilities visible as rights-holders and to detail the state's obligations to ensure that people with disabilities enjoyed their human rights on an equal basis with others. This motivation is codified in Article 1 of the treaty, which asserts that the purpose of the Convention is to ensure the full and equal enjoyment of all human rights by all persons with disabilities. During the negotiations on the treaty text, parties settled on the wording of 'equality' and 'equal treatment' in order to facilitate agreement on matters where dispute over the substantive issue could not be resolved: for example, whether it should be lawful to override treatment refusals under certain circumstances and, if so, what those circumstances are. Whilst no agreement could be reached on a rule that would clearly permit or prohibit compulsory mental health care, agreement could be reached on the idea that people with psychosocial disabilities have the right to enjoy liberty, integrity and legal capacity on an equal basis with others. This reference to the equal enjoyment of rights reassured concerned state delegates that disabled people would not be accorded rights over and above those afforded to other segments of the population. The very same phrase enabled others to interpret the text in a progressive, even radical, way.

[84] JL Corsi, 'Article 5 Equality and Non-Discrimination' in I Bantekas, MA Stein, and D Anastasiou (eds), *The UN Convention on the Rights of Persons with Disabilities: A Commentary* (Oxford, Oxford University Press, 2018) 155–57.

[85] This is recognised in the preamble of the CRPD. See in particular (d) and (k).

[86] Resolution on Comprehensive and Integral International Convention to Promote and Protect the Rights and Dignity of Persons with Disabilities, UNGA Res 57/229 (18 December 2002).

The notion of the equal enjoyment of rights may be traced to the fundamental idea that all human beings are equal in dignity and worth and thereby entitled to the same rights and the effective enjoyment of these rights – an ideal that cannot easily be rejected. What this notion means in terms of concrete state obligations is, however, more difficult to pin down. As many commentators have observed, equality is a complex and dynamic concept that has no fixed or settled definition in international human rights law.[87] Equality can mean, and has been taken to mean, many things, including formal equality (that is, treating like cases alike), equality of opportunity, equality of results and respect for dignity. Equality of opportunity is listed among the general principles that are to inform the interpretation of the Convention.[88] Equality of opportunity can be understood as a response to the limitations inherent in a formal understanding of equality that focuses on ensuring sameness of treatment and fails to properly consider contextual factors. Marginalisation, economic hardship, past discrimination and public prejudice affect a person's ability to enjoy her rights. To illustrate this point, authors often draw on the metaphor of competitors in a race.[89] True equality can only be achieved if individuals begin the race from the same starting point. To achieve this, states must remove all obstacles that prevent the advancement of marginalised groups and take positive measures to ensure that members of these groups are genuinely in a position to access their rights.[90]

In the mental health context, this implies that states must remove all legal and institutional barriers preventing people with psychosocial disabilities from making valid health care decisions and provide appropriate support to facilitate such decision-making. Whether compulsory psychiatric care is compatible with an obligation to ensure equality of opportunity is, however, a matter of debate. The answer will essentially depend on how one understands the concept of an equal starting point or, to be more precise, on how variations in decision-making ability and in levels of risk (of harm to self or others) affect our understanding of what constitutes an equal starting point. Are people who, despite having access to support, have a limited ability to understand and appreciate their health needs and the negative implications of refusing medical treatment starting from the same position as people who – with or without support – are able to appreciate the implications of their health care decisions? Further, are people who, despite having access to support, at an increased risk of harming themselves or others starting from the same position as people who (with or without support) do not find themselves in a situation of increased risk? Answering these questions

[87] J Clifford, 'Equality' in D Shelton (ed), *The Oxford Handbook of International Human Rights Law* (Oxford, Oxford University Press, 2013) 420–45.

[88] CRPD Art 3(e).

[89] S Fredman, 'Substantive Equality Revisited' (2016) 14 *International Journal of Constitutional Law* 712, 723.

[90] *Ibid*.

requires that we carefully consider the value of decision-making ability and that of risk-taking, matters on which the principle of equal opportunity is silent. An affirmative answer to the first question implies that diminished decision-making abilities ought to be no barrier to legally valid decision-making within the health care context, and a negative answer suggests the opposite. Similarly, an affirmative answer to the second question suggests that risk assessments should not be used in such situations to override the patient's expressed preferences, whilst a negative reply speaks in favour of permitting such assessments. Equality of opportunity requires that everyone have a fair chance of success in making legally valid treatment decisions, but it does not guarantee such success.

In the CRPD literature, it is often held that the Convention is anchored in another form of equality, namely transformative equality or equality as transformation.[91] This form of equality is characterised by its focus on tackling the root causes of discrimination and marginalisation through structural reform. Transformative equality involves changing social structures and institutions rather than simply providing support and accommodation in individual cases to facilitate social inclusion. Individual support and accommodation are appropriate ways of ensuring equality in individual cases, but only in situations where access to social goods cannot be properly ensured through an inclusive system genuinely open to all. Andrea Broderick describes the transformative approach to equality as obliging states to implement a range of positive measures to change stereotypes, customs and practices that prevent marginalised groups from enjoying their rights; to transform social structures that perpetuate disadvantage and exclusion; to raise awareness about the capabilities of disabled people; and to involve people with disabilities in every aspect of such reform.[92] This focus on societal transformation is also visible in the outputs of the CRPD Committee. In many of its views on individual complaints, the Committee stresses that states parties have an obligation to adapt systems and procedures, including, for example, ATM services,[93] information systems for public transport,[94] voting procedures[95] and procedures relating to jury duty,[96] to make them accessible and suitable for people with disabilities. In its general

[91] A Broderick, *The Long and Winding Road to Equality and Inclusion for Persons with Disabilities: The United Nations Convention on the Rights of Persons with Disabilities* (Cambridge, Intersentia, 2015) 36–38; T Degener, 'Disability in a Human Rights Context' (2016) 5 *Laws* 35; Corsi, 'Article 5' 141.

[92] Broderick, *ibid* 36–37.

[93] CRPD Committee, 'Communication No 1/2010' *Szilvia Nyusti and Péter Takács v Hungary* (2013) UN Doc CRPD/C/9/D/1/2010 paras 9.5–9.6.

[94] CRPD Committee, 'Communication No 21/2014' *F v Austria* (2015) UN Doc CRPD/C/14/D/21/2014 paras 8.4–8.7.

[95] CRPD Committee, 'Communication No 19/2014' *Fiona Given v Australia* (2018) UN Doc CRPD/C/19/D/19/2014 paras 8.5, 8.8–8.10; CRPD Committee, 'Communication No 4/2011' *Bujdosó et al v Hungary* (2013) UN Doc CRPD/C/10/D/4/2011 paras 9.5–9.6.

[96] CRPD Committee, 'Communication No 13/2013' *Michael Lockrey v Australia* (2016) UN Doc CRPD/C/15/13/2013 para 8.6.

comment on equality and non-discrimination, the CRPD Committee further asserts that the CRPD is based on a concept of inclusive equality, which is similar to transformative equality.[97] The Committee describes this form of equality as a four-dimensional model of substantive equality. The four dimensions are:

> (a) a fair redistributive dimension to address socioeconomic disadvantages; (b) a recognition dimension to combat stigma, stereotyping, prejudice and violence and to recognize the dignity of human beings and their intersectionality; (c) a participative dimension to reaffirm the social nature of people as members of social groups and the full recognition of humanity through inclusion in society; and (d) an accommodating dimension to make space for difference as a matter of human dignity.[98]

The originator of the multi-dimensional concept of equality relied upon by the CRPD Committee, Sandra Fredman, explains that the four dimensions help us to understand the link between the equality that human rights law strives to achieve and 'non-discrimination grounds'.[99] Inequality is not the same as socioeconomic hardship. Socioeconomic disadvantage becomes an inequality concern when such disadvantage disproportionately affects a group that also suffers from public prejudice and/or a lack of voice in public affairs. Typically this would be a group that is protected under the prohibition of discrimination.[100] Fredman also highlights that the different dimensions can conflict with each other in concrete situations, which is why there is a need for compromise and for a comprehensive approach to equality.[101] Transforming our societies into more inclusive ones will, for example, take resources. States will have to make choices concerning how much money to spend in order to achieve such transformation and how much to reserve for other legitimate purposes. Precisely how such policy choices should be made is a matter for debate. As Oddný Mjöll Arnardóttir has noted, there remain quite a few questions that must be answered before multidimensional approaches to equality can be translated into non-discrimination law and justiciable rights.[102] Chapter four of this book develops a model for dealing with such conflicts of interest within discrimination analysis.

A. The Prohibition of Discrimination

The debate over what kind, or kinds, of equality should inform an interpretation of the CRPD's notion of the equal enjoyment of rights will continue. Few would

[97] CRPD Committee, 'General Comment No 6' para 11.
[98] CRPD Committee (n 64) para 11.
[99] Fredman, 'Substantive Equality' 734ff.
[100] Fredman (n 89) 735.
[101] Fredman (n 89) 736.
[102] O Mjöll Arnardóttir, 'A Future of Multidimensional Disadvantage Equality?' in O Mjöll Arnardóttir and G Quinn (eds), *The UN Convention on the Rights of Persons with Disabilities: European and Scandinavian Perspectives* (Leiden, Martinus Nijhoff, 2009) 65.

dispute, however, that the principle of the equal enjoyment of rights outlaws state policies and practices that are discriminatory. If compulsory mental health interventions violate the prohibition of discrimination, then they cannot be lawful under the CRPD. Article 2 of the CRPD defines discrimination as follows:

> 'Discrimination on the basis of disability' means any distinction, exclusion or restriction on the basis of disability which has the purpose or effect of impairing or nullifying the recognition, enjoyment or exercise, on an equal basis with others, of all human rights and fundamental freedoms in the political, economic, social, cultural, civil or any other field. It includes all forms of discrimination, including denial of reasonable accommodation.

The definition is almost identical to its counterparts in previous UN human rights instruments, such as the Convention on the Elimination of Discrimination against Women (CEDAW) and the Convention on the Elimination of Racial Discrimination (CERD).[103] The text points to certain state practices (acts or omissions), namely disability-based distinctions, exclusions or restrictions, that have certain (illegitimate) purposes or negative effects on the recognition, enjoyment or exercise of human rights and fundamental freedoms. This prohibition of discrimination has been interpreted to include not only rights-restricting policies that are expressly based on a prohibited discrimination ground, but also policies that are based on other grounds but have a disparate impact on members of a protected group. The latter is often called indirect discrimination.[104] This means that the prohibition of discrimination applies to domestic policies that restrict the use of compulsory health care interventions to people with psychosocial disabilities only. This is in addition to policies that authorise the coercive care of both people with psychosocial disabilities *and people without* psychosocial disabilities if such policies nevertheless affect the former group disproportionately.

The CRPD treaty text is silent on whether policies and practices that come within the ambit of the definition of disability-based discrimination can be justified. Other UN human rights treaties are similarly silent on whether discriminatory practices can be justified. Still, these treaties have been interpreted so as *not* to prohibit every policy that adversely affects individuals for reasons connected with their sex, ethnicity, religion, social origin, etc. Policies and practices that pursue legitimate aims and are based on 'objective and reasonable criteria' do not violate the prohibition of discrimination under these treaties. There are good arguments for supposing that the CRPD allows for a similar justification of domestic policies. Such an interpretation ensures that the Convention's protection against disability-based discrimination matches corresponding prohibitions of discrimination in other international human

[103] CEDAW Art 1; CERD Art 1.

[104] CRPD Committee (n 64) para 18(b); Human Rights Committee, 'Communication No 998/2001' *Althammer et al v Austria* (2003) UN Doc CCPR/C/74/D/803/1998 para 10.2.

rights treaties. This accords with the purpose of the Convention (that is, to ensure *equal* enjoyment of the right not to be discriminated against by people with disabilities) and with the drafters' intentions. The initial draft of the definition of discrimination expressly excluded from its ambit practices that were 'objectively and demonstrably justified by the State Party by a legitimate aim and where the means of achieving that aim are reasonable and necessary'.[105] Negotiating states favouring such a clause held that it codified the normative content of the prohibition of discrimination under current international human rights law and thereby helped to clarify the scope of state obligations in relation to this prohibition.[106] The majority of the negotiating parties, however, rejected this argument. They disagreed not because they thought that it misrepresented what constitutes unlawful discrimination. Instead, they believed that the explicit reference to the possibility of justifying prima facie discriminatory practices would signal that disability-based discrimination was different from other types of discrimination and, therefore, more easily justified.[107] To avoid this, overt references to the possibility of justifying disability-related, rights-restricting practices were omitted.[108] I cannot but interpret this as expressing an intention for the CRPD to be viewed in the light of existing human rights standards.

Moreover, it can be argued that interpreting the prohibition of discrimination as a prohibition of *all* state action that qualifies as direct or indirect discrimination produces highly questionable – if not manifestly unreasonable – results. To see this, consider the following example. Suppose that the fire service is seeking to hire new staff and that it requires all job applicants to take a number of physical tests. Such a requirement is likely to have a disparate impact on people with certain disabilities. If the fire service is looking for administrative staff, then great physical strength and ability may not be an essential qualification for the job. If, on the other hand, the fire service is looking for firefighters, few would say that rejecting applicants who do not meet a minimum standard of physical fitness is unlawful because it discriminates on the basis of disability. A prohibition of *all* actions that have a disparate impact on the rights of people with disabilities, however, would imply that rejecting

[105] Compilation of Proposed Revisions and Amendments Made by the Members of the Ad Hoc Committee to the Draft Text Presented by the Working Group as a Basis for Negotiations by Member States and Observers in the Ad Hoc Committee, Annex II to the Report of the Third Session of the Ad Hoc Committee on a Comprehensive and Integral International Convention on the Protection and Promotion of the Rights and Dignity of Persons with Disabilities (9 June 2004) UN Doc A/AC.265/2004/5 Art 7. See also fn 26 of the Report.

[106] Ad Hoc Committee, 'Daily Summary of Discussion at the Fourth Session' (2 September 2004) www.un.org/esa/socdev/enable/rights/ahc4sum02sep.htm (see in particular recorded statements by the Netherlands (on behalf of the EU), Israel, Canada and the Coordinator).

[107] *Ibid* (see statements by Mexico, New Zealand, Norway, Israel and the Coordinator).

[108] Report of the Coordinator to the Ad Hoc Committee at its Fourth Session, Annex IV to the Fourth Session Report of the Ad Hoc Committee on a Comprehensive and Integral International Convention to Promote and Protect the Rights and Dignity of Persons with Disabilities (14 September 2004) UN Doc A/59/360 paras 25–26.

such applicants was unlawful.[109] This does not cohere with how the prohibition of discrimination is understood in human rights law in international and domestic jurisprudence.[110] The UN treaty bodies have developed a standard for distinguishing between lawful and unlawful discriminatory state practices. This standard in discussed in the next section.

B. The Objective and Reasonable Standard

The CRPD Committee has recognised that state policies falling within the ambit of the prohibition of disability-based discrimination may under certain circumstances be justified, but it has devoted little attention to the question of what standard such justifications must meet.[111] According to jurisprudence from other UN treaty bodies, prima facie discriminatory laws and practices that serve 'legitimate aims' and are based on 'objective and reasonable criteria' do not violate the prohibition of discrimination laid down in the UN human rights treaties.[112] Legitimate aims are aims that are 'compatible with the provisions, aims and objectives' of the treaty in question.[113] None of the UN treaty bodies have elaborated on how such compatibility is to be determined. However, a number of public interests have been acknowledged as legitimate aims: for example, public health,[114] public order,[115] public safety[116] and the protection of the rights of others,[117] to name but a few.

Besides pursuing legitimate aims, rights restrictions must be based on objective and reasonable criteria. Domestic laws and practices that are based on objective criteria are those that contribute to their (legitimate) aims. The fact that Canadian regulations that mandated safety headgear for railway workers contributed to worker safety led the Human Rights Committee to

[109] I do not rule out the possibility that the use of physical tests for prospective firefighters may be discriminatory under certain circumstances – for example, if the test requires the applicant to demonstrate *more* physical fitness than is necessary for the job.

[110] The same argument is made by Dawson (n 30) 75.

[111] CRPD Committee, 'Communication No 9/2012' *AF v Italy* (2015) UN Doc CRPD/C/13/D/9/2012 para 8.5; CRPD Committee, 'Communication No 39/2017' *Iuliia Domina and Max Bendtsen v Denmark* (2018) UN Doc CRPD/C/20/D/39/2017 para 8.3; CRPD Committee, 'Communication No 3/2011' *HM v Sweden* (2012) UN Doc CRPD/C/7/D/3/2011 para 8.3.

[112] A Nilsson, 'Objective and Reasonable? Scrutinising Compulsory Mental Health Interventions from a Non- discrimination Perspective' (2014) 14 *Human Rights Law Review* 459, 463f.

[113] Human Rights Committee, 'Communication No 1932/2010' *Fedotova v the Russian Federation* (2012) UN Doc CCPR/C/106/D/1932/2010 paras 10.4–10.5.

[114] *Ibid* para 10.6.

[115] Human Rights Committee, 'Communication No 854/1999' *Wackenheim v France* (2002) UN Doc CCPR/C/75/D/854/1999 para 7.4.

[116] Human Rights Committee, 'Communication No 1493/2006' *Williams Lecraft v Spain* (2009) UN Doc CCPR/C/98/D/1493/2006 para 7.2.

[117] Human Rights Committee, 'Communication No 566/1993' *Somers v Hungary* (1996) UN Doc CCPR/C/53/D/566/1993 para 9.8.

accept the policy, even though it prevented Sikh workers from wearing a turban and thereby interfered with their freedom of religion.[118] The degree of contribution required – meaning 'how much' the policy or practice must promote the aim – remains an open question. In many of the cases brought before the UN treaty bodies, this question was not discussed. For example, in the Canadian case, no one asked how much protective helmets contribute to worker safety. However, if the effectiveness of the policy under review is disputed, then states parties need to demonstrate its connection with the achievement of the legitimate aim. As a minimum requirement, the policy must not be irrelevant to the achievement of the aim.[119] What is more, if the policy stipulates differential treatment on the basis of a protected non-discrimination ground, and can thus be characterised as directly discriminatory, it does not suffice to demonstrate that the policy contributes to the aim pursued. States parties also need to explain why *differentiation* based on any of the non-discrimination grounds is relevant vis-à-vis the aim pursued. The Human Rights Committee has, for example, examined and rejected an immigration policy that treated men and women differently. The policy aimed at protecting national security and restricted migrants' rights to enter and reside in the country. The rights of male migrants were restricted to a greater extent than those of female migrants. The Committee held that, although security considerations may justify constraints on migration rights, this aim could not justify the differential treatment of men and women.[120] It should be noted that, in this case, the fact that the policy in question had been introduced following a number of events in which male migrants (and not female migrants) were suspected of subversive activities, was not considered to be a sufficient reason to differentiate based on gender.[121] Returning to the mental health context, this means that CRPD states parties that want to retain national legislation providing for compulsory interventions against people with psychosocial disabilities *but not against other health care users* must not only demonstrate that coercive intervention is relevant to the protection of health and prevention of violence; they have a more challenging task, namely to demonstrate that, in order to achieve these aims, there are valid reasons for authorising the use of compulsion against people with psychosocial disabilities that do not exist in the case of people without psychosocial disabilities.

The other component of the objective and reasonable standard is more elusive: whether the policy or practice under scrutiny is 'reasonable'. What

[118] Human Rights Committee, 'Communication No 208/1986' *Bhinder v Canada* (1981) UN Doc CCPR/C/37/D/208/1986 para 6.2.

[119] See Human Rights Committee's reasoning in 'Communication No 2172/2012' *G v Australia* (2017) UN Doc CCPR/C/119/D/2172/2012 paras 7.7–7.9 and 'Communication No 1361/2005' *X v Colombia* (2007) UN Doc CCPR/C/89/D/1361/2005 para 7.2.

[120] Human Rights Committee, 'Communication No 35/1978' *Mauritian Women v Mauritius* (1981) UN Doc CCPR/C/OP/1 para 9.2(b) 2 (ii) 3.

[121] *Ibid* para 5.1.

constitutes a reasonable policy, or how a reasonable policy can be distinguished from an unreasonable one, has not been discussed in general terms. It is clear from the jurisprudence of the treaty bodies, however, that a plurality of reasons may be taken into account when seeking to determine whether a policy is reasonable. The *effects* of the policy under review should be considered. Laws or practices that have very serious consequences for those concerned are less likely to be deemed reasonable. The first individual complaint brought before the CRPD Committee illustrates this point. The case concerned the rejection of a building permit for an indoor hydrotherapy pool. The reason for refusing the building permit was that the proposed pool violated the local plan for the built environment. For the claimant, the pool was her only hope of continuing to live at home. Without it, she would have had to move to a specialist health care institution. Under such circumstances, the Committee concluded, refusing the building permit was disproportionate and in violation of the prohibition of discrimination.[122] Other cases in which the negative effects of a policy appear to have played an important role in the Committee coming to the conclusion that the prohibition of discrimination had been violated include *Marlon James Noble v Australia* and *X v Argentina*. The first case concerned an unfitness to plead policy that allowed people with intellectual disabilities to be incarcerated for unlimited periods of time and prevented those detained from having their cases tested on the merits. These negative effects, in combination with the state's failure to provide the claimant with the support and accommodation he requested to exercise his legal capacity, led the Committee to conclude that the policy in question was discriminatory.[123] In the second case, the Committee found that the substandard conditions of a detention facility, in which the claimant was unable to access, on his own, the bathroom, shower, recreation yard and nursing service, violated the right to respect for personal integrity on an equal basis with others.[124]

In the treaty bodies' jurisprudence, there are also examples of cases in which state practices that severely restricted individuals' entitlements under human rights law have been accepted. In a case concerning the restitution of confiscated property, the Human Rights Committee concluded that a system allowing tenants the option to buy the property they were living in (a 'first-buy option') was reasonable even though it severely restricted the rights of previous owners. This conclusion was motivated by the fact that the current tenants had been living there for years and had contributed to the maintenance of the property. Their interests as tenants therefore deserved protection, the Committee held.[125]

[122] *HM v Sweden* (n 111) paras 8.5 and 8.8.

[123] CRPD Committee, 'Communication No 7/2012' *Marlon James Noble v Australia* (2016) UN Doc CRPD/C/16/D/7/2012 para 8.4.

[124] CRPD Committee, 'Communication No 8/2012' *X v Argentina* (2014) UN Doc CRPD/C/11/D/8/2012 paras 8.5–8.6.

[125] *Somers v Hungary* (n 117) para 9.8.

The Committee also found that a total ban on an activity that constituted the claimant's main source of income was reasonable because it was *necessary* to protect public order.[126] Another factor that was taken into account was whether those affected by the rights restriction had a reasonable *choice*, that is, whether they could be expected to choose alternatives to avoid the negative effects of the state practice in question. For example, the differential treatment of married and unmarried cohabiting couples, to the detriment of the latter, has been accepted as reasonable as long as marriage is an option open to those subject to the disadvantageous treatment.[127] In situations in which national law does not provide same-sex partners with the right to marry, disadvantageous treatment of this group based on their status as unmarried has been judged unreasonable.[128]

Apart from state practices that aim to advance de facto equality or equality of results, the UN treaty bodies have been reluctant to accept state action that explicitly differentiates members of groups protected under non-discrimination law from other persons.[129] They have been more reluctant to accept such direct discrimination than they have been to accept state practices that operate with other criteria but that nevertheless have a disparate impact on a protected group. At the time of writing, the CRPD Committee has outlawed all domestic systems that differentiate on the basis of disability/impairment. In its general comment on equality and non-discrimination, the Committee went as far as to say that Article 5(1) of the Convention, on equality before the law, implies that 'there should be no laws that allow for specific denial, restriction or limitation of the rights of persons with disabilities'.[130] Precisely how this will affect policies that differentiate on the basis of disability in practice remains to be seen. The Human Rights Committee has gone into slightly more detail about the reasons behind its reluctance to accept differential treatment based on discrimination grounds. Considering a piece of legislation that made it difficult for spouses to take the wife's (as opposed to the husband's) surname as the family name, the Human Rights Committee reasoned as follows:

> A differentiation based on reasonable and objective criteria does not amount to prohibited discrimination within the meaning of Article 26. A different treatment based on one of the specific grounds enumerated in Article 26, clause 2 of the

[126] *Wackenheim v France* (n 115) para 7.4. The Committee concluded that the means in question (in this case a prohibition of a public activity in which the claimant, wearing protective gear, would allow himself to be thrown onto an air bed) was necessary to protect public order and thus (objective and) reasonable, without, however, discussing and rejecting alternative ways of achieving the aim.

[127] T Choudhury, 'Interpreting the Right to Equality under Article 26 of the International Covenant on Civil and Political Rights' (2003) 1 *European Human Rights Law Review* 24, 44.

[128] *X v Colombia* (n 119) para 7.2.

[129] This is often referred to within the discrimination literature as 'affirmative action' and within human rights law as 'special measures', 'temporary special measures' or 'specific measures'. See CERD Art 1(4); CEDAW Art 4(1); CRPD Art 5(4).

[130] CRPD Committee (n 64) para 14.

> Covenant, however, *places a heavy burden* on the State party to explain the reason for the differentiation.[131]

Neither the fact that the law reflected the prevailing custom in that society nor the fact that the wish to assume the wife's surname as the family name could be accommodated using special procedures constituted a sufficient justification for the law. The conclusion was reached 'in view of the importance of the principle of equality between men and women'.[132] The statement concerning the heavy burden of justification can be interpreted in at least two ways: descriptively or prescriptively. It can be understood as an empirical claim about the fact that disadvantageous treatment based on sex (or any of the other discrimination grounds) rarely contributes to a legitimate aim and is often unreasonable. Indeed, the history of discrimination is replete with examples of segregation, subordination and exclusion based on ideas of women and marginalised groups as not qualified or worthy of participation in politics or other public arenas.[133] Alternatively, the statement can be understood as a normative claim to the effect that rights restrictions based on discrimination grounds are different from rights restrictions based on other reasons: they are (morally) worse. The past and present comparative social disadvantage experienced by women, people of colour, people with disabilities and other groups covered by the list of non-discrimination grounds makes such differentiation particularly bad. It trades on these patterns of injustice and tends to exacerbate conditions of inequality. This coheres with the treaty bodies' approach to what is often referred to as racial or ethnic profiling, that is, the use by law enforcement of ethnic characteristics (skin colour, clothing, etc) as a basis for suspecting certain individuals of unlawful behaviour.[134] The Human Rights Committee and the Committee on the Elimination of Racial Discrimination have on several occasions expressed the view that such profiling violates the prohibition of discrimination. In a case concerning an identity check on a black woman at a train station, the Human Rights Committee concluded that identity checks carried out for public security purposes or to control immigration serve legitimate aims but that identity checks must not be based on 'physical or ethnic characteristics' alone and that they should not 'be carried out in such a way as to target only persons with specific physical or ethnic characteristics'.[135] To act otherwise, in the Committee's

[131] Human Rights Committee, 'Communication No 919/2000' *Müller and Engelhard v Namibia* (2002) UN Doc CCPR/C/74/D/919/2000 para 6.7 (emphasis added). See also *Mauritian Women v Mauritius* (n 120) para 9.2(b) 2 (ii) 3.

[132] *Müller and Engelhard v Namibia*, ibid para 6.8.

[133] For example, the many laws that, in the past, prevented women from voting, owning property or pursuing certain professions. D Hellman, *When is Discrimination Wrong?* (Cambridge, Massachusetts, Harvard University Press, 2008) 133.

[134] O De Schutter and J Ringelheim, 'Ethnic Profiling: A Rising Challenge for European Human Rights Law' (2008) 71 *The Modern Law Review* 358, 361f. Such profiling is commonly used proactively to prevent criminal acts.

[135] *Williams Lecraft v Spain* (n 116) para 7.2.

view, is not only an affront to the dignity of the person concerned, but also a way of contributing to the spread of xenophobic attitudes among the public at large; it thus runs counter to an effective policy aimed at combating racial discrimination.[136]

The UN treaty bodies have sometimes couched their reasoning about the reasonableness of certain rights restrictions for the individuals concerned in terms of *proportionality*. In the case concerning the rejection of an application for a building permit, mentioned above, the CRPD Committee held that domestic authorities had not given due weight to the specific circumstances of the case (namely to the disability-related needs of the applicant). This lack of proportionality between the negative effects of the decision and the aim behind the decision 'produced a discriminatory effect' in violation of the Convention.[137] In a case concerning laws restricting the voting rights of persons under guardianship, the CRPD Committee argued, among other things, that such laws are not 'proportional to the aim of preserving the integrity of the State party's political system'.[138] Other treaty bodies have made similar references to proportionality.[139] Whether proportionality ought to be understood as a *tool* for reasoning about the reasonableness of rights restrictions or as a *criterion* that is either part of or an addition to the reasonableness criterion is a matter for debate, and the committees' brisk reasoning on these matters does not allow us to draw definite conclusions. Their proportionality reasoning typically includes a description of the state practice under review that details its aim(s) and some of its effects, and the committees commonly proceed to a conclusion about whether the law or practice is proportionate or disproportionate on the basis of such descriptions of the facts, without clearly explaining the relevance and weight of the factual circumstances in relation to the outcome.[140]

VII. THE CRPD'S APPROACH TO MENTAL HEALTH CARE IN BRIEF

In this chapter, I have demonstrated that much of the originality in the CRPD's approach to mental health care lies in its emphasis on the principle that people with disabilities have an entitlement to *equal* enjoyment of rights and in the

[136] *Williams Lecraft v Spain* (n 116) para 7.2.

[137] *HM v Sweden* (n 111) paras 8.5 and 8.8.

[138] *Bujdosó et al v Hungary* (n 95) para 9.6.

[139] See, eg, Human Rights Committee, 'Communication No 932/2000' *Gillot et al v France* (2002) UN Doc CCPR/C/75/D/932/2000 paras 13.2 and 13.17; Committee on the Elimination of Racial Discrimination, 'Communication No 42/2008' *DR v Australia* (2009) UN Doc CERD/C/75/D/42/2008 para 7.3; Committee on Economic, Social, and Cultural Rights, 'General Comment 20 on Non-Discrimination in Economic, Social and Cultural Rights (Art 2, para 2)' (10 June 2009) UN Doc E/C.12/GC/20 para 13.

[140] See, eg, *Bujdosó et al v Hungary* (n 95) para 9.6. As described above, the CRPD Committee is slightly more detailed in its reasoning on the merits in *HM v Sweden* (n 111) paras 8.5 and 8.8. See also *Gillot et al v France* (n 139) paras 13.2 and 13.17.

fact that the treaty text contains no provisions explicitly permitting compulsory mental health interventions. This marks a break from previous human rights law and provides a much-needed means to challenge the inequalities inherent in much domestic mental health legislation. An interpretation of the treaty text according to the rules for the interpretation of international treaties enables us to label certain practices as unlawful without having to engage in equality analysis. This includes mental health laws according to which the existence of a 'disability' – understood to mean the presence of a psychosocial condition – is a sufficient reason to deprive an individual of her liberty. This clearly violates Article 14(1)(b) of the Convention. In addition, Article 12 grants people with psychosocial disabilities the same right as people without such disabilities to reject clinical treatment. The mere fact that someone has a psychiatric diagnosis can never justify disregarding that person's treatment preferences. Article 12 further asserts that the primary response to situations in which someone has difficulty exercising his or her legal capacity should be to provide support. In some situations, support will indeed be sufficient to enable free and informed health care decisions to be made. In such situations, the mere fact that a failure to treat entails a risk of harm to the health or life of the individual concerned does not constitute sufficient reason to impose treatment. People who, with or without support, are able to make free and informed decisions about their medical treatment are, in principle, free to reject treatment even in situations in which such a decision may have fatal consequences.[141] Last but not least, the prohibition of inhuman or degrading treatment sets a basic limit on what kind of medical treatment can be imposed on people. Under no circumstances may states subject people to medical or scientific experimentation without their consent.[142] Neither may states detain people in psychiatric facilities in deplorable conditions or without sufficient protection against ill treatment from medical staff or others.[143] Such ill treatment can take many forms, but it includes the use of outdated treatment methods that are no longer accepted as evidence-based treatment and the administration of medication and treatment for illegitimate purposes, for instance to punish or intimidate the person concerned. Article 17 complements the prohibition of inhuman and degrading treatment by outlawing abusive practices with less severe implications.

The answers to many other questions concerning the lawfulness of compulsory mental health interventions depend essentially on equality or non-discrimination analysis. One such question is: are states permitted to authorise the compulsory care of people with psychosocial disabilities in situations where the person concerned is considered to lack the ability to make free and informed health care decisions? Another is: are states permitted to authorise

[141] See Section V.
[142] CRPD Art 15.
[143] See section IV. See also *X v Argentina* (n 124) paras 8.5–8.6.

such compulsion where there is a risk that a person with a psychosocial disability will harm themselves or others? The CRPD prohibits discrimination based on disability and defines such discrimination as any act (or omission) that has the purpose or effect of limiting the equal enjoyment of human rights and fundamental freedoms by persons with disabilities. Compulsory mental health interventions typically circumscribe the rights of people with psychosocial disabilities to liberty, integrity, and legal capacity more than they do those of health care users without disabilities. Consequently, compulsory mental health interventions fall within the CRPD's definition of discrimination, so a justification is required if these interventions are to be deemed lawful.

The CRPD Committee has paid little attention to the question of what the relevant standard is when it comes to the justification of disability-based discrimination. I argue that the objective and reasonable standard defines the limits of lawful state action in this case. As I conceptualise it in this book, this standard requires that the mental health regime in question have a *legitimate aim*, that it *contribute* to the achievement of its aim, and that it be *reasonable* in light of the aim. The standard includes a requirement that the rationale behind laws that differentiate on the basis of a protected ground or that have a disparate impact on protected groups be explained or justified. The precise scope and content of the third criterion (reasonableness) is disputed. The UN treaty bodies have not explained in general terms what constitutes a reasonable measure or how a reasonable measure ought to be distinguished from an unreasonable one. It is clear that a plurality of reasons may be taken into account in determining reasonableness and that the effects of the measures under consideration must not be unduly burdensome for those concerned. Moreover, attention must be paid to the 'necessity' of the measure in light of the aim. The next chapter applies the objective and reasonable standard to typical domestic authorisations of civil detention and compulsory psychiatric care. This will provide a more concrete account of the legal implications of the rights to enjoy legal capacity, liberty and respect for integrity on an equal basis with others for domestic mental health legislation.

2

Putting Mental Health Laws to the Test

I. APPLYING THE OBJECTIVE AND REASONABLE STANDARD

THIS CHAPTER APPLIES the objective and reasonable standard at the domestic level. The purpose of this exercise is to give a more concrete account of the legal implications of the UN Convention on the Rights of Persons with Disabilities (CRPD)[1] for domestic mental health legislation. The next section, section II, provides some preliminary background information, describing key elements of mental health laws that permit compulsory psychiatric care. The assessment starts in section III with a discussion of whether compulsory mental health interventions serve legitimate aims. I provide an analysis of whether domestic systems for compulsory care can be said to be based on objective criteria. This analysis includes a discussion of relevant empirical data on the contribution made by these systems to the common aims of compulsory care, that is, the protection of the health and life of the patient and the protection of others. This section also considers common justifications for subjecting people with psychosocial disabilities, but not people without such disabilities, to coercive care, in light of these aims. Section V addresses the third criterion of the objective and reasonable standard, that is, the reasonableness of the laws and policies under review. As I concluded in the previous chapter, assessments of reasonableness take a plurality of reasons into account and balance these against one another. The main findings of this application of the objective and reasonable test to domestic laws are summarised in section VI. It will come as no surprise that an application of this fairly abstract and vague standard to concrete examples of authorisations of compulsory care gives rise to additional questions that have not been dealt with by the UN treaty bodies.

II. DOMESTIC MENTAL HEALTH LEGISLATION

Compulsory intervention is a common element of mental health regimes around the world. Civil detention is a common response to situations in which people

[1] Convention on the Rights of Persons with Disabilities (adopted 13 December 2006, entered into force 3 May 2008) 2515 UNTS 3 (CRPD).

with psychosocial conditions of a certain kind or severity refuse care that they are believed to require and at least one of four additional criteria is satisfied. These are that the individual:

- lacks decision-making ability;
- is at risk of serious deterioration of health;
- is at risk of self-harm; or
- is at risk of harming others (sometimes formulated as posing a 'danger' to others).[2]

The precise combination of conditions for compulsory admission to a psychiatric hospital and the meaning and scope of these criteria vary across jurisdictions. For example, Swedish law limits the group of people who may be hospitalised against their will to people with 'severe psychiatric conditions' and excludes people diagnosed only with intellectual disabilities.[3] Other jurisdictions delineate the target group differently. Elizabeth Fistein and colleagues have compared mental health law in diverse Commonwealth jurisdictions. They identify five categories of diagnosis criteria applied across the jurisdictions. These range from jurisdictions that have 'no legal definition' of the mental conditions that may justify the imposition of compulsory care, to those that have medical approaches based on internationally recognised systems of classification such as the International Classification of Diseases, published by the World Health Organisation, or the Diagnostic and Statistical Manual for Mental Disorders, published by the American Psychiatric Association.[4] In several jurisdictions, the conditions for civil detention do not explicitly refer to a lack of decision-making ability.[5] Rather, it is implicit in the diagnostic criteria in the sense that only conditions that have a certain impact on the individual's ability to make treatment decisions will qualify as psychosocial conditions that may justify compulsory intervention under the law in question.[6] When it comes to requirements relating to the risk of certain adverse effects or events (deterioration of health, self-harm and harm to others), there are variations among jurisdictions as regards how likely it must be that the adverse event will occur and how serious the adverse event must be to warrant intervention. The risk of self-harm is

[2] The language of risk has replaced that of dangerousness in much mental health law. 'Dangerousness' was seen as a trait possessed by certain individuals. 'Risk' has different connotations: we can all, at least in principle, be placed on a continuum of risk. Nevertheless, risk assessments within psychiatry are focused on identifying those at high risk of problematic behaviour. For a discussion of this point, see G Szmukler and N Rose, 'Risk Assessment in Mental Health Care: Values and Costs' (2013) 31 *Behavioral Sciences and the Law* 125, 131ff.

[3] Act (SFS: 1991:1128) on Compulsory Psychiatric Care, Sweden, para 3.

[4] EC Fistein et al, 'A Comparison of Mental Health Legislation from Diverse Commonwealth Jurisdictions' (2009) 32 *International Journal of Law and Psychiatry* 147, 149–50.

[5] See, eg, Swedish Act on Compulsory Psychiatric Care (n 3) para 3.

[6] In the Swedish context, this is explicated in the bill 1990/91:58 on compulsory psychiatric care, at 86 and 238.

sometimes conceptualised in a narrow sense that includes suicide and serious forms of self-harming behaviour (self-mutilation, self-cutting, ingestion of toxic substances, etc) or in a broader sense that includes the neglect of basic personal needs (sleep, food, hygiene, etc) and even the loss of social networks. Similarly, the risk of harm to others may refer only to physical harm or include emotional harm and financial loss.[7] Finally, many jurisdictions treat civil detention as a means of last resort, reserved for situations in which no voluntary or less restrictive alternatives are available.[8]

Domestic law usually makes clear that any clinical treatment during hospitalisation should, in principle, be based on the free and informed consent of the patient. Nonetheless, most jurisdictions authorise the compulsory administration of medication and other forms of clinical treatment under certain circumstances. Under Swedish law, people admitted for compulsory psychiatric care cannot refuse medication that is deemed to be necessary to protect the patient's health and achieve the aims of the coercive care.[9] Treatment decisions should be taken in consultation with the person concerned (and close relatives, if appropriate), but it is the attending psychiatrist who makes the final decision.[10] The mental health legislation of several other EU Member States incorporates similar obligations for health care staff to involve the patient in decisions about the care provided, coupled with the power to impose treatment if no agreement is reached.[11] Some jurisdictions lay down specific restrictions on certain treatment methods that are of a particularly painful, intrusive or irreversible nature. For example, the Mental Health Act 1983, which applies in England and Wales, contains restrictions on the use of electroconvulsive therapy and on the use of courses of medication that continue for more than three months.[12] If such treatments are to be administered without the consent of the person concerned, a second opinion from another appointed psychiatrist is necessary. Electroconvulsive therapy cannot be forced on someone who possesses decision-making ability or who has rejected such interventions in a valid and applicable advance directive.[13] The legal system in Ontario (Canada) attaches more weight to the presence of decision-making ability. According to the Health Care Consent Act 1996, which also applies to people who are subject

[7] Fistein et al, 'A Comparison' 149–50.

[8] See, eg, European Union Agency for Fundamental Rights, *Involuntary Placement and Involuntary Treatment of Persons with Mental Health Problems* (Luxembourg, Publications Office of the European Union, 2012) 33; Initial Reports Submitted by States Parties under Article 35 of the Convention from Australia (submitted 3 December 2010, published 7 June 2012) UN Doc CRPD/C/AUS/1 para 76 and Argentina (submitted 6 October 2010, published 28 June 2011) CRPD/C/ARG/1 para 200.

[9] Swedish Act on Compulsory Psychiatric Care (n 3) para 17.

[10] Swedish Act on Compulsory Psychiatric Care (n 3) para 17.

[11] European Union Agency for Fundamental Rights, *Involuntary Placement* 34.

[12] Mental Health Act 1983 (England and Wales) ss 58 and 58A.

[13] *Ibid* and J Dawson, 'A Realistic Approach to Assessing Mental Health Laws' Compliance with the UNCRPD' (2015) 40 *International Journal of Law and Psychiatry* 71, 76.

to compulsory inpatient care, free and informed treatment refusals cannot be overridden.[14] Even in emergency situations, such wishes must be respected if the person is above 16 years old and able to communicate his or her decision to reject treatment.[15]

The Mental Capacity Act (Northern Ireland) 2016 goes one step further. The law states that compulsory health interventions (detention and treatment alike) involving people aged 16 and older may only proceed if the person concerned is unable to make an informed decision on the matter. Such inability is at hand if the health care user fails to understand the information relevant to the decision, retain that information for the time required to make the decision, appreciate the relevance of that information, use and weigh it as part of the process of making the decision, or is unable to communicate his or her decision.[16] Health care users who struggle with treatment decisions are entitled to support, and no one can be considered to lack decision-making ability unless all practicable help and support have been provided.[17] This means that, in Northern Ireland, everyone with decision-making ability can effectively refuse treatment and that adults with psychosocial conditions can no longer be hospitalised and treated against their expressed preferences on the basis of the risk of harm to health, of suicide, or of violent behaviour alone. People who lack decision-making ability can still be detained and treated against their will if such interventions are considered to be in their 'best interests', taking into account the past and present wishes of the person concerned and any relevant written statement made by the person when he or she had decision-making ability.[18] This law has been supported by many as a progressive piece of legislation based on the principle of non-discrimination.[19] It has also been criticised as not going far enough to eliminate every element of discrimination from the mental health system. Authorisations of compulsory care that use decision-making ability as a central criterion, it has been argued, will have a disproportionate impact on people with psychosocial disabilities and, because of the relatively loose nature of the current tests for assessing decision-making ability, may even increase the use

[14] Health Consent Act (Ontario) 1996 (Canada) SO ch 2, sch A, ss 10, 25(3) and 26. Under this law, an emergency situation is one in which 'the person for whom the treatment is proposed is apparently experiencing severe suffering or is at risk, if the treatment is not administered promptly, of sustaining serious bodily harm'. See s 25(1).

[15] *Ibid* s 10.1(b).

[16] Mental Capacity Act (Northern Ireland) 2016 pt 1, s 4.

[17] *Ibid* ss 1(3)(b) and 5.

[18] *Ibid* ss 2 and 7. To establish 'best interests', decision-makers are also required, as far as is practicable, to encourage the individual concerned to participate as fully as possible in determining his or her best interests and to support the individual in doing so.

[19] eg G Szmukler and J Dawson, 'Reducing Discrimination in Mental Health Law: The "Fusion" of Incapacity and Mental Health Legislation' in T Kallert, J Mezzich, and J Monahan (eds), *Coercive Treatment in Psychiatry* (Chichester, Wiley-Blackwell, 2011) 98ff.

of compulsory health care intervention.[20] Some jurisdictions in Australia have implemented similar reforms to limit the use of compulsory care to people who are considered to lack the ability to express valid consent, and there are many other examples of jurisdictions that have brought in such reforms, but I will not discuss these here.[21]

To sum up, compulsory interventions are commonly permitted under mental health legislation at the national level around the world. Civil detention is a common response to situations in which people with psychosocial disabilities refuse treatment and a failure to treat is considered likely to put the health or life of the person concerned at risk. Many jurisdictions also provide for compulsory care to prevent violence against others. Mental health laws often conceptualise civil detention as a means of last resort, reserved for situations in which no voluntary or less restrictive alternatives are available. During the hospitalisation that follows civil detention, mental health laws generally provide for compulsory clinical interventions, should they be deemed necessary to avoid the deterioration of the patient's health. Following the entry into force of the CRPD, there has been a growing trend towards granting individuals who are deemed to possess adequate decision-making abilities the right to reject clinical treatment. In what follows, I will discuss whether compulsory care regimes can be justified under the objective and reasonable standard, that is, whether they serve legitimate aims, contribute to the legitimate aims, and are reasonable.

III. DO COMPULSORY INTERVENTIONS SERVE LEGITIMATE AIMS?

Compulsory mental health interventions typically aim to prevent harm to the health and life of the person concerned and to prevent violence against others. Some mental health laws also seek to promote the autonomy of the person concerned by enhancing certain of their capabilities,[22] and some domestic statutes permit interventions for the purposes of avoiding social and financial harms.[23] In this study, I have chosen to focus on three aims in particular, namely the protection of health, the protection of life and the protection of third parties. To qualify as legitimate under the objective and reasonable standard, these aims must not conflict with the CRPD's purpose or substantive rights provisions.[24] All three aims arguably satisfy this criterion. One must distinguish

[20] eg E Flynn, 'Mental (In)Capacity or Legal Capacity? A Human Rights Analysis of the Proposed Fusion of Mental Health and Mental Capacity Law in Northern Ireland' (2013) 64 *Northern Ireland Legal Quarterly* 485, 490f.

[21] eg Mental Health Act 2013 (Tasmania) s 40(e); Mental Health Act 2016 (Queensland) s 12(1)(b).

[22] See, eg, Swedish Act on Compulsory Psychiatric Care (n 3) para 2.

[23] See, eg, the Dutch Act (1992) on Psychiatric Hospitals (Compulsory Admissions) Arts 1, 2, and 14a.

[24] See ch 1, section VI.B.

here between aims and means. Whilst the use of coercive means may clash with the general principle to respect autonomous choices (CRPD, Article 3), there is no necessary or inherent conflict between the protection of health and life and the principle of respect for autonomy and self-determination. Quite the opposite, in fact: Articles 10 and 25 concern the rights to health and life of people with disabilities and obliges states parties to implement a range of measures to ensure that people with disabilities have access to general health care services, as well as to the services they need because of their impairments. This supports the claim that the protection of life and health constitute legitimate aims under the Convention. The CRPD Committee has even interpreted Article 10, on the right to life, to include an obligation to prevent suicide, an interpretation that accords with how this right is conceptualised by the Human Rights Committee.[25]

Moreover, the CRPD endorses measures to prevent violence. Article 14 obliges states parties to ensure that people with psychosocial disabilities can enjoy security on an equal basis with others, and Article 16 includes an obligation to provide protection from violence and abuse. Article 4(1)(d) and (e) make explicit that the obligation to prevent violence and abuse extends to violent acts carried out by private actors. While Article 16 was drafted with certain abuses in mind, namely abuses taking place within institutional settings, including psychiatric hospitals, the general language of the Article means that it also covers situations in which people with disabilities are at risk of harming other people with disabilities.[26] Even if it does not extend to potential victims without disabilities, the Article implies that states have an obligation to combat violent crime. It would be absurd to hold that the CRPD obliges states parties to protect people with disabilities against violence from third parties but prohibits them from pursuing the same goal with respect to people without disabilities.[27] In conclusion, none of the protective aims underpinning most domestic authorisations of civil detention and compulsory clinical treatment conflict with the

[25] See, eg, CRPD Committee, Concluding Observations on the Initial Report of Sweden (adopted 11 April 2014) UN Doc CRPD/C/SWE/CO/1 paras 29–30; Human Rights Committee, 'General Comment No 36: Article 6 Right to Life' (3 September 2019) UN Doc CCPR/C/GC/36 para 9. See also *Reynolds v the United Kingdom* App no 2694/08 (European Court of Human Rights (ECtHR), 13 March 2012) paras 61–63.

[26] See Ad Hoc Committee on a Comprehensive and Integral International Convention on Protection and Promotion of the Rights and Dignity of Persons with Disabilities (Ad Hoc Committee), 'Daily Summary of Discussion at the Fourth Session' (26 August 2004) www.un.org/esa/socdev/enable/rights/ahc4sum26aug.htm (recorded statements by New Zealand, the Netherlands (on behalf of the EU), Japan and the International Disability Caucus); Ad Hoc Committee, 'Daily Summary of Discussion at the Fifth Session' (31 January 2005) www.un.org/esa/socdev/enable/rights/ahc5sum31jan.htm (statements by Thailand, New Zealand, Canada, Republic of Korea).

[27] This claim is supported further by the fact that the International Covenant on Civil and Political Rights (adopted 16 December 1966, entered into force 23 March 1976) 1999 UNTS 171 Art 9, by which many of the states parties to the CRPD are bound, requires its states parties to take appropriate measures to protect their inhabitants from foreseeable threats to life or health stemming from private actors.

purpose or provisions of the CRPD. On the contrary, the Convention endorses these aims.

IV. ARE COMPULSORY INTERVENTIONS BASED ON OBJECTIVE CRITERIA?

Domestic regimes of coercive care are commonly defended with arguments about the serious harms that would occur in the absence of such care. A closer look at such arguments gives rise to a number of questions that need further consideration before any conclusions may be drawn about the objectivity (and reasonableness) of compulsory mental health interventions. A critical question is whether compulsory interventions do indeed *contribute* to their aims.[28] Do civil detention and compulsory clinical interventions protect the health and life of those subjected to such practices, and do such interventions prevent violence against others? A related but separate question concerns the relevance of subjecting people with psychosocial disabilities, but not people without such disabilities, to coercive care in order to achieve these aims. Many states have systems of compulsory mental health care that apply to people with psychosocial disabilities only and thereby fit the definition of direct discrimination. As I explained in chapter one, these states must provide a justification for differentiating between these two groups.[29] In what follows, I address these matters in relation to each of the aims of compulsory intervention separately, starting with the aim of protecting health.

A. The Protection of the Health of the Person Concerned

Do compulsory interventions contribute to the aim of protecting the health of those subjected to such practices? The existing research conveys a nuanced picture: in short, compulsory care helps some but not others. A literature review of studies of the outcomes of compulsory mental health care concludes that, although most inpatients showed signs of clinical improvement upon discharge, the proportion of study participants who considered their hospitalisation to have been helpful varied greatly between studies (from 39 per cent to 81 per cent), and a substantial proportion of them (between 6 per cent and 33 per cent) reported no benefits from the treatment provided.[30] One plausible explanation for why compulsory care tends to be less effective than voluntary treatment is that perceived coercion creates negative expectations of treatment and undermines trust in the doctor–patient relationship, which in turn has a

[28] See ch 1, section VI.B.
[29] *Ibid.*
[30] C Katsakou and S Priebe, 'Outcomes of Involuntary Hospital Admission: A Review' (2006) 114 *Acta Psychiatrica Scandinavica* 232.

negative impact on treatment outcomes.[31] The negative experience of being detained and coerced may also hamper the process of recovery. Other factors that are associated with lower levels of satisfaction with care include repeated admissions for compulsory care, being diagnosed with a severe psychiatric condition, having a high level of education, being relatively young and lacking close social relationships.[32] In addition, the health improvements observed upon discharge or shortly thereafter do not seem to persist in the longer term. Studies suggest that most people subjected to coercive inpatient care report only limited improvement in their condition one year later.[33] One year after hospitalisation, their condition was generally back to how it was before intervention.

The next question to consider is whether there are valid reasons for restricting the use of compulsory care to people with psychosocial disabilities only. Needless to say, the presence of a psychosocial condition does not in itself constitute a sufficient reason for imposing such care on this group. The question is rather whether other factors, associated with psychosocial conditions, constitute sufficient reason for the use of coercion against this group only. Most contemporary mental health laws are based on the assumption that such a justification is possible, and the main arguments concern the association of certain psychosocial conditions with diminished decision-making ability. The entry into force of the CRPD calls this presumption into question. States parties to the CRPD will need to specify which abilities they believe a person must possess in order to be able to reject medical treatment (for example the ability to understand and weigh relevant information and to communicate the choice to reject care) and explain why these abilities are necessary to this end. When engaging with this question, it must be borne in mind that a certain degree of irrationality seems to permeate all, or almost all, human decision-making. Work on the psychology of decision-making has demonstrated, for example, that we are generally poor at probability reasoning and commonly fail to weigh complex costs and benefits in a rational manner.[34] Research into irrational beliefs, including delusions and memory distortions as well as superstition and racism, has found that the irrationality present in people with psychiatric diagnoses is not different in kind

[31] See, eg, R Kaltiala-Heino, Pekka Laippala, and Raimo Salokangas, 'Impact of Coercion on Treatment Outcome' (1997) 20 *International Journal of Law and Psychiatry* 311; A Theodoridou et al, 'Therapeutic Relationship in the Context of Perceived Coercion in a Psychiatric Population' (2012) 200 *Psychiatry Research* 939. See also G Meynen and D Swaab, 'Why Medication in Involuntary Treatment May Be Less Effective: The Placebo/Nocebo Effect' (2011) 77 *Medical Hypotheses* 993.

[32] V Bird et al, 'Factors Associated with Satisfaction of Inpatient Psychiatric Care: A Cross Country Comparison' (2020) 50 *Psychological Medicine* 284.

[33] S Priebe et al, 'Predictors of Clinical and Social Outcomes Following Involuntary Hospital Admission: A Prospective Observational Study' (2011) 261 *European Archives of Psychiatry and Clinical Neuroscience* 377; G Newton-Howes and R Mullen, 'Coercion in Psychiatry Care: Systematic Review of Correlates and Themes' (2011) 62 *Psychiatric Services* 465.

[34] See, eg, the influential work of Daniel Kahneman and Amos Tversky. A Tversky and D Kahneman, 'Judgment under Uncertainty: Heuristics and Biases' (1974) 185 *Science* 1124.

from the irrationality present in others.[35] All humans make mistakes in reasoning and hold beliefs that are either badly supported by evidence or resistant to counter-evidence. Any argument concerning the supposed lack of decision-making abilities on the part of people with psychosocial disabilities must take these facts into consideration. Only deficiencies in decision-making ability that go beyond the limitations inherent in all human decision-making are relevant here.

There are a number of studies that discuss the significant impact that certain psychosocial conditions have on decision-making. For example, work on psychotic conditions has demonstrated how such conditions can distort an individual's perception of reality and his or her ability to appreciate the pros and cons of clinical treatment and the consequences of non-treatment.[36] Having said that, we also know that psychosocial conditions do not always affect such abilities negatively. A systematic review of studies of decision-making ability among people with psychosocial disabilities admitted for inpatient treatment concludes that the majority were able to consent to medical treatment.[37] What is more, people with psychosocial disabilities are not the only ones whose decision-making abilities may be affected from time to time. Although there is relatively little research into the issue, it has been suggested that a fair number of people hospitalised because of acute *somatic* conditions fail mental capacity tests when they are assessed.[38] These people include not only patients who are unconscious or, for some other reason, unable to express a preference, but also patients who, because of diminished cognitive ability (and/or a lack of support), pain, fever or other factors, have difficulties in reasoning about treatment alternatives or making choices in line with personal values.[39] Such conditions may affect decision-making abilities to varying degrees and for longer or shorter periods of time. This is as true of pain, fever, shock and apathy as it is of psychosis.

Moreover, treatment decisions are value sensitive, in the sense that the 'right' choice in a concrete situation depends on personal preferences. Therefore, it is

[35] J Craigie and L Bortolotti, 'Rationality, Diagnosis, and Patient Autonomy in Psychiatry' in JZ Sadler, KWM Fulford, and C Werendly van Staden (eds), *The Oxford Handbook of Psychiatric Ethics* (Oxford, Oxford University Press, 2015) 390–92.

[36] For a systematic review see, eg, RM Russien et al, 'A Systematic Review of the Literature about Competence and Poor Insight' (2012) 125 *Acta Psychiatrica Scandinavica* 103.

[37] D Okai et al, 'Mental Capacity in Psychiatric Patients: Systematic Review' (2007) 191 *British Journal of Psychiatry* 291. See also T Grisso and PS Appelbaum, 'The MacArthur Treatment Competence Study III: Abilities of Patients to Consent to Psychiatric and Medical Treatments' (1995) 19 *Law and Human Behavior* 149.

[38] See Raymont et al, 'Prevalence of Mental Incapacity in Medical Inpatients and Associated Risk Factors: Cross-Sectional Study' (2004) 364 *The Lancet* 1421. See also GS Owen et al, 'Decision-making Capacity for Treatment in Psychiatric and Medical In-patients: Cross-sectional, Comparative Study' (2013) 203 *The British Journal of Psychiatry* 461. The latter study is to my knowledge the first study that compares the ability to consent of persons in need of somatic and those in need of psychiatric care.

[39] Owen et al, *ibid*.

important to distinguish between a person's ability to reason about treatment alternatives and his or her personal values and preferences. In principle, so-called mental capacity tests, which test a person's ability to understand and reason about relevant information in view of personal preferences, can be applied in a manner that is neutral with respect to the content of these personal preferences. The tests require the individual to be able to make decisions that accord with his or her personal values but they do not challenge these values *as such*. Many jurisdictions, for example, accept treatment refusals based on religious beliefs. Jehovah's Witnesses need not defend the personal beliefs underpinning their rejection of blood transfusions as rational or reasonable. It is enough to demonstrate an ability to make decisions that accord with one's view of what is right. However, few, if any, jurisdictions are equally tolerant of all the personal preferences that may shape treatment choices. Self-destructive preferences are, for example, often disqualified as personal preferences and categorised as the results of psychosocial conditions. Anorexia is a case in point: valuing 'thinness' and wishing to avoid food are viewed as indications of an inability to make valid treatment decisions rather than as personal preferences that might justify informed treatment rejections.[40] Dismissing certain preferences as simply the effects of a psychosocial condition in this way raises difficult questions about whether it is possible or desirable to distinguish personal preferences from illness-influenced preferences. Even if we assume that such a distinction can be made satisfactorily, it must also be borne in mind that experiences of severe pain and acute need may alter personal preferences, regardless of whether the patient's condition is labelled as somatic or psychiatric.[41]

To summarise the above, existing research supports the conclusion that compulsory mental health interventions do contribute to the aim of protecting the health of some of those subjected to such practices in the short-term. Rather few studies have been carried out on the subject, and those that have been indicate that a majority of those subjected to such intervention experience health improvement upon discharge but also that a significant proportion do not. The empirical evidence for the long-term health benefits of compulsory intervention seems to be particularly weak. Our next question was whether there are sound reasons for singling out people with psychosocial disabilities for compulsory health interventions. There can be little doubt that certain psychosocial conditions affect a person's decision-making ability and personal preferences. But so do certain other factors. In fact, empirical studies indicate that everyone's decision-making abilities fluctuate. Moreover, there is little evidence that

[40] See, eg, S Boyle, 'How Should the Law Determine Capacity to Refuse Treatment for Anorexia?' (2019) 64 *International Journal of Law and Psychiatry* 250.

[41] B Kelly et al, 'Terminally Ill Cancer Patients' Wish to Hasten Death' (2002) 16 *Palliative Medicine* 339; J-J Georges et al, 'Requests to Forgo Potentially Life-Prolonging Treatment and to Hasten Death in Terminally Ill Cancer Patients: A Prospective Study' (2006) 31 *Journal of Pain and Symptom Management* 100, 103f.

psychosocial conditions affect decision-making abilities in a way that differs in any essential respect from the way certain severe somatic illnesses or cognitive conditions affect these abilities. Whether the above should lead us to conclude that compulsory interventions do contribute to the aim of health protection and that the differential treatment of people with psychosocial disabilities is justified is a judgement call; the objective and reasonable standard provides insufficient guidance to facilitate definitive conclusions on this matters.

B. The Protection of the Life of the Person Concerned

As in the previous section, I begin by asking whether compulsory interventions contribute to the aim in question: here, the protection of life, through the prevention of acts of suicide. The prevailing view in the literature is that the clinical treatment of depression and similar conditions is key to the prevention of suicide.[42] Hospitalisation serves to facilitate such treatment; it also discourages or constrains self-destructive behaviour before the treatment takes effect. However, the effectiveness of continued hospitalisation in cases in which clinical treatment has been tried but has not achieved the desired results, and in which the individual continues to suffer from suicidal ideations and behaviour, has been questioned. Although it may prevent self-destructive activities temporarily, long-term prevention requires other measures.[43]

A problem with interventions targeting individuals at risk of suicide is that, in individual cases, it is very difficult to predict that such acts will take place in the near future. This difficulty is due to several factors, among which two in particular are worth pointing out. First, we do not know what distinguishes people who actually engage in serious self-harm from those who do not (other than committing the act itself, of course). Empirical research suggests that certain factors are associated with suicide across the world, such as having recently experienced a negative life event, having depression, having a severe somatic illness, being male, and having relatives or friends who have exhibited suicidal behaviour.[44] This information makes it possible to identify groups that, compared to the general population, are at an elevated risk of self-harm, but it does not enable us to effectively identify *who* (within a group of people

[42] JJ Mann et al, 'Suicide Prevention Strategies: A Systematic Review' (2005) 294 *Journal of the American Medical Association* 2064, 2069; CM van der Feltz-Cornelis et al, 'Best Practice Elements of Multilevel Suicide Prevention Strategies: A Review of Systematic Reviews' (2011) 26 *Crisis* 327.

[43] K Hawton et al, 'Psychosocial Interventions for Self-harm in Adults (Review)' (2016) 5 *Cochrane Database of Systematic Review* 2. In this review, 'self-harm' includes acts intended to result in death (attempted suicide), those without suicidal intent and those with a mixed motivation. See also B Skodlar, M Tomori and J Parnas, 'Subjective Experience and Suicidal Ideation in Schizophrenia' (2008) 49 *Comprehensive Psychiatry* 482, 485f.

[44] L Vijayakumar and S Rajkumar, 'Are Risk Factors for Suicide Universal? A Case-control Study in India' (1999) 99 *Acta Psychiatrica Scandinavica* 407.

at increased risk) will actually engage in serious self-harm within the coming days, weeks or months.[45] Second, suicides are rare events, even among those at elevated risk.[46] Only a small number of people diagnosed with depression and/or other conditions associated with serious self-harm will go on to attempt to commit suicide. This means that, even if people with certain psychosocial conditions are at an increased risk of self-harm, the likelihood of such acts occurring is still low. A systematic review of the clinical factors associated with suicide has calculated the predictive value of risk assessments of inpatient suicide to be below two per cent when the estimated risk of suicide within the group assessed is one in 300. This means that even if 100 individuals are classified as being at risk of committing suicide, more than 98 of them will not take their own lives.[47] Consequently, decisions about whether to intervene for preventive purposes are necessarily based on incomplete information, and the risk of error is significant. Erring on the side of caution entails that coercion will be used against individuals who would not actually have harmed themselves seriously even if no intervention took place. Erring on the side of non-intervention will inevitably mean not intervening in cases in which individuals will go on to harm themselves seriously. Mental health laws may give the impression that we can effectively identify individuals at 'immediate risk' of suicide and prevent them from ending their lives through compulsory care, but this seems impossible in practice.

I now turn to the question of whether there are sound reasons for targeting people with psychosocial disabilities for compulsory intervention for the purposes of protecting life. There can be little doubt that people with psychosocial disabilities are over-represented among the group of those who commit suicide.[48] However, people with psychosocial disabilities are not the only ones who engage in serious self-harm; people without such conditions also end their lives by their own hands. Empirical studies suggest that, in high-income Western countries, up to 90 per cent of people who die from suicide are people with psychosocial conditions and that depressive symptoms and other related symptoms are present among the remaining 10 per cent.[49] In low- and middle-income

[45] M Large et al, 'Systematic Review and Meta-analysis of the Clinical Factors Associated with the Suicide of Psychiatric In-patients' (2011) 124 *Acta Psychiatrica Scandinavica* 18; J Powell et al, 'Suicide in Psychiatric Hospital In-patients: Risk Factors and their Predictive Power' (2000) 176 *British Journal of Psychiatry* 266; AD Pokorny, 'Prediction of Suicide in Psychiatric Patients: Report of a Prospective Study' (1983) 40 *Archives of General Psychiatry* 249.

[46] Suicide rates vary considerably between countries. The World Health Organisation (WHO) has estimated that close to 800,000 people die by suicide every year. WHO, 'Suicide in the World: Global Health Estimates' (WHO, 2019) 7.

[47] Large et al, 'Systematic Review' 26.

[48] JTO Cavanagh et al, 'Psychological Autopsy Studies of Suicide: A Systematic Review' (2003) 33 *Psychological Medicine* 395, 399; EC Harris and B Barraclough, 'Suicide as an Outcome for Mental Disorders: A Meta-Analysis' (1997) 170 *British Journal of Psychiatry* 205, 210ff.

[49] WHO, *Preventing Suicide: A Global Imperative* (Luxembourg, WHO, 2014) 40.

countries, where the total number of suicides is higher (about three times higher), the proportion of those who commit suicide who are diagnosed with a psychosocial condition is less significant.[50] In certain states parties to the CRPD it is around 60 per cent.[51] These numbers need to be treated with caution. Both under-reporting and over-reporting may occur in the process of distinguishing suicide from other causes of death and in the process of establishing the underlying causes of deaths by suicide. Not all states have good-quality data that can be used to estimate suicide rates, and suicide registration is a complicated procedure that involves several actors and authorities. In countries in which suicide is still illegal, or socially and religiously unacceptable, acts of suicide tend to be classified as 'accidents' and the like. In addition, separating human distress from depression is difficult. Some authors argue that there is a tendency in the West to explain suicide as an expression of depression, or a similar psychosocial condition, even in cases in which the person who has ended his or her life was not diagnosed with such a condition before committing suicide.[52] This tendency is less visible in other parts of the world, where suicide is more often explained with reference to other factors, such as interpersonal conflict, substance abuse and alcoholism, financial problems or unemployment.[53]

To summarise, then, the clinical treatment of depression, bipolar disorder and some other psychosocial conditions does prevent suicide and thereby contribute to the protection of life. A problem with authorising compulsory interventions as preventive means, however, is that suicide is very difficult to predict in the near future in individual cases. The limitations of current risk assessment tools mean that, in order to prevent one or more acts of suicide, many people who would not have ended their lives even if their treatment refusals had been respected would need to be hospitalised. This raises questions about the reasonableness of such interventions (see section V, below). As regards the reasons for focusing on people with psychosocial disabilities, there is ample evidence that people with certain psychosocial disabilities are in a majority among those who engage in serious self-harm. They are, however, not the only ones who resort to such acts. Again, whether the over-representation of people with psychosocial disabilities among those who commit suicide constitutes a sufficient reason for restricting coercive care to this group, is a finely balanced judgement to which the objective and reasonable standard provides little guidance.

[50] *Ibid.*

[51] See, eg, R Radhakrishnan and C Andrade, 'Suicide: An Indian Perspective' (2012) 54 *Indian Journal of Psychiatry* 304; M Phillips et al, 'Risk Factors for Suicide in China: A National Case-control Psychological Autopsy Study' (2002) 360 *The Lancet* 1728. For other examples see A Millner, J Sveticic and D De Leo, 'Suicide in the Absence of Mental Disorder? A Review of Psychological Autopsy Studies Across Countries' (2013) 59 *International Journal of Social Psychiatry* 545.

[52] Cavanagh et al, 'Psychological Autopsy Studies' 401.

[53] eg SD Manoranjitham et al, 'Risk Factors for Suicide in Rural South India' (2009) 196 *British Journal of Psychiatry* 26, 29.

C. The Protection of Others

The protection of others is the third and final aim of compulsory mental health intervention considered in this book. Of course, civil detention prevents the detained person from engaging in violent acts directed against people outside the hospital walls. Whether such hospitalisation, in combination with treatment, has preventive effects that persist after discharge from the hospital raises highly contentious issues regarding the relationship – if there is one – between psychosocial conditions and violence. Those defending the use of coercive measures within mental health care often contend that there is a link between the two. The link is sometimes described as a direct connection; symptoms of certain psychosocial conditions are thought to trigger violent behaviour.[54] A typical example would be a person with paranoid delusions attacking a perceived persecutor. Sometimes the link is described as more indirect. Certain psychosocial conditions are associated with other factors that research in criminology has identified as general risk factors for violence, such as substance abuse, antisocial personality traits or behaviour[55] and socioeconomic factors. For example, people with psychosocial disabilities are over-represented among people with substance abuse problems, and people with substance abuse problems are over-represented among those who resort to violence. People with psychosocial disabilities and people with substance abuse problems are, in turn, over-represented among the homeless and unemployed, factors that are statistically correlated with having been convicted of a violent crime.[56] These factors form a complex web of correlations within which causal factors, if they exist, are difficult to distinguish from confounding factors.

There are clinical studies showing that at least some forms of psychiatric treatment (for example, medication with antipsychotics and mood stabilisers) reduce not only clinical symptoms but also the frequency of violent crimes. Two cohort studies of people with psychosocial diagnoses compared the crime rates for periods during which they were prescribed medication to crime rates for periods during which they were not receiving medication. Both studies indicated

[54] See, eg, R Keers et al, 'Association of Violence with Emergence of Persecutory Delusions in Untreated Schizophrenia' (2014) 171 *American Journal of Psychiatry* 332; J Coid et al, 'The Relationship Between Delusions and Violence: Findings from the East London First Episode Psychosis Study' (2013) 70 *JAMA Psychiatry* 465.

[55] In the context of risk prediction, antisocial behaviour commonly refers to any action that violates cultural standards of appropriate behaviour. It includes, but is not limited to, violent criminal behaviour. See, eg, DA Andrews and J Bonta, *The Psychology of Criminal Conduct*, 5th edn (New Providence, Matthew Bender & Company, 2010) 17.

[56] JL Skeem, S Manchak, and JK Peterson, 'Correctional Policy for Offenders with Mental Illness: Creating a New Paradigm for Recidivism Reduction' (2011) 35 *Law and Human Behaviour* 110, 117; E Silver, 'Understanding the Relationship Between Mental Disorder and Violence: The Need for a Criminological Perspective' (2006) 30 *Law and Human Behaviour* 685; J Bonta, M Law and K Hanson, 'The Prediction of Criminal and Violent Recidivism among Mentally Disordered Offenders: A Meta-Analysis' (1998) 123 *Psychological Bulletin* 123.

that the crime rate was significantly lower during the times when medication was prescribed (25–45 per cent lower).[57] It is tempting to interpret the lower crime rate as a positive effect of the treatment, but one should avoid immediately concluding that there is a causal connection here. The studies establish an association between the prescription of medication and the frequency of violent behaviour. It is possible that some of the prescribed medication was, in fact, not taken, and the studies do not rule out that other factors, besides medication, could have contributed to the effect. In addition, there are other studies that show that people with psychosocial diagnoses act violently for a variety of reasons and that offence patterns and 'triggers' for violence are relatively similar for perpetrators with and without psychosocial conditions.[58] Jillian Peterson and colleagues studied parolees with and without serious psychosocial conditions, and found that only a small minority of the participants with psychosocial conditions (about seven per cent) acted violently for reasons that were directly related to clinical symptoms (for instance delusions). The vast majority of the participants in this study (90 per cent of those with a psychosocial diagnosis and 68 per cent of those without) described their violent acts as driven by hostility and impulsivity and as reactions to provocation.[59]

There are also studies of violent behaviour that occurs within psychiatric hospitals and the impact of medical treatment on such behaviour. Two studies from Germany point in different directions. A small observational study conducted in a psychiatric department in south-west Germany compared the frequency of violent incidents – defined as the disruptive behaviour of a patient leading to painful or harmful physical contact with another patient or member of staff – in periods during which medication was forced on patients with the frequency of such incidents in periods during which medication was administered on a voluntary basis.[60] The study found that violence did not increase in the period during which medication was administered voluntarily. It should, however, be noted that the use of compulsory medication in this hospital was rare: about two–five cases per year, affecting less than 0.5 per cent of the inpatients. The psychiatric department was characterised by its therapeutic culture; it operated with no closed wards and with staff committed to keeping the use

[57] S Fazel et al, 'Antipsychotics, Mood Stabilisers, and Risk of Violent Crime' (2014) 384 *The Lancet* 1206; Z Chang, P Lichtenstein and N Långström, 'Association Between Prescription of Major Psychotropic Medications and Violent Reoffending after Prison Release' (2016) 316 *Journal of the American Medical Association* 1798. Both studies are based on Swedish national registers and compare the rate of violent criminality for the same individual during periods when he or she is on and off medication. Both studies involved large numbers of people. The study undertaken by Fazel et al involved 82,547 individuals who had been prescribed antipsychotics or mood stabilisers, and the study conducted by Chang et al involved 22,275 released prisoners.

[58] See, eg, Skeem, Manchak, and Peterson, 'Correctional Policy' 117.

[59] J Peterson et al, 'Analyzing Offense Patterns as a Function of Mental Illness to Test the Criminalization Hypothesis' (2010) 61 *Psychiatric Services* 1217.

[60] M Zinkler, 'Germany without Coercive Treatment in Psychiatry: A 15 Month Real World Experience' (2016) 5 *Laws* 15, s 3.2.

of compulsion to a minimum.[61] In contrast, another study, of seven psychiatric hospitals in south-west Germany, found a significant increase in inpatient violence in clinical settings where medication was provided on a voluntary basis only compared with settings where medication was on occasion administrated with force.[62] Studies from the Netherlands reveal similar results.[63] In sum, the available evidence suggests that psychiatric treatment may prevent violent behaviour in some cases. What remain matters of dispute are how many cases it can prevent, why it has this effect, and whether the compulsory administration of medication is necessary to achieve its effects.

Furthermore, like self-harm, violence against others is difficult to predict in individual cases. Serious violence is rare, and we do not know how to distinguish effectively in advance between people who will commit seriously violent acts and those who will not. Therefore, if compulsory interventions are to contribute to the prevention of violence, they would have to be applied not only to those individuals who would actually go on to harm others (unless preventive action was taken) but also to many others who would not. A systematic review of nine commonly used risk assessment tools concludes that (at least) two persons 'at risk' have to be detained to prevent one violent act, such as an assault.[64] An earlier study, covering a smaller number of risk assessment instruments, estimated that six 'high risk' people needed to be detained to prevent one violent event.[65] In order to prevent rarer violent acts, for example homicides, the numbers are much higher. A study covering people diagnosed with schizophrenia suggests that the numbers of people who would need to be detained to prevent one homicide range from 151 to 35,000.[66] The latter figure (ie 35,000) refers to how many would need to be detained to prevent one act of homicide

[61] *Ibid.*

[62] E Flammer and T Steinert, 'Association Between Restriction of Involuntary Medication and Frequency of Coercive Measures and Violent Incidents' (2016) 67 *Psychiatric Services* 1315.

[63] T Steinert, EO Noorthoorn and CL Mulder, 'The Use of Coercive Interventions in Mental Health Care in Germany and the Netherlands: A Comparison of the Developments in Two Neighboring Countries' (2014) 2 *Frontiers in Public Health* 141.

[64] S Fazel et al, 'Use of Risk Assessment Instruments to Predict Violence and Antisocial Behaviour in 73 Samples Involving 24,827 People: Systematic Review and Meta-Analysis' (2012) 345:e4692 *British Medical Journal* 4. The study examined the predictive validity of violence risk assessment tools from 73 samples involving 24,847 individuals in 13 countries (all high-income Western countries). It focused on two statistical measures of diagnostic accuracy when reviewing the tools: sensitivity (the proportion of offenders that a risk assessment tool predicted would offend) and specificity (the proportion of non-offenders that a risk assessment tool predicted would not offend). It concluded that of those individuals who went on to harm others, about 92% had been classified as at a 'moderate' or 'high risk' of future violence (sensitivity). Of those participants who did not go on to violently offend, about 36% had been classified as 'low risk' (specificity). This implies a positive predictive value of 41%, which is equivalent to a median 'number needed to detain' of two.

[65] A Buchanan and M Leese, 'Detention of People with Dangerous Severe Personality Disorders: A Systematic Review' (2001) 358 *The Lancet* 1955.

[66] M Large et al, 'The Predictive Value of Risk Categorization in Schizophrenia' (2011) 19 *Harvard Review of Psychiatry* 25, 30.

committed against someone unknown to the offender. A further complication here concerns the fact that risk assessment tools are sometimes not used in an optimal manner in practice, which further undercuts the preventive effect of incarceration based on the use of such assessment tools.[67]

I turn now to the question of whether there are convincing reasons to single out those with psychosocial disabilities for compulsory intervention. The defenders of this practice typically argue that the (direct or indirect) link between violent behaviour and psychosocial conditions justifies the focus on people with psychosocial disabilities. Empirical studies do confirm that people with certain psychosocial conditions act violently somewhat more often than 'the average person'. Population-based studies have, for example, shown that people with psychotic conditions commit violent acts somewhat more often than people without such conditions.[68] However, people with psychosocial disabilities are not the only group with an increased propensity for violence. It is still not entirely clear how psychotic symptoms compare with other risk factors in terms of the strength of the association with violence, and this issue is still a matter of debate.[69] Today, there is broad agreement, however, on the fact that other factors – including male gender, antisocial personality, history of violent behaviour, and substance abuse problems – are at least as closely associated with violence as certain psychosocial conditions and that they are better predictors of future aggressive behaviour than the fact that a person has a psychosocial condition.[70]

Summing up, civil detention prevents those detained from committing violent acts against people outside the hospital, and there are empirical studies indicating that, in some cases, clinical treatment results in reduced levels of aggressive behaviour, but just how many instances of violent behaviour compulsory care might be able to prevent remains uncertain. In addition, violent crimes are more frequently committed by people with psychosocial disabilities than by the 'average person', but they are not the only group more likely to commit such acts. Violent crimes are at least as common among middle-aged males with a

[67] JL Viljoen, DM Cochrane and MR Johnson, 'Do Risk Assessment Tools Help Manage and Reduce Risk of Violence and Reoffending? A Systematic Review' (2018) 42 *Law and Human Behaviour* 181.

[68] See, eg, E Elbogen and S Johansson, 'The Intricate Link Between Violence and Mental Disorder: Results from the National Epidemiologic Survey on Alcohol and Related Conditions' (2009) 66 *Archives of General Psychiatry* 152; S Fazel and M Grann, 'The Population Impact of Severe Mental Illness on Violent Crime' (2006) 163 *American Journal of Psychiatry* 1397.

[69] K Douglas, Laura Guy and Stephen Hart, 'Psychosis as a Risk Factor for Violence to Others: A Meta-Analysis' (2009) 137 *Psychological Bulletin* 679, 692.

[70] eg JL Skeem et al, 'Offenders with Mental Illness Have Criminogenic Needs, Too: Toward Recidivism Reduction' (2014) 38 *Law and Human Behaviour* 212; A Buchanan and M Leese, 'Quantifying the Contributions of Three Types of Information to the Prediction of Criminal Conviction Using the Receiver Operating Characteristic' (2006) 188 *British Journal of Psychiatry* 472; and T Nilsson et al, 'Violent Recidivism: A Long-Time Follow-Up Study of Mentally Disordered Offenders' (2011) 6:e25768 *PLoS One*.

history of violent behaviour and substance abuse problems. Again, whether the over-representation of people with psychosocial disabilities among those who commit violent crimes constitutes a justification for states to impose coercive care only on members of this group is a judgement call.

V. ARE COMPULSORY INTERVENTIONS REASONABLE?

The third element of the objective and reasonable standard concerns the reasonableness of the policy under consideration. Again, what makes a policy reasonable remains an open question. In seeking to determine whether a policy is reasonable, it is clear that a number of considerations may be taken into account and balanced against one another.[71] One important consideration is the *effect* of the state practice under review on those concerned: this effect should not be unduly burdensome for these individuals. Few would deny that compulsory psychiatric care is burdensome. Civil detention in a psychiatric ward severely restricts the personal liberty of those subjected to it, and it is hard to imagine an intervention that interferes more directly with personal integrity and self-determination than the introduction of mind-altering chemicals into someone's body against his or her will. The adverse effects of antipsychotic medication are well documented. Haloperidol, which is one of the most frequently used antipsychotic drugs around the world, causes sleeping problems, extrapyramidal side effects, tremors, and restlessness in more than one in ten patients. Other common side effects include depression, hallucinations, weight gain (or weight loss), tardive dyskinesia (involuntary rhythmic movements, usually of the tongue, lips, face, hands and feet) and Parkinsonian symptoms (slowness of movement, rigidity and tremors).[72] These effects can be permanent. Depression is commonly treated with tricyclic medication or selective serotonin re-uptake inhibitors (SSRIs), which also have undesirable effects, including drowsiness, nausea, blurred vision and sexual problems (changes in sexual desire and/or impotence).[73]

In addition, the very fact that hospitalisation and treatment with medication is imposed and not chosen voluntarily causes emotional harm and distress for those subjected to such practices. Patients describe their experiences of being forced to undergo certain treatments as physically and emotionally painful, degrading, humiliating and terrifying. A systematic review from 2016 of

[71] See ch 1, section VI.B.

[72] The medical information in this section is drawn from the Swedish national formulary (FASS), produced by Läkemedelsföreningen, which is the trade association for the research-based pharmaceutical industry in Sweden. The adverse effects listed here relate to the medication Haldol (produced by Janssen-Cilag AB), which is the trade name for the substance Halperidol.

[73] See, eg, the adverse effects of the tricyclic antidepressant Anafranil (the trade name for Clomipramine, produced by Novartis Pharma AG) and of the SSRIs Fontex (the trade name for Fluoxetine, produced by Eli Lilly & Company Ltd) and Zoloft (the trade name for Sertraline, produced by Pfizer Inc).

qualitative studies of the experience of civil detention in acute psychiatric care in western European countries demonstrates huge variations in how participants experience coercive care.[74] Whilst all participants initially resisted treatment, some came to recognise that they had behaved in a self-destructive way and experienced a sense of relief when professionals had taken control.[75] Others described feelings of disempowerment, fear and trauma. Such feelings were associated with several factors, including past negative experiences of coercive care and a lack of information about the adverse effects of medication. Having to wait before being allowed to undertake basic activities, such as going for a walk, left some feeling punished. On the other hand, being listened to and being involved in treatment decisions were associated with more positive views on compulsory care.[76]

The legal design of mental health regimes also affects how burdensome they are for those concerned. Legal authorisations of civil detention that provide for long-term (even indefinite) incarceration in a restrictive setting interfere more with the right to liberty than do legal regimes that limit the length of the detention to weeks and keep the use of coercive means during detention to a minimum. Similarly, domestic regimes that prohibit treatment methods that are particularly painful or intrusive interfere less with the right to integrity than systems that do not include such prohibitions. The degree to which domestic systems involve individuals in decisions about their treatment is also important. Mental health laws that grant individuals with decision-making ability the right to reject clinical treatment are less onerous than laws that give the responsible doctor the final word. In addition, generic laws – that is, laws that do not refer directly to 'disability' or psychiatric diagnoses – are more likely to be judged to be reasonable than laws that apply to people with psychosocial conditions only.[77]

The reasonableness of a domestic regime depends not only on its negative implications for human rights entitlements but also on its positive effects, that is, on the amount of health protection and harm prevention provided by the regime. In a jurisprudential context, attention must also be paid to the degree to which compulsion is necessary to achieve these positive outcomes and to the relevance of targeting people with psychosocial disabilities to achieve

[74] T Seed, J Fox and K Berry, 'The Experience of Involuntary Detention in Acute Psychiatric Care: A Review and Synthesis of Qualitative Studies' (2016) 61 *International Journal of Nursing Studies* 82. This study is a review of studies that took place from 2006 to 2014 that involved, in total, 254 individuals subjected to compulsory mental health care in Austria, Ireland, the Netherlands, Norway, Sweden and the United Kingdom. The review is an 'update' of the review conducted by Katsakou and Priebe in 2006, which covered the five qualitative studies on the topic available at that point. See C Katsakou and S Priebe, 'Patients' Experiences of Involuntary Hospital Admission and Treatment: A Review of Qualitative Studies' (2007) 16 *Epidemiologia e Psichiatria Sociale* 172.

[75] Seed, Fox, and Berry, *ibid* 90.

[76] Seed, Fox, and Berry, *ibid* 90.

[77] See ch 1, section VI.B.

these aims.[78] We know from the above that compulsory intervention contributes to the protection of health and life. However, can it be said to be necessary in the pursuit of these aims? Furthermore, supposing that we could establish with certainty that compulsion is necessary to protect health and life in *some* situations, would this suffice to justify the maintenance of a system of compulsory care? What we have to bear in mind here is that, because of epistemic uncertainties and weaknesses in the available risk prediction tools, such a system applies to a much larger group of people than just those who would actually have gone on to harm themselves or others, and it thereby undermines the personal liberty, integrity and self-determination of large numbers of people. Put differently, does the fact that some people benefit from compulsory care justify its negative effects, the adverse effects not only for those who are actually subjected to such practices but also for those who risk being subjected to such practices because of their psychosocial disabilities? Answers to these questions cannot be deduced from treaty body jurisprudence, and for this reason the outcome of the discussion of the reasonableness of compulsory mental health intervention cannot be settled with certainty. The reasonableness of compulsory care regimes becomes a matter of (value) judgement. The objective and reasonable standard indicates the factors to be taken into account, but it offers little guidance on how to determine the outcome.

VI. CONCLUSIONS ON THE OBJECTIVITY AND REASONABLENESS OF DOMESTIC REGIMES

Currently, most domestic mental health laws restrict the compulsory care of adults to members of certain groups: people with psychiatric conditions, people with intellectual disabilities and people with substance abuse problems. To comply with the prohibition of disability-based discrimination in the CRPD, such differential treatment of people with and people without disabilities must be justified. The entry into force of the CRPD has led some states to revise their health legislation and formulate the criteria for compulsory care in disability-neutral terms. The Mental Capacity Act (Northern Ireland) 2016 and health legislation in several jurisdictions in Australia, for example, apply to everyone above a certain age and limit the use of compulsion to people who lack decision-making skills.[79] The application of such legislation will, however, most likely have a disparate impact on people with psychosocial disabilities, so it also needs to be justified if it is to comply with the CRPD's prohibition of indirect discrimination.

To justify compulsory care regimes that fall within the definition of disability-based discrimination, states parties must demonstrate that their care regimes

[78] *Ibid.*

[79] See section II, above.

serve legitimate aims, contribute to their aims, and are reasonable. The extent to which such regimes satisfy the first criterion is easy to assess. The protection of the health and life of patients and the protection of third parties are legitimate aims that are compatible with the CRPD.[80] Evaluation of compliance with the second criterion (contribution to the aim) is less straightforward. The available research suggests that many domestic systems of compulsory mental health care contribute to their aims, at least in a substantial number of cases and in the short-term. Research also indicates that a significant number of people treated by means of coercive psychiatry do not, however, feel that they have been helped by the treatment provided.[81] This raises the question of 'how much' domestic regimes must contribute to their aims to comply with the objective and reasonable standard. Is full realisation of the aim(s) necessary, or is a marginal contribution sufficient? Or – and this seems more plausible – is the standard somewhere in between? Further, if a certain level of contribution to the aim(s) is necessary, how are we to deal with the fact that such (empirical) facts can be difficult to determine reliably? Our knowledge about 'how much' our laws or policies contribute to a given aim tends to be limited, and the laws and policies discussed in this study are no exception.[82] The effectiveness of domestic systems of compulsory mental health intervention is poorly understood, if it is understood at all. This raises the question of whether the objective and reasonable standard implies that, in order to establish whether a given law or practice contributes to its aim, the relevant empirical evidence should have to meet a certain threshold of reliability. The UN treaty bodies have not (yet) taken a general position on these matters.

States with a domestic system of compulsory care that applies only to people with psychosocial disabilities (and hence qualifies as directly discriminatory) must also explain the need to differentiate on the basis of psychosocial disability. The UN treaty bodies have given very little guidance on what sort of explanation will suffice. A minimum requirement seems to be that differentiation between people with and without psychosocial conditions must be relevant in light of the aim behind the regime under consideration – that differentiation must make some contribution to the achievement of this aim.[83] Imagine that new evidence were to emerge proving that there was no correlation between violence and psychosocial conditions: people with such conditions committed violent acts just as often as did people without psychiatric diagnoses, and any overrepresentation of this group among people convicted of violent crimes could be fully explained in terms of the biased behaviour of law enforcement. In other words, police officers, prosecutors and judges were influenced by stereotypical

[80] See section III, above.
[81] See section IV.A, above.
[82] JJ Rachlinsk, 'Evidence-based Law' (2011) 96 *Cornell Law Review* 901, 910ff.
[83] See ch 1, section VI.B.

views of people with psychosocial disabilities, which led to more arrests and convictions of people belonging to this group. Under such circumstances, domestic authorisations of the civil detention of members of this group *but not others* to prevent violent crime would certainly fall foul of the prohibition of discrimination. That a policy complies with this minimum requirement of means–ends relevance is not necessarily sufficient for it to comply with the prohibition of discrimination. The Human Rights Committee has rejected laws that set out different rules for men and women, even though the differentiation between the genders could be viewed as means–ends relevant. The *Mauritian Women v Mauritius* case concerned immigration policies restricting the rights of male, but not female, immigrants for the purposes of preventing subversive activities. In view of the fact that men are clearly over-represented in statistics on violent crimes, it seems reasonable to assume that men, as a group, are more likely to engage in such activities. The Mauritanian policy had indeed been introduced following a number of events in which male migrants (but not female migrants) were suspected of such crimes. The Human Rights Committee nevertheless held that the state had not demonstrated the need for a gender-differentiated policy.[84] The Committee has, however, accepted domestic policies that differentiate on the basis of a protected ground in cases where such differentiation was motivated by other or additional reasons. The Committee has, for example, accepted a policy that targeted a specific group of people with disabilities because it was considered to be 'necessary' to achieve the aim of maintaining public order.[85]

In terms of the topic of this study, we may conclude that many domestic systems that involve differential treatment of persons with and people without psychosocial disabilities will comply with the minimum requirement of means–ends relevance. Diminished decision-making ability, suicide and violent behaviour are more prevalent among people with psychosocial disabilities (as a group) than among people without such disabilities. This may 'explain' a focus on persons with psychosocial disabilities in coercive care policies. But, as noted above, this will not necessarily suffice to justify differential treatment. In view of the very burdensome negative effects compulsory mental health care has on the personal liberty, integrity, and legal capacity of people with psychosocial disabilities, a full justification of differential treatment will most likely require additional reasons in its favour. Whether there are such additional reasons and whether they are sufficiently strong, in relation to a given regime, to compensate for the negative effects of these practices are difficult questions. It could certainly be argued that there are situations in which compulsory care appears to be necessary to protect an individual's health and life and to protect others.

[84] Human Rights Committee, 'Communication No 35/1978' *Mauritian Women v Mauritius* (1981) UN Doc CCPR/C/OP/1 para 9.2 (b) 2 (ii).

[85] Human Rights Committee, 'Communication No 854/1999' *Wackenheim v France* (2002) UN Doc CCPR/C/75/D/854/1999 paras 2.1 and 7.4.

It is easy to imagine a situation in which an individual is in urgent need of care, but rejects such care. In such a situation, overriding the individual's preferences seems to be the most effective way to protect health and life. However, could these aims also be achieved with generic laws, applicable both to people with psychosocial conditions *and* to people without such conditions? If they could, would we still be able to say that systems of coercive care applicable only to people with psychosocial disabilities are 'necessary'?

When reasoning about the reasonableness of compulsory mental health care, we must not ignore the positive effects of such care. States parties have obligations not only to refrain from discriminatory intrusions into personal liberty and integrity but also to protect the health and lives of people with disabilities and of others.[86] The fact that the use of compulsion is not prohibited by the treaty text implies that there may be some room for the legitimate use of coercive means. Rather than excluding all forms of compulsory hospitalisation and forced administration of treatment from the ambit of lawful state action, the prohibition of discrimination implies that such interventions can only be lawful in certain circumstances. The references to proportionality in the treaty bodies' reasoning suggest that a balance needs to be struck between the positive and negative implications of the domestic system under consideration. In the next chapter, I explore whether a form of proportionality reasoning based on Robert Alexy's framework may provide a way forward.

[86] Convention on the Rights of Persons with Disabilities (adopted 13 December 2006, entered into force 3 May 2008) 2515 UNTS 3 Arts 10, 16, and 25.

3

Proportionality Reasoning

I. A WAY FORWARD?

THE PREVIOUS CHAPTERS have shown that, in seeking to determine the lawfulness of compulsory mental health interventions under the UN Convention on the Rights of Persons with Disabilities (CRPD),[1] important questions are left unanswered if we proceed simply on the basis of a discrimination analysis guided by the jurisprudence of the UN human rights treaty bodies. These questions include: how much must compulsory interventions contribute to their aims to comply with the objective and reasonable standard? Is a certain level of contribution required, or can the level vary depending on the circumstances of the particular case? If the level can vary, then what circumstances determine the level of contribution required in a particular case? Furthermore, what reasons are relevant to determining whether a particular authorisation of compulsory care is reasonable under discrimination law? Apart from the fact that coercive care may be necessary to protect health and life, and apart from the positive and negative effects of the coercive care regime, what other considerations, if any, are to be taken into account? What would it take to fully explain or justify differential treatment on the basis of disability as reasonable? How do we evaluate the strength of the considerations that speak in favour of and against the reasonableness of coercive care? Another set of questions concerns how decision-makers should deal with the epistemic uncertainty that pervades mental health law. As I explained in the previous chapter, the positive effects of domestic practices of compulsory care on the health of the patient are poorly understood, as is the connection between such practices and the prevention of suicide and violence against others. Does this uncertainty about the actual contribution of these practices to their aims render them non-compliant with the objective and reasonable standard? If it does not, does it affect the outcome of the discrimination assessment in some other way?

This chapter explores whether proportionality reasoning, according to Robert Alexy's model of such reasoning, offers a way forward by providing answers to questions that the analysis of the objective and reasonable standard

[1] Convention on the Rights of Persons with Disabilities (adopted 13 December 2006, entered into force 3 May 2008) 2515 UNTS 3 (CRPD).

leaves open. It begins with a brief overview of the theoretical foundation upon which Alexy's model is based (section II), as a brief account of Alexy's view of the normative characteristics of constitutional rights will, I believe, help us to understand his proportionality assessment model. This is followed by a description of the basic steps and rules that govern proportionality argumentation (section III), and a discussion of the compatibility of Alexy's model with the objective and reasonable standard (section IV). Thereafter, I describe and reflect on the kind of legal argumentation and judgement involved in the last step of proportionality assessment: balancing (section V). This stage of a proportionality assessment is arguably the most demanding, and it is the stage that has attracted the most criticism from legal scholars. Section VI describes how Alexy's model deals with epistemic uncertainty, including uncertainty about the positive and negative effects of a given state practice. When reasoning about the lawfulness of compulsory mental health care, it is important to approach such questions in a principled manner, as arguments about the effectiveness of such interventions, as well as about the relevance of focusing interventions solely on people with psychosocial disabilities, rest on uncertain empirical assumptions. This chapter ends with a discussion of the advantages and disadvantages of drawing on Alexy's work to determine the lawfulness of compulsory mental health interventions under the CRPD.

II. THEORETICAL UNDERPINNINGS

Robert Alexy's model of proportionality argumentation is part of a theory of constitutional rights that he lays out in his *Theorie der Grundrechte* (*A Theory of Constitutional Rights*).[2] The model is developed as a reconstruction and theorisation of the jurisprudence of the German Federal Constitutional Court (*Bundesverfassungsgericht*).[3] Although this means that the model is only directly applicable, strictly speaking, in that context, its procedural nature and high level of abstraction allows for it to be more widely applied. Indeed, Alexy's rules for proportionality argumentation are widely discussed, and they have inspired human rights and constitutional rights adjudication around the world.[4] A central feature of Alexy's theory of constitutional rights is the distinction between rules and principles. Rules are legal norms that, when applicable to the case at hand, constitute *definitive* reasons for a certain action. If a rule is valid, and if its criteria are fulfilled, then what it prescribes must be done – no more

[2] As I noted in the introduction, I will refer to the English translation: R Alexy, *A Theory of Constitutional Rights* (translated by J Rivers) (New York, Oxford University Press, 2010).

[3] *Ibid* 13f.

[4] GC Webber, 'Proportionality, Balancing, and the Cult of Constitutional Rights Scholarship' (2010) 23 *Canadian Journal of Law and Jurisprudence* 179; TA Aleinikoff, 'Constitutional Law in the Age of Balancing' (1987) 96 *The Yale Law Journal* 943, 944.

and no less.[5] Principles, on the other hand, are norms that can be satisfied to varying degrees and that ought to be satisfied to the greatest extent possible given the legal and factual possibilities. They are, to use Alexy's words, optimisation requirements.[6]

Alexy's distinction between rules and principles ties in with the work of the German legal theorist Josef Esser on the same topic[7] and shares some similarities with the American philosopher Ronald Dworkin's conceptualisation of legal rules and principles.[8] It should be noted, however, that Alexy's distinction between rules and principles is not based on a norm's level of generality (principles tend to be general, rules more specific), origin (rules tend to be codified in statutory provisions), or status in the legal canon (rules often take precedence over principles if there is a conflict between the two types of norms). While Alexy accepts that there is something to the distinctions made by Dworkin and other scholars, he finds them unhelpful in explaining the role of principles in constitutional rights adjudication.[9] For Alexy, the key to understanding such adjudication lies in the idea of constitutional rights norms as optimisation precepts. This (structural) difference between rules and principles implies that conflicts between rules and conflicts between principles warrant different kinds of solution. Conflicts between rules are solved by creating an exception to one of the rules, or through the application of meta-rules, such as *lex superior derogat legi inferiori* or *lex specialis derogat legi generali*, giving one of the conflicting rules priority over the other. Conflicts between principles, on the other hand, are settled through proportionality argumentation. There is thus a close connection between principles theory and proportionality argumentation; proportionality reasoning, and balancing in particular, presupposes the existence of norms that have the structure of principles, and vice versa.[10] In Alexy's view, most, if not all, constitutional rights include norms that have the character of principles. The legal provisions that codify these rights are phrased in abstract and ideologically loaded language, providing limited guidance to those applying the law in concrete cases.[11] Their typically wide scope of application means that the individual entitlements and corresponding state obligations prescribed by these norms often conflict with claims protected under other legal norms. When they do, the statutory provisions seldom dictate the outcome of the conflict. Instead,

[5] Alexy, *A Theory of Constitutional Rights* 48.

[6] Alexy (n 2) 47–48.

[7] R Alexy, 'On the Structure of Legal Principles' (2000) 13 *Ratio Juris* 294.

[8] R Dworkin, *Taking Rights Seriously* (Cambridge, Massachusetts, Harvard University Press, 1977) 22ff.

[9] Alexy (n 2) 57.

[10] R Alexy, 'Constitutional Rights and Proportionality' (2014) 22 *Revus* 51, 52 and 57. For a critique of the thesis that principles theory implies proportionality argumentation and vice versa, see, eg, K Möller, 'Balancing and the Structure of Constitutional Rights' (2007) 5 *International Journal of Constitutional Law* 453, 459–60.

[11] Alexy (n 2) 84–86, 371.

such conflicts are settled in a context-sensitive manner, which involves proportionality reasoning and balancing. Alexy does not deny that constitutional rights provisions also incorporate rules and that rights adjudication includes the application of such rules. His point is rather that, in many cases, the idea of the subsumption of facts under general rules does not accurately reflect the entire process of constitutional rights adjudication, which typically involves weighing legal arguments for and against a given outcome.[12]

Alexy's conceptualisation of balancing as a rational method of solving conflicts between competing claims in constitutional law ties in with his discourse-theoretic view of legal argumentation. In *Theorie der Juristischen Argumentation: Die Theorie des Rationalen Diskurses als Theorie der Juristischen Begründung* (*A Theory of Legal Argumentation*), Alexy is concerned with the question of whether – and, if so, how – legal argumentation can be rational.[13] He starts from the assumption that the interpretation and application of legal norms involves more than the subsumption of concrete circumstances ('facts') under abstractly formulated norms.[14] The transition from a legal norm to a legal decision also involves judgement. The rules for legal argumentation are not entirely conclusive: they do not produce a single correct answer in every situation.[15] In many situations, more than one outcome can be backed by well-grounded legal argument, and there is no meta-rule powerful enough to deliver a conclusive answer. In such situations, decision-makers have to make a choice that is based on some other factor.[16] A key question for Alexy is whether such choices, such (value) judgements, can be rationally grounded and justified.[17] Alexy's answer to this question is that they can. Briefly, a legal proposition is justified if it is the result of a practical discourse that adheres to a set of rules and forms of legal argumentation. To defend this claim, Alexy constructs a system of 28 of these rules and forms of argumentation. These include the rule that legal propositions must be anchored in universal norms and the rule that they must adhere to basic rules of logic (for example demands of non-contradiction and consistency). Legal propositions must also comply with rules governing the use of certain forms of legal argument (for example analogy and *e contrario* arguments), rules governing the allocation of the burden of proof, and so on.[18] Proportionality reasoning is not mentioned as one of the forms of argument to

[12] Alexy (n 2) 84–86, 371. See also R Alexy, 'Constitutional Rights, Balancing, and Rationality' (2003) 16 *Ratio Juris* 131.

[13] R Alexy, *Theorie der Juristischen Argumentation: Die Theorie des Rationalen Diskurses als Theorie der Juristischen Begründung* (Frankfurt am Main, Suhrkamp, 1978). I refer to the English translation: R Alexy, *A Theory of Legal Argumentation* (translated by R Adler and N MacCormick) (Oxford, Oxford University Press, 2010).

[14] *Ibid* 1f.

[15] *Ibid* 287f.

[16] *Ibid* 3ff.

[17] *Ibid* 7.

[18] A list of Alexy's rules can be found in the Appendix to *A Theory of Legal Argumentation*.

be used in legal argumentation. In more recent writings, Alexy has confirmed that the proportionality test is the proper form of rational legal argumentation for settling conflicts between constitutional rights and between constitutional rights and legitimate public interests.[19] In such situations, a plurality of (legal) arguments must be taken into account, and the strength of the reasons in favour of one constitutional norm must be balanced against the strength of the reasons in favour of the competing norm. Proportionality argumentation, and balancing in particular, provides a structure within which the weights of legal arguments can be assessed and balanced against each other.[20]

The idea that rights norms should be understood as optimisation requirements and the idea that proportionality reasoning, and balancing in particular, can be rational are both highly controversial claims.[21] In this book, I do not adopt a particular position on these matters. My reason for drawing on Alexy's work is to find a way of reasoning about the lawfulness of compulsory mental health intervention under the CRPD. As I have demonstrated in the previous chapters, in many cases the lawfulness of such interventions hinges on discrimination analysis, which, in turn, requires judgements about the objectiveness and reasonableness of such interventions. Such judgements involve reasoning about the strength of the arguments for and against compulsory care from the perspective of the CRPD. As will be demonstrated in the remainder of this chapter and in chapter four, Alexy's proportionality assessment model provides a structure for making such judgements that allows us to reach more predictable conclusions about these matters.

III. THE RUDIMENTS OF PROPORTIONALITY ASSESSMENT

This section explains the content and structure of Alexy's proportionality assessment model. As we will see, Alexy divides proportionality assessments into four stages, and at each stage there is a criterion that has to be fulfilled.[22] These stages concern the legitimacy of the aim(s) of the law or practice under review, the suitability of the law or practice for achieving the aim(s), the necessity of the law or practice and the proportionality, in the narrow sense, of the law or practice. I discuss each stage in turn below, paying particular attention to the last stage, which involves balancing.

[19] See, eg, R Alexy, 'On Balancing and Subsumption' (2003) 16 *Ratio Juris* 433, 448 and Alexy, 'Constitutional Rights and Proportionality' 52.

[20] Alexy (n 10) 54f.

[21] For an overview of the different criticisms of principles theory, see R Poscher, 'The Principles Theory: How Many Theories and What Is Their Merit?' in M Klatt (ed), *Institutionalized Reason: The Jurisprudence of Robert Alexy* (Oxford, Oxford University Press, 2012). Regarding the criticism that balancing tries to compare the incommensurable, see section VII.A below.

[22] Alexy (n 2) 66.

A. Legitimate Aim(s)

In Alexy's model, the first question to be asked is whether the law or practice under scrutiny has a legitimate aim. Any aim that does not conflict with the aims, objectives or provisions of the relevant legal framework is legitimate.[23] There is no doubt that this provides states and legislators with ample room for manoeuvre; a common critique of Alexy is precisely that he offers policy-makers too much leeway to introduce laws and policies that interfere with individual entitlements under human rights law.[24] Alexy's standard of legitimacy, however, corresponds to that applied by the UN treaty bodies in their discrimination jurisprudence.[25] For this reason, I will not discuss whether a higher standard ought to be set.

B. Suitability

This stage of the proportionality assessment asks an empirical question: does the policy or practice under review contribute to its aim(s)? Only means that *in fact* contribute to their aims are acceptable.[26] For Alexy, this requirement follows from the conceptualisation of constitutional rights norms as optimisation requirements and the idea of Pareto optimality. Pareto optimality describes a situation in which one position (here, an individual entitlement protected under the CRPD) cannot be improved without making another position worse off (that is, without interfering with another individual entitlement protected under the Convention or with a legitimate public or collective interest).[27] The suitability criterion expresses this idea by ruling out policies and practices that interfere with individual rights without making any contribution to their aims. Abolishing such a policy clearly improves the level of protection for the rights at stake without having any negative impact on its stated aims, to which it does not contribute anyway. This criterion is easy to accept in the human rights context. Interferences with international human rights norms require justification; if a practice does not make any real contribution to the aim it was intended to serve, it surely cannot be justified.

[23] Alexy (n 2) 395. For Alexy, the relevant legal framework is the German Constitution. In this book, it is the CRPD.

[24] See, eg, S Tsakyrakis, 'Proportionality: An Assault on Human Rights?' (2009) 7 *International Journal of Constitutional Law* 468, 474.

[25] See ch 1, section VI.B.

[26] Alexy (n 2) 397–98.

[27] The concept of Pareto optimality, or Pareto efficiency, was developed by the Italian economist, sociologist and philosopher Vilfredo Federico Damaso Pareto. The idea is widely used in welfare economics and game theory. Alexy discusses its application in relation to constitutional rights jurisprudence in Alexy (n 2) 105, fn 222 and 398–99.

Assessing whether a given law or practice actually furthers an (often abstractly formulated) aim can, however, be difficult. Our knowledge about the capacity of a specific piece of legislation (and of law in general) to bring about desired results is often uncertain and incomplete.[28] The topic of this study is no exception. The effects of coercive care are poorly understood. Though there is empirical support for the view that compulsory mental health interventions lead to health improvements and prevent suicide and violent acts in some cases, and in the short-term, we also have evidence that such positive effects are absent in other cases.[29] This conflicting evidence raises questions about how much a particular policy or practice must contribute to its aims to count as suitable and how certain the empirical facts underpinning suitability assessments must be. Is it enough that a particular regime of compulsory psychiatric care contributes to its aims in a few cases? Must it serve its aims in at least a majority of the situations to which it applies? Or is the suitability criterion an even higher threshold? Also, what kind of evidence is necessary to establish that the regime in question is suitable? Regarding the first question ('how much'), Alexy argues that, unless the constitution says otherwise, policy-makers are free to decide on the degree to which they wish to pursue a legitimate aim.[30] Applied to the topic of this study, this means that, unless the CRPD says otherwise, states parties are free to decide on the extent to which they want to protect the health and lives of people with psychosocial disabilities and to prevent violent crimes among this group. The CRPD limits this room for discretion by requiring its states parties to ensure that people with psychosocial disabilities can enjoy these rights 'on an equal basis with others'.[31] This means that if a state party to the CRPD has the ambition of reducing the number of suicides or the number of people who have certain negative health outcomes, then such an ambition must cover people with disabilities as well. The state cannot set a less ambitious target for people with disabilities.

The second question concerns how certain suitability assessments must be. According to Alexy, policy-makers may rely on uncertain but not 'evidently false' data about the effectiveness of their policies.[32] In the CRPD context, this means that a state party to the Convention may rely on the claim that X per cent of those subjected to compulsory psychiatric care see health improvements, but no state can rely on the claim that everyone subjected to such care benefits from it. This rather low threshold is a compromise between two – in Alexy's view – extreme positions on the epistemic quality of justifications for infringements

[28] JJ Rachlinsk, 'Evidence-based Law' (2011) 96 *Cornell Law Review* 901, 910ff.

[29] See ch 2, section IV.

[30] Alexy (n 2) 395. Alexy calls this freedom 'end-setting discretion'.

[31] CRPD Arts 10, 16, and 25. Art 25 uses the formulation 'without discrimination on the basis of disability' instead of 'on an equal basis with others'.

[32] Alexy (n 2) 418–20. Alexy affirms this position in more recent writings; see, eg, R Alexy, 'Formal Principles: Some Replies to Critics' (2014) 12 *International Journal of Constitutional Law* 511, 520–22.

of rights norms. The first position is connected to principles theory and the idea that constitutional rights are optimisation requirements. If legislatures (or states parties to the CRPD) were allowed to act on uncertain empirical knowledge, there would be a risk that these norms would not be realised to the greatest extent that is factually possible, and, ideally, this risk should be avoided. This suggests that laws and policies that interfere with constitutional or human rights ought to rely on empirical premises that can be established with certainty, that is, on the basis of reliable data.[33] Given that such empirical knowledge is seldom available, and may even be impossible to come by, this position would paralyse a legislature. This is clearly undesirable: democratic institutions must be able to pursue their political agendas. The opposite position emphasises the value of democracy: legislatures must be free to set national policies even in situations of uncertainty. The problem with this position is that it permits interferences with constitutionally protected individual entitlements based on uncertain and possibly incorrect information. Thereby, it undermines the protection provided by constitutional rights.[34] Alexy's solution to this problem is to set a low threshold at the suitability stage and defer final answers to the balancing stage, at which point the degree of certainty required to justify an interference will depend on the severity of the interference. The more serious the interference with a rights norm, the more reliable the underlying empirical evidence in its favour must be (see further below, in section III.D and section VI).

C. Necessity

The third stage of Alexy's proportionality test concerns the necessity of the means under consideration. This criterion prohibits restrictions of constitutional norms that go *beyond* what is required to achieve the aim of the law. If a legitimate aim can be achieved by two or more (broadly) equally suitable means, then the law or policy that interferes the least with rights norms must be chosen.[35] This standard is sometimes referred to as the requirement of 'least restrictive means' and also expresses the idea of Pareto optimality. If, for example, compulsory care and voluntary care were to produce similar therapeutic outputs for people at risk of committing suicide, then voluntary approaches would have to be preferred. Authorising compulsion under such circumstances would interfere with personal integrity without compensating for this interference by saving more lives. Far-reaching and indiscriminate policies and practices will typically fall foul of this threshold. Think, for instance, of the Swedish

[33] Alexy (n 2) 416.
[34] Alexy (n 2) 417–18.
[35] Alexy (n 2) 67–68, 398–99.

system of coercive care, in which people admitted for compulsory psychiatric care cannot refuse medication that is deemed to be necessary to protect the individual's health and achieve the aims of coercive care, regardless of their ability to make a free and informed treatment decision in a particular situation.[36] If the aim of this policy is to avoid decisions about treatment options being made by patients who do not understand and cannot weigh up the relevant information, then the policy is overly broad, covering many cases where compulsion is not necessary to achieve the aim. As noted above, a systematic review of research into the decision-making ability of people with psychosocial disabilities admitted for inpatient treatment has concluded that the majority possessed the ability to make treatment decisions.[37]

The necessity requirement does not, however, imply that laws and policies with the smallest negative impact on the protection of human rights should always be preferred. Its application is restricted to cases in which an aim can be achieved by equally suitable means that do not have a negative impact on some *third* legitimate interest (for instance public resources or the rights of third parties).[38] Hence, the mere fact that there are ways to protect health and prevent suicide and violence against others that interfere less with the fundamental rights of people with psychosocial disabilities than the policy in question does not automatically imply a violation of the necessity criterion. First, it must be determined whether such alternative policies and practices are equally efficient ways of achieving their aims: that they produce 'as much' protection of health and life as compulsory care. In addition, they should not interfere with the other rights protected under the CRPD or with other legitimate public interests.

Just like the suitability criterion, the necessity criterion asks an empirical question: can the aim be pursued through other means that are equally suitable but less restrictive? For example, some states parties to the CRPD provide for so-called compulsory community-based treatment as an alternative to compulsory inpatient treatment. However, the evidence shows that this treatment method is not particularly effective. Compulsory community-based treatment does not seem to produce better therapeutic outcomes than standard voluntary care.[39] If this is correct, then maintaining a coercive element in community-based treatment for people with psychosocial disabilities, which clearly interferes with the entitlement to respect for personal integrity, is unnecessary and therefore unlawful. To determine the class of relevant alternatives to compulsory inpatient care, one has to know how much a particular domestic

[36] Act (SFS: 1991:1128) on Compulsory Psychiatric Care, Sweden, para 17.

[37] See ch 2, section IV.A. D Okai et al, 'Mental Capacity in Psychiatric Patients: Systematic Review' (2007) 191 *British Journal of Psychiatry* 291.

[38] Alexy (n 2) 400.

[39] S Kisely and L Campbell, 'Compulsory Community and Involuntary Outpatient Treatment for People with Severe Mental Disorders (Review)' (2014) 12 *Cochrane Database of Systematic Reviews*.

system contributes to its aims, and one has to be able to assess the ability of possible alternatives to match this level of contribution. As far as compulsory mental health interventions are concerned, both of these endeavours are problematic. As discussed above, our knowledge of the effectiveness of compulsory care is uncertain.[40] The same is true of our knowledge of the effectiveness of potential alternatives.

Certain possible alternatives to compulsory mental health care are often highlighted in the literature. These include Soteria projects,[41] Open Dialogue,[42] family group conferencing,[43] personal ombudsman systems,[44] community crisis care[45] and advance treatment directives.[46] Common features of these alternatives are that they focus on developing the abilities and promoting the well-being of the individual concerned through dialogue, support and advance planning. Another common feature is that they view conventional medical treatment as just one route to improved well-being among others. The existing research does not

[40] See ch 2, section IV.

[41] The Soteria treatment model was developed by the American psychiatrist Loren Mosher in the early 1970s. Under this model, treatment services are provided in a community-based setting and all clinical treatment is administered on a voluntary basis. The model has been replicated in a number of European countries. See T Calton et al, 'A Systematic Review of the Soteria Paradigm for the Treatment of People Diagnosed with Schizophrenia' (2008) 34 *Schizophrenia Bulletin* 181.

[42] Open Dialogue is a form of support for adults experiencing emotional distress or crisis that was pioneered in Finland. The process begins with an initial meeting that brings together mental health professionals, the patient, and people who are important to the patient, such as family and friends. Decisions on future care and treatment are made on the basis of a consensus of everyone participating in the dialogue. See J Seikkula and M Olson, 'The Open Dialogue Approach to Acute Psychosis: Its Poetics and Micropolitics' (2003) 42 *Family Process* 403. A Cochrane review to systematically evaluate its merits for people with psychosis and serious clinical conditions is underway. See R Pavlovic, A Pavlovic and S Donaldson, 'Open Dialogue for Psychosis or Severe Mental Illness (Protocol)' (2016) 10 *Cochrane Database of Systematic Reviews*.

[43] Family group conferencing is another form of decision-making based on dialogue between the person experiencing mental health problems and his or her family, friends and professional network. It was developed in the Netherlands, and it differs from the Open Dialogue approach in that medical professionals provide information and advice but do not participate in the meetings in which treatment decisions are made by the person concerned and his or her social network. G de Jong, G Schout and T Abama, 'Prevention of Involuntary Admission through Family Group Conferencing: A Qualitative Case Study in Community Mental Health Nursing' (2014) 70 *Journal of Advanced Nursing* 2651, 2653.

[44] As described in ch 1, section II, an ombudsman is a publicly employed professional whose only task is to support his or her clients in various matters, including in their contacts with health care authorities. The ombudsman has no special legal powers, and can neither consent to nor reject clinical treatment on behalf of clients. Instead, the potential of the system lies in the ombudsman's ability to develop trusting relationships with individuals and to help them to make their own decisions.

[45] The idea behind community crisis care is to respond to people with psychosocial conditions experiencing acute stress with swift, short-term treatment in their homes or in a community setting to avoid hospitalisation. S Murphy et al, 'Crisis Intervention for People with Severe Mental Illnesses (Review)' (2015) 12 *Cochrane Database of Systematic Reviews* 5.

[46] P Weller illustrates how such directives can be used to support people with psychosocial disabilities when making health care choices in *New Law and Ethics in Mental Health Advance Directives: The Convention on the Rights of Persons with Disabilities and the Right to Choose* (Hove, Routledge, 2015), in particular 2–3, 9–11 and 159–61.

allow us to draw definitive conclusions about the efficacy of these alternatives. A systematic review of Soteria projects identified three randomised controlled trials involving a total of 223 participants diagnosed with schizophrenia.[47] The review concluded that, for this group, treatment according to the Soteria model produced therapeutic outputs that were as good as and, in certain areas, better than those produced by compulsory inpatient treatment. Yet the paucity of reliable evidence for the efficacy of this method prevented the research team from recommending Soteria as a standard treatment method. Researchers have drawn similar conclusions about community crisis care[48] and 24-hour care in hostel-type houses staffed with psychologists and nurses.[49]

To sum up, there seems to be ample evidence that, in many cases, including in some complex ones, voluntary care and support can be just as effective as compulsory care. But it remains uncertain whether alternative and less restrictive forms of care can cater for the needs of the *entire group* of people who are currently subject to compulsory care. Alexy handles such problems in the same way that he handles problems of empirical uncertainty at the suitability stage. States may rely on uncertain empirical facts but not on claims that are 'evidently false'.[50] Further considerations are postponed to the balancing stage, which is discussed below (see sections III.D and VI.A).

D. Proportionality in the Narrow Sense

The last stage of Alexy's proportionality model involves a balancing exercise to ensure that the legally relevant reasons in favour of the policy or practice under scrutiny are, broadly speaking, 'on balance with' the reasons against it. Whilst the suitability and necessity stages in Alexy's model establish fixed but low threshold criteria, the standard set at this stage is different. It depends on how much the policy under scrutiny (here, the system of compulsory mental health care) interferes with rights norms. Alexy formulates this in the (first) law of balancing, which reads: 'The greater the degree of non-satisfaction of, or detriment to, one principle, the greater must be the importance of satisfying the other [principle].'[51] The first 'principle' referred to in this law of balancing is a rights norm and the second, the 'other' principle, represents a competing norm protecting a legitimate public interest or another constitutional or human right.

[47] Calton et al, 'A Systematic Review'.

[48] Murphy et al, 'Crisis Intervention'. Under certain circumstances, such interventions have been proven to be as effective as compulsory inpatient care.

[49] R Macpherson et al, 'Twenty-four Hour Care for Schizophrenia (Review)' (2009) 2 *Cochrane Database of Systematic Reviews*. When compared with compulsory inpatient care, care in hostel-like settings tended to result in more social activities and similar therapeutic outcomes. However, the limited number of studies available means that conclusions cannot be drawn with any certainty.

[50] See section III.B above.

[51] Alexy (n 2) 102.

The process for determining whether the legally relevant reasons in favour of a policy are on balance with the reasons against it is called balancing. It can be broken down into three steps.[52] The first step is to estimate the degree to which a policy interferes with an entitlement protected under constitutional law in the circumstances at hand. Second, a similar estimation is made with regard to the competing entitlement or public interest (the 'other' principle) by looking at the degree to which the abolition of the policy would interfere with the individual entitlement or public interest it aims to protect. Third, the two estimates of degrees of interference are compared with one another. Take civil detention to prevent suicide, for example. To assess the proportionality (in the narrow sense) of a particular domestic regime that provides for such an intervention, the first step is to estimate its negative implications for the entitlement to personal liberty. Then, one estimates the negative implications of abolishing that regime and replacing it with a system that interferes less with the personal liberty of those concerned. Depending on the design of the regime under review, the less restrictive alternative could be a system with higher thresholds for hospitalisation, shorter time frames, more generous conditions for leaves of absence, and so on. The closure of all closed psychiatric wards and the redeployment of resources to voluntary mental health services might also be an alternative. The loss incurred by modifying or repealing the regime under review essentially depends on its effectiveness in preventing suicide vis-à-vis the ability of alternative systems to prevent such acts. The last step compares the weight or seriousness of these negative implications – that is, the significance of the infringement of liberty brought about by the system under review and the harm that would be caused to life if the system were modified or abolished. If the negative consequences of permitting civil detention are greater than the negative implications of prohibiting such detention, then civil detention to prevent suicide is disproportionate and unlawful. If the opposite is the case, such detention is permitted (and may even be obligatory). If the negative consequences are of broadly equal weight, the state is free to choose whether to provide for civil detention to prevent suicide. This is the same as saying that this practice is permitted.

These steps are captured in Alexy's weight formula, which also illustrates the form of argument that balancing represents.[53] In its simplest form, the formula reads:

$$W_{i,j} = \frac{I_i}{I_j}$$

[52] R Alexy, 'The Weight Formula' in J Stelmach, B Brożek and W Załuski (eds), *Studies in the Philosophy of Law: Frontiers of the Economic Analysis of Law* (Cracow, Jagiellonian University Press, 2007) 9, 10f. See also Alexy, 'On Balancing and Subsumption' 436f.

[53] The weight formula is first introduced in the postscript to Alexy's book on constitutional rights theory. See Alexy (n 2) 408ff.

I_i represents the degree to which the policy or practice under consideration interferes with an entitlement protected under the constitution (or, in this book, the CRPD); I_j represents the degree to which abolition of the policy or practice would interfere with the competing entitlement or public interest. The indices '$_i$' and '$_j$' serve to make clear which norm the interference relates to. $W_{i,j}$ represents the weight of the reasons *against* a given policy or practice in the circumstances at hand.[54] Alexy suggests that a triadic scale may be used to classify the interferences as 'light', 'moderate' or 'serious'.[55] Other terminology is possible. For example, 'minor' or 'weak' might be used instead of 'light', and 'high' or 'strong' instead of 'serious'. To continue with the example of civil detention to prevent suicide, we should classify the degree to which such detention interferes with liberty as light, moderate or serious, and the same goes for the degree to which the abolition or modification of this form of compulsory hospitalisation would interfere with the protection of life. These estimates can then be replaced with numbers so that they form a sequence, for instance 1, 2 and 3.[56] A light interference is given the number 1, a moderate interference the number 2, and a serious interference the number 3. Once numbers are introduced into the formula, a numerical outcome is produced. A result above 1 means that the law or practice under review is disproportionate. If the result is below 1, then the law or practice is permitted, and may even be obligatory. If the outcome is 1, this represents a stalemate in which the legislature (or state) has discretion; it may choose to keep or repeal the policy. Both courses of action can be justified as proportionate.[57]

To cater for the fact that the rights and public interests at stake might differ in their legal importance, Alexy introduces another set of variables into the formula:

$$W_{i,j} = \frac{W_i \; x \; I_i}{W_j \; x \; I_j}$$

W_i represents the abstract weight of the individual entitlement that is interfered with by the policy or practice under review and W_j the abstract weight of the competing entitlement or public interest. Whilst I_i and I_j are tied to

[54] Expressed in more accurate but also more abstract terms, $W_{i,j}$ represents the concrete weight of the principle P_i (ie a constitutional rights norm protecting an individual entitlement) relative to the conflicting principle P_j (ie the competing norm protecting another constitutional rights norm or a legitimate collective interest). Alexy (n 2) 409.

[55] Alexy (n 2) 412–13.

[56] Alexy, The Weight Formula' 21, though Alexy uses the sequence 1, 2, 4. Given that any selection of three numbers in which the succeeding number is greater than the preceding one will do the job, I prefer to use 1, 2, 3 here. See L Lindahl, 'On Robert Alexy's Weight Formula for Weighing and Balancing' in AS Dias et al (eds), *Liber Amicorum de José de Sousa e Brito em Comemoração do 70.° Aniversário: Estudos de Direito e Filosofia* (Coimbra, Almedina, 2009) 183, fn 31.

[57] Alexy (n 2) 417–18.

the circumstances at hand, W_i and W_j refer to the weights of the competing entitlements or public interests relative to each other according to the constitution (here, the CRPD), but independently of their weight or importance in the concrete case.[58] In the example of civil detention to prevent suicide, W_i refers to the entitlement to personal liberty, and W_j to the competing public interest in preventing suicide and thereby protecting life. One can certainly discuss whether life is more important than liberty, or vice versa. I will revisit this question below.[59] The rationale behind the inclusion of abstract weights becomes clearer if we exchange life for property and imagine mental health legislation that provides for compulsory care to prevent damage to the property of the person concerned or of third parties.[60] Under such circumstances, most human rights lawyers would agree that a 'serious' interference with property rights is not as important as a 'serious' interference with personal liberty, even broadly speaking. The weight formula caters for this by allowing its users to assign a higher abstract weight to the protection of liberty.

To complete the weight formula, Alexy argues, a third pair of variables must be inserted, namely those representing the *reliability* of the assumptions upon which the legal argumentation rests.[61] The extended weight formula reads:

$$W_{i,j} = \frac{W_i \; x \; I_i \; x \; R_i}{W_j \; x \; I_j \; x \; R_j}$$

R_i and R_j represent the degree of reliability of the assumptions upon which the estimates about the abstract weights (W_i and W_j) and degrees of interference (I_i and I_j) rest. Consider again the example of civil detention to prevent suicide. How should we classify the degree to which abolishing such a regime would interfere with the interest in protecting life? Would it constitute a 'serious', 'moderate' or 'light' interference? Our choice of classification depends on how efficient a particular domestic system of compulsory mental health care is at preventing suicide and on how much protection voluntary services could offer. As we know from the above, we lack certain knowledge about both of these matters. Empirical uncertainty of this kind is taken into account when balancing, and it influences the outcome by undercutting the weight given to arguments founded on such uncertain assumptions.[62] A triadic scale can be used to classify the degree of reliability of the underlying assumptions. The three classes are 'certain', 'plausible' and 'not evidently false'. Just like classifications

[58] Alexy, The Weight Formula' (n 52) 16.
[59] See section V.A below.
[60] Some mental health laws incorporate such provisions. See, eg, Dutch Act (1992) on Psychiatric Hospitals (Compulsory Admissions) Art 1(f)(3).
[61] Alexy (n 2) 419.
[62] Alexy (n 2) 418–19.

of abstract weights and degrees of infringement, classifications of reliability can be represented by numbers. In Alexy's model, 'certain' assumptions are assigned the number 1, 'plausible' assumptions the number 0.5, and 'not evidently false' assumptions the number 0.25.[63] This means that estimates about abstract weights (W_i and W_j) and degrees of interference (I_i and I_j) that are based on reliable empirical data retain their weight when balanced against the competing entities in the weight formula. Estimates that rest on uncertain data, on the other hand, are undercut. Suppose that a particular mental health regime constitutes a serious (s) interference with the entitlement to liberty under the CRPD and that this assessment is based on empirically reliable (r) information about the relevant characteristics of the regime. The law authorises civil detention for long periods of time in closed wards in psychiatric hospitals, and the treating clinician has discretion to decide about leaves of absence and the like. Assume further that the protection of liberty and the protection of life are considered to be equally important ($W_i = W_j$). Translated into the weight formula, this reads as follows:

$$W_{i,j} = \frac{(W_i\ x)\ I_i\ x\ R_i}{(W_j\ x)\ I_j\ x\ R_j} = \frac{s\ x\ r}{} = \frac{3\ x\ 1}{}$$

Under such circumstances, states parties to the CRPD would need to demonstrate that the abolition of the regime under review would seriously interfere with the protection of life and that this estimate could be backed by reliable data. The fact that the effects of compulsory regimes and their alternatives tend to be poorly understood complicates this task. If we modify the example so that the system only authorises the compulsory hospitalisation of people who lack the ability to make free and informed treatment choices, and we classify the infringement on liberty brought about by such a system as moderate (m), states parties are in a better position to justify their practices. Translated into the weight formula, this would read:

$$W_{i,j} = \frac{(W_i\ x)\ I_i\ x\ R_i}{(W_j\ x)\ I_j\ x\ R_j} = \frac{m\ x\ r}{} = \frac{2\ x\ 1}{}$$

States parties could argue, for example, that any system similar to the one under review could be expected to prevent X number of suicides. A regime with higher thresholds or shorter time frames is bound to be less effective, and so it would lead to increased numbers of suicides.[64] This would interfere at least moderately (m) with the protection of life, and this estimate rests on empirical facts that are reliable (r). The weight formula can illustrate that the weights of the

[63] Alexy, The Weight Formula' (n 52) 25.
[64] See ch 2, section IV.B.

arguments for and against a compulsory regime that limits its scope of application to people who lack decision-making ability are the same:

$$W_{i,j} = \frac{(W_i\ x)\ I_i\ x\ R_i}{(W_j\ x)\ I_j\ x\ R_j} = \frac{m\ x\ r}{m\ x\ r} = \frac{2\ x\ 1}{2\ x\ 1}$$

When all the numbers are inserted into the weight formula, the outcome follows as a matter of arithmetic, but the weight formula should not be understood as a way of turning balancing into calculation.[65] The outcome is not 'true' or precise in the sense we usually associate with the results of multiplication and division. The truth of the outcome depends on the truth of the premises upon which the arguments are based, and the weight formula helps us to see this clearly. The numbers represent the strength of the arguments, and they help make explicit the internal workings of balancing reasoning. They do not imply mathematical exactitude. If the outcome of balancing is 2, this means that the law or practice in question is disproportionate and therefore unlawful. It does not imply that the reasons for respecting the individual entitlement represented in the numerator are precisely twice as strong or weighty as the reasons in favour of the competing entitlement or public interest. What the weight formula does is to make clear the relationships between the different factors that must be taken into account. It demonstrates that the balancing process can rest on a rational legal argument.[66] In so far as the classification choices are legally sound (or whatever term one prefers to use to express the fact that they are acceptable from a legal point of view) and no calculation errors are made, the outcome of the weight formula is equally legally sound. But balancing is still a matter of legal argumentation – not mathematics.

IV. COMPATIBILITY WITH THE OBJECTIVE AND REASONABLE STANDARD

This section examines whether Alexy's proportionality assessment model is compatible with the objective and reasonable standard developed in the jurisprudence of the UN treaty bodies – that is, whether these two frameworks for assessing justifications of interferences with human rights norms express similar or different standards. Were they to express different standards, Alexy's work would be less helpful to us in pursuing the aims of this study. As I explained in chapter one, the objective and reasonable standard requires that the state action under consideration has a *legitimate aim*, that it *contributes* to its aim, and that it be *reasonable* (in relation to the aim).[67] It is obvious that there is a significant overlap between this standard and Alexy's proportionality model. First, Alexy's

[65] R Alexy, 'On Constitutional Rights to Protection' (2009) 3 *Legisprudence* 1, 9.
[66] See section II, above, on Alexy's position on legal argumentation.
[67] See ch 1, section VI.B.

conceptualisation of a legitimate aim is identical to that of the UN treaty bodies.[68] Legitimate aims are aims that are compatible with the provisions, aims and objectives of the legal framework in question. Second, both the objective and reasonable formula and Alexy's model stipulate that domestic policies and practices that interfere with human rights norms must contribute to their aims. In Alexy's model, this is expressed in the suitability threshold.[69] The objective and reasonable standard does not provide a clear answer to the question of 'how much' domestic practices must contribute to their aims.[70] Alexy's model sets a low threshold for policies to pass at the suitability stage and defers the ultimate resolution of the issue to the balancing stage.[71] In addition, both the objective and reasonable standard and Alexy's model ask whether the domestic policy under review is necessary to achieve its aims, and both involve an examination of its positive and negative effects in light of the relevant normative framework. For the UN treaty bodies, the relevant framework is whichever treaty they are set up to monitor; for Alexy, the relevant framework is found in the German Constitution.

In Alexy's model, 'necessity' has a specific meaning. As I explained above, the necessity criterion expresses the idea of Pareto optimality. If there are means of pursuing legitimate aims that are equally suitable and that do not affect other legitimate interests in a negative way, states and legislatures must use the least restrictive means to pursue the aims. More concretely, Alexy's model prohibits systems that authorise compulsory care in situations where the same outputs (that is, an equivalent amount of therapeutic benefits and a corresponding level of prevention of suicide and violent crime) could be achieved with voluntary care and support or without any intervention at all.[72] In the jurisprudence of the UN treaty bodies, talk of 'necessity' is often connected to arguments about the reasonableness of the law or practice under review. The fact that a domestic policy (that infringes on a human right) is indiscriminate, covering a range of situations where it arguably makes no real contribution to its aim, constitutes a strong reason against it.[73] Conversely, the fact that a domestic regime is held to be 'the only' or 'the only effective' way to achieve an aim constitutes a strong, though not conclusive, reason in favour of its reasonableness and lawfulness.[74] This implies that the existence of alternative ways of pursuing the same aim is of relevance when determining reasonableness. If such alternative regimes can be

[68] See section III.A.
[69] See section III.B.
[70] See section I and ch 1, section VI.B.
[71] See section III.B.
[72] See section III.C.
[73] Human Rights Committee, 'Communication No 2807/2016' *Hebbadj v France* (2018) UN Doc CCPR/C/123/D/2807/2016 para 7.7. See also joint opinion of Committee members I Brands Kehris, S Cleveland, C Heyns, MVJ Kran and Y Shany (concurring) in 'Communication No 2747/2016' *Yaker v France* (2018) UN Doc CCPR/C/123/D/2747/2016 para 3.
[74] See ch 1, section VI.B.

said to interfere less with individual entitlements protected under human rights law, then they ought to be preferred, unless stronger reasons speak against using the alternatives. In other words, the UN treaty bodies also deploy, in effect, the ideas of Pareto optimality and balancing. Thus, even if Alexy's model and the jurisprudence of the UN treaty bodies differ in their use of terminology and their levels of precision, Alexy's necessity criterion does not conflict with the objective and reasonable standard. On the contrary, it may help us to understand the outcomes of the treaty bodies' decisions in individual cases.

The next question to consider is whether Alexy's proportionality (in the narrow sense) criterion corresponds to the reasonableness criterion in the objective and reasonable standard. Both criteria take a plurality of reasons into account and weigh reasons against counter-reasons. The key question for this study is whether the relevant parameters for reasoning about reasonableness under the objective and reasonable standard are fully captured by Alexy's balancing process. There are reasons to believe that they are, and thus that each process has the same impact on the outcome. The reasonableness criterion under the objective and reasonable standard takes into account the importance of the rights and interests at stake,[75] the negative effects of the law or practice under review, and alternative ways of achieving the same aim(s).[76] So too does Alexy's balancing process. The importance of the rights and interests at stake is clearly represented in the weight formula by the variables W_i and W_j (abstract weights).[77] The negative effects of a law or practice are represented in the numerator of the formula by the variable I_i (degree of interference with an individual entitlement); reasoning about alternative ways to achieve legitimate aims relates to the classification of I_j (degree of interference with a competing entitlement or public interest). It should be noted that, in Alexy's model, alternative ways of achieving the aim of a particular policy are relevant both at the necessity stage and at the proportionality stage. The existence of *equally efficient* and *less restrictive* alternative ways of achieving the same aim in question means the regime fails to comply with the necessity criterion and therefore cannot be justified. The existence of *less* efficient (and less restrictive) means does not entail that the policy is ruled out as unnecessary, but it does mean that there is less reason to keep it. Within the weight formula, the existence of such less efficient alternatives speaks against classifying I_j as a 'serious' interference. The operation of this meta-rule is also evident in the treaty bodies' reasoning about the reasonableness of certain policies and practices. The CRPD Committee's

[75] See *ibid*. Illustrative of this point is the Human Rights Committee's reasoning in 'Communication No 919/2000' *Müller and Engelhard v Namibia* (2002) UN Doc CCPR/C/74/D/919/2000. In para 6.8, the Committee points to 'the importance of the principle of equality between men and women' and holds that the reasons put forward in defence of a policy treating men and women differently are not of 'sufficient importance in order to outweigh' the reasons against the policy.

[76] See ch 1, section VI.B.

[77] See section III.D.

reasoning in *Bujdosó et al v Hungary* is illustrative. The case concerned restrictions on voting rights for persons under guardianship that had been introduced in order to protect the integrity of the state party's political system. As the Committee correctly noted, there are alternative ways to pursue this aim, ways that are even suggested in the treaty text. Voting procedures could be adapted to ensure that they are accessible and easy to understand and use for people with intellectual and psychosocial disabilities, and states could allow people with disabilities to be assisted in voting.[78] This constituted a strong, although not conclusive, reason against the state's restrictive approach.

The objective and reasonable standard was developed as part of discrimination analysis, and it implies a definite reluctance to accept direct discrimination, that is, laws, policies and practices that involve the *differential* disadvantageous treatment of protected groups on the basis of sex, race, disability and similar discrimination grounds. To justify such differential treatment, states must 'explain' the need to differentiate based on a ground protected under the discrimination scheme. Alexy's model contains no such rule. Given that Alexy's model operates at a high level of abstraction and is not tied to discrimination analysis in particular, this is only to be expected. In the next chapter, I will show that the requirement to justify differential treatment can be included within Alexy's model of proportionality reasoning.[79]

There remains the important question of whether 'reasonableness' and 'proportionality in the narrow sense' are equally demanding criteria. Proportionality is determined according to the law of balancing, which states that the policy that interferes less with the relevant entitlements or interests at stake is to be preferred. If there is a stalemate, states may decide at their discretion.[80] The UN treaty bodies have not been explicit about the rule governing the outcome of reasonableness assessments under the objective and reasonable standard. For this reason, it is possible that the objective and reasonable standard sets a higher standard than Alexy's proportionality criterion. We cannot rule out the possibility that the objective and reasonable standard requires that the reasons in favour of a given domestic regime must *outweigh* the reasons against it. This would imply that, in the case of a stalemate, as Alexy calls it, the state action under review would be unlawful. In fact, the Human Rights Committee has, on occasion, indicated that this is the case. Reviewing a piece of legislation that differentiated on the basis of sex, the Committee concluded that it violated the prohibition of discrimination because the reasons in favour of this distinction did not 'outweigh' the reasons in favour of a gender-neutral approach.[81] On other occasions, its reasoning has, however, implied that states

[78] CRPD Committee, 'Communication No 4/2011' *Bujdosó et al v Hungary* (2013) UN Doc CRPD/C/10/D/4/2011 para 9.6.

[79] See ch 4, section II.

[80] See section III.D.

[81] *Müller and Engelhard v Namibia* (n 75) para 6.8.

have discretion in so-called stalemate situations. In a case concerning gender quotas, the Committee found no violation of the prohibition of discrimination because 'a reasonable proportionality' was maintained between the aim and the means.[82] This suggests that states have some leeway when assessing proportionality in the narrow sense. The CRPD Committee's declaration, in several of its discrimination cases, that states enjoy a certain margin of appreciation when determining issues of reasonableness and proportionality suggests the same conclusion.[83]

The term 'margin of appreciation' is borrowed from the jurisprudence of the European Court of Human Rights (ECtHR) and expresses the idea of state discretion.[84] So far, the CRPD Committee's references to state discretion have been limited to assessments of the reasonableness and proportionality of accommodation measures[85] and to the determination of the specific procedural arrangements that would facilitate the exercise of legal capacity in the domestic context.[86] Although the Committee does not give any reasons for its acceptance of state discretion in these areas, it seems reasonable to assume that its motivations are similar to those of the ECtHR. The European Court grants state discretion on several grounds, most notably because views of the precise scope and content of states' obligations under human rights law vary between countries as a result of differences in legal traditions, constitutional values and historical developments. A certain degree of discretion is therefore granted out of respect for the democratic process and to facilitate the pluralism associated with democratic societies. Discretion is also granted on the basis that, because of their first-hand knowledge of the facts and values at stake in individual cases, domestic authorities are often better placed than the Court to make certain decisions.[87] This fits well with Alexy's model, which permits domestic legislators to base their justifications of interferences with human rights on uncertain (but not evidently false) empirical data when reliable information

[82] Human Rights Committee, 'Communication No 943/2000' *Jacobs v Belgium* (2004) UN Doc CCPR/C/81/D/943/2000 para 9.5.

[83] See the CRPD Committee's reasoning in 'Communication No 5/2011' *Jungelin v Sweden* (2014) UN Doc CRPD/C/12/D/5/2011 paras 10.5–10.6; 'Communication No 35/2016' *JH v Australia* (2018) UN Doc CRPD/C/20/D/35/2016 para 7.4; 'Communication No 26/2014' *Bacher v Austria* (2018) UN Doc CRPD/C/19/D/26/2014 para 9.7.

[84] Much has been written on this topic. See, eg, A Legg, *The Margin of Appreciation in International Human Rights Law: Deference and Proportionality* (Oxford, Oxford University Press, 2012).

[85] *Ibid*. Accommodation measures refer to the modifications and adjustments of the built environment, public services, and information and communication systems needed in a particular case to ensure that persons with disabilities can enjoy their human rights on an equal basis with others. Denial of reasonable accommodation measures constitutes a form of discrimination (CRPD Art 2).

[86] CRPD Committee, 'Communication No 7/2012' *Marlon James Noble v Australia* (2016) UN Doc CRPD/C/16/D/7/2012 para 8.6; 'Communication No 30/2015' *Marakov v Lithuania* (2017) UN Doc CRPD/C/18/D/30/2015 para 7.6.

[87] G Lestas, *A Theory of Interpretation of the European Convention on Human Rights* (Oxford, Oxford University Press, 2007) 80–98.

is not available.[88] It also accords with Alexy's stalemate rule. In one sense, granting states discretion in stalemate situations is uncontroversial. If there are equally strong (legal) reasons in favour of two competing interpretations of what the law demands in a certain situation, then neither interpretation is better than the other. In Alexy's theory of legal argumentation, both interpretations would therefore be legally correct.[89] In relation to the topic of this study, Alexy's position is tantamount to claiming that, in situations in which there are equally strong (legal) reasons for the proposition that a domestic regime of compulsory care is proportionate (and therefore ought to be permitted) as there are reasons backing the opposite proposition (that is, that the regime violates the CRPD), the prohibition of discrimination leaves states parties with a choice: they can maintain the regime or abolish it. Neither is required by the treaty. What the CRPD neither obliges nor prohibits, states parties are free to do or not to do. At this abstract level, the claim is convincing. The question will be how, precisely, the stalemate situation is delineated in Alexy's model. I will return to this matter in section VII.A.

V. ASSESSING AND WEIGHING ARGUMENTS

As this chapter has illustrated, the first three stages of Alexy's proportionality model set rather low thresholds for the policy under review to meet. They weed out domestic regimes that serve offensive aims, that are extremely ineffective in achieving their aims, and that are excessive and permit more coercion than necessary to achieve their aims. All other regimes will pass to the balancing stage, where most of the intellectual heavy lifting takes place. As Kai Möller points out, balancing is a concept that is used not only in constitutional and human rights law but also in moral philosophy and in everyday language.[90] It is a flexible concept that can mean several things. Balancing makes us think of a set of scales: we put competing rights, interests, or reasons for and against a certain decision on either side of the scale in order to determine which right or interest ought to prevail. Recall the example involving Nancy from the Introduction to this book. When deciding to reject treatment, she probably reflected on her alternatives: accept the doctor's recommendation of inpatient treatment, or go home. She might have balanced, on the one hand, the unpleasant effects of hospitalisation and medical treatment (eg distress and the side effects of medication) and, on the other hand, the possibility of improved health and well-being as a result of the proposed treatment and the risk of the further

[88] See sections III.B and D.

[89] Alexy (n 13) 287f.

[90] K Möller, *The Global Model of Constitutional Rights* (Oxford, Oxford University Press, 2012) 137.

deterioration of her health and other problems if she declined treatment. Or her decision to decline treatment might have been a spontaneous response, based on her previous bad experiences of psychiatric care. Similarly, the physician who recommended that Nancy accept inpatient treatment probably identified and weighed the pros and cons of different treatment alternatives before discussing them with Nancy.

When balancing takes place as a part of legal reasoning, the image of a set of scales can be misleading. The outcome does not hinge on the concrete effects of a single decision alone. Legal rules inform and constrain balancing in the sense that they constitute weighty reasons for or against a particular course of action regardless of the positive and negative effects of this course of action in an individual case. The right to free and informed consent means that medical staff must not impose medical care on people who reject care and who, with or without support, are able to make free and informed treatment decisions. The obligation to refrain from imposing care also applies in situations in which a failure to treat may appear unreasonable if we focus on the concrete effects alone. A case in point is an (adult) Jehovah's Witness refusing a blood transfusion and thereby denying him- or herself lifesaving treatment. In most jurisdictions, if someone in Nancy's situation declined hospitalisation, the physician would be authorised to make an initial decision about whether to respect the decision or to commit the person to compulsory care. Domestic laws create a framework for decision-making; they determine the factors that should be taken into account and those that should be left out. In most jurisdictions, physicians would be expected to assess the risks of non-intervention. In Nancy's case, her condition would probably deteriorate further. She might neglect basic needs (food and hygiene), and she might engage in self-harming behaviour, even suicide. These risks would have to be balanced against the prospect of avoiding such harms through inpatient care. It is possible, however, to set a different standard for lawful compulsion. The Mental Capacity Act (Northern Ireland) 2016 provides an example here. Under this law, people who (with or without support) are able to make free and informed treatment decisions are protected from compulsory care, regardless of whether respecting a treatment refusal would involve risks to health and life.[91]

In this study, balancing takes place at the level of domestic policy and law-making. The primary question is not whether coercive care is proportionate and in accordance with the CRPD in an individual case. Instead, the question is whether a specific system of coercive care is proportionate, and thereby compatible with the CRPD, in a particular domestic context. When considering the proportionality of legal rules and regimes, legislators have to estimate and compare the effects of such systems on the individuals concerned. How many have their personal liberty, integrity, and legal capacity restricted by

[91] See ch 2, section II.

alternative versions of compulsory care, and how much do these systems interfere with the rights of those concerned? Further, how many would experience health harms, end their lives, or commit violent crimes against others if one system were replaced with a less restrictive one? Answering these questions means reasoning about the system's clinical benefits and about the ability of the system to prevent harmful behaviour. It also means reasoning about the adverse effects of psychiatric medication, including when coercively administered. The risk of decision-makers misapplying these rules in individual cases and the risk of abuse in closed settings must also be taken into account. There are many reports of abuse, neglect and ill treatment within mental health settings, particularly in closed wards. The severity of such malpractice ranges from the use of condescending language and minor but disproportionate coercive incidents (eg unwarranted searches) to abuses of unfathomable cruelty, such as patients being chained, whipped and raped.[92] Obviously, if there is a high risk that treatment tantamount to torture will take place under a particular system, this would constitute a conclusive reason against maintaining the system. On the other hand, a lower risk of, for instance, erroneous decision-making or minor abuses might be acceptable if appropriate legal safeguards were in place and the overall positive effects of the system compensated for such negative effects.

This form of balancing is quite similar to practical reasoning.[93] What we are doing is developing a legal argument for whether compulsory mental health care is lawful under the CRPD, taking all legally relevant circumstances into account.[94] This is a form of balancing in the sense that we are considering the trade-offs of permitting and prohibiting compulsory care, and one can describe the process as striking a balance between the entitlements and interests at stake in light of the weight attached to these entitlements and interests under the CRPD. But, as will be seen in the rest of this book, the process is far from a mechanical exercise, and Alexy's weight formula is merely a tool to remind decision-makers of the different factors that must be taken into account and of their mutual relationships. The rest of this section is devoted to the key components of the balancing process. Section V.A discusses the abstract weights of the relevant entitlements and interests. Section V.B discusses the extent to which compulsory care interferes with the entitlements to personal liberty,

[92] Non-governmental organisations like Human Rights Watch and Validity (formerly the Mental Disability Advocacy Centre) do groundbreaking work in this area, disclosing information about the use of 'net beds' and chains to prevent people from leaving, sexual abuses, malnutrition and overmedication. Information is available on their websites: www.hrw.org and www.validity.ngo.

[93] By practical reasoning, I mean reasoning about what ought to be done in the circumstances. Unlike practical reasoning in general, law is formal in the sense that norms codified in authoritative sources of law provide reasons to act in accordance with these norms *because of their origin*. F Schauer, 'Balancing, Subsumption, and the Constraining Role of Legal Text' in M Klatt (ed), *Institutionalized Reason: The Jurisprudence of Robert Alexy* (Oxford, Oxford University Press, 2012) 315.

[94] See Möller, *The Global Model* 140.

integrity and legal capacity and asks what would be lost if such systems were modified or abolished.

A. Abstract Weights

Abstract weights are the weights attached to the individual entitlements and public or collective interests that conflict in the situation under consideration. Domestic mental health laws determine the circumstances under which compulsory care is lawful within that jurisdiction. They thereby set out how the conflict between the entitlements to personal liberty, integrity and legal capacity, on the one hand, and the interest in protecting health and life and promoting public safety, on the other, should be solved within this area of law. In the weight formula, the weights of these entitlements and interests are represented by the variables W_i and W_j.[95] These weights may differ, and when they do this ought to affect the outcome of balancing.[96] I know of no international human rights treaty that ranks its norms in a particular order of importance, but some entitlements are considered to be of particular importance, such that no individual or collective interest may justify their infringement, not even in times of emergency. The prohibition of torture is a case in point. It is often held that this prohibition is 'absolute' in the sense that there are no circumstances in which interests such as public or personal safety may justify acts of torture, or inhuman or degrading treatment or punishment. No safety gains may compensate for the harm caused by such acts and/or the fact that such acts have been permitted; respect for the prohibition of torture is simply, and always, more important.[97] If we were considering domestic health legislation that permitted interventions that violated the prohibition of torture, there would be no need to resort to discrimination and proportionality argumentation. Such legislation would clearly violate the CRPD and would have to be repealed.[98] None of the other norms at stake in this study have such an elevated status within human rights law.

The question then becomes whether there are other reasons to consider the enjoyment of personal liberty, integrity and legal capacity to be more important than the protection of health and life and the promotion of public safety, or vice versa. The treaty text provides no clear-cut answer to this question. As I noted in chapter one, the CRPD sets out some general principles that are to guide the interpretation of the treaty. One of these principles is respect for dignity and

[95] See section III.D.

[96] If the competing rights and interests are considered to be of equal weight, abstract weights can be disregarded in balancing. The weight formula clearly illustrates this: assigning the same number to the variables W_i and W_j does not affect the outcome of the equation.

[97] According to Alexy, this implies that the prohibition of torture is a *rule* of high legal ranking. Alexy (n 2) 82–83.

[98] CRPD Art 15.

individual autonomy, including the freedom to make one's own choices.[99] The connection between the principle of respect for human dignity and the right to respect for physical and mental integrity, as well as the connection between the principle of respect for autonomy and the right to legal capacity (and, though more indirectly, the right to respect for integrity and for personal liberty), could be taken to imply that these principles and individual entitlements are of particular importance under the CRPD – that they are *more* important than other interests and individual entitlements enshrined in the Convention. If so, then this might justify assigning a higher abstract weight to liberty, integrity and legal capacity when balancing them against the protection of health and life and the promotion of public safety. The merit of this argument, I believe, becomes clear in light of the reasons behind the Convention's emphasis on dignity and autonomy. In chapter one, I suggested that the prominence given to these principles in the treaty text is best explained by the fact that the denial of the right to make personal decisions, both everyday decisions and major life choices, is one of the most pressing human rights concerns for people with disabilities, and this is one of the central concerns that the CRPD seeks to address.[100] This does not mean that protecting autonomy is always more important than protecting other rights and interests or, to put it another way, that moderate interferences with the entitlement to legal capacity are in principle worse, from the point of view of the CRPD, than moderate interferences with the interest in protecting life or health. Rather, the CRPD's emphasis on autonomy-related entitlements serves as a reminder that such concerns should be given priority when implementing the treaty obligations at the domestic level and, more generally, that they should better inform domestic policy-making in areas where they have not been emphasised sufficiently and where the value of personal decision-making for people with disabilities has been underestimated.

It is possible to adopt a different position on this matter. The fact that neither the treaty text nor any other legal source provides conclusive answers to these questions implies that commentators will reasonably disagree about them. In the end, judgements about the normative importance of the entitlements and interests at stake in compulsory care depend on moral and ideological assumptions about what is 'good' about the entitlements and interests at stake and how these 'goods' compare with each other from the perspective of the CRPD. The legal debate over the lawfulness of compulsory psychiatric care under the CRPD has paid relatively little attention to such matters. Rather, the critique of compulsory care has focused on its ineffectiveness in achieving its aims, its adverse effects, and its focus on people with psychosocial disabilities.

In chapter four of this book, I adapt Alexy's proportionality assessment model to fit the non-discrimination context. As we will see, Alexy's weight

[99] *Ibid* Art 3(a). See also ch 1, section I.
[100] See ch 1, section I.

formula helps us to make explicit the considerations that underlie the process of balancing interests in discrimination analysis. In the adapted model, the abstract weight variable plays a slightly different role; it assists us in understanding the value of consistency (or formal equality) within discrimination analysis.[101]

B. Degrees of Infringement

I turn now to the question of how we should determine the degrees of interference with the entitlements and interests at stake in a given system of compulsory mental health care. In contrast to abstract weights, degrees of infringement are not determined in relation to each other, but separately. The variable I_i in the weight formula represents a situated estimate of the degree to which a domestic practice interferes with an individual entitlement; I_j stands for a corresponding estimate regarding the degree to which refraining from this practice would interfere with the competing entitlement or interest.[102] These estimates are made in relation to a given legal framework – in our case, the CRPD. These two variables are the focus, I believe, of most of the legal argumentation that takes place in the balancing process. In order to determine how much a domestic authorisation of civil detention in a psychiatric hospital interferes with the entitlement to personal liberty under the CRPD, a number of factors are relevant. These include the domestic thresholds for civil detention, the time frames for detention, and how restrictive the regime is for those who are hospitalised against their will. Regimes that permit compulsory inpatient treatment for very long periods of time (years) interfere more with personal liberty than regimes that only permit short-term hospitalisation. Furthermore, it may be argued that domestic regimes that completely cut off the individual from his or her social network interfere more with personal liberty than regimes that provide for leaves of absence and allow for visits from family and friends. Full and effective participation and inclusion in society is an important principle that permeates the CRPD. It is given the status of a general principle of the Convention in Article 3(c) and forms the normative basis of many of the substantive provisions in the treaty, including Article 19, which obliges states parties to ensure that people with disabilities have equal opportunities to choose their places of residence. It also requires that they have access to in-home and community-based services to support living in the community and prevent isolation and segregation.

Another relevant factor to consider is whether the regime permits detention in situations in which free and informed treatment decisions can be obtained. Whilst all forms of detention entail an element of disregard for personal preferences (eg preferences about where to stay), it can be argued that the

[101] See ch 4, section III.
[102] See section III.D.

interference with personal self-determination is most pronounced in cases in which the detained are able (with or without support) to make free and informed decisions about their care. Given the Convention's emphasis on personal self-determination, we can say that the compulsory hospitalisation of people who are able to make free and informed treatment decisions interferes more with the CRPD than the compulsory hospitalisation of people who lack this ability. Respect for individual autonomy, including the freedom to make one's own choices, is another general principle undergirding the CRPD.[103] Article 12(2) affirms people with disabilities' entitlement to equal respect for personal choices. The precise implications of the lack of decision-making ability for these entitlements are not explicated in the treaty text but have to be worked out using discrimination analysis. Nonetheless, few would disagree that overriding 'truly' free and informed health care rejections is worse, from the point of view of the Convention, than ignoring treatment refusals that are unduly influenced by external factors or clinical symptoms.[104] Further parameters could be added to this list to make it more detailed and to tailor it to specific contexts. An estimate of how much the abolition of a regime would interfere with the protection of life requires an assessment of its effectiveness. How many benefit from the system under review, and how much do they benefit? The answers to these questions would then be compared with the amount of protection that could be generated by a system that interferes less with the personal liberty of those affected, for example a system with shorter time frames or one that is restricted to situations in which free and informed treatment decisions cannot be obtained.

Alexy's model of balancing asks us to classify the degrees of interference as 'serious', 'moderate' or 'light' on the basis of such considerations.[105] In some cases, this is feasible and helpful. Imagine a system that commits large numbers of people to compulsory care in closed facilities in a remote area for long periods of time. Few would contest that such a regime interferes with the entitlement to personal liberty to a 'serious' degree. Imagine further that proponents of the system claim that it prevents suicide and thereby protects the lives of those committed to compulsory care. Nevertheless, compulsory care has a poor record when it comes to treating symptoms of depression and averting self-destructive acts. In fact, acts of suicide occur on a regular basis during coercive care.[106] Determining how much the abolition of the compulsory regime would interfere with the protection of life in such circumstances is harder than determining the

[103] CRPD Art 3(a).
[104] See ch 1, section II.
[105] Alexy (n 2) 409.
[106] Results from a 2015 meta-analysis show that suicide rates in psychiatric inpatient settings vary considerably between hospitals, from as high as one death by suicide in 113 admissions to as low as one in 1,300 admissions. G Walsh et al, 'Meta-analysis of Suicide Rates among Psychiatric In-patients' (2015) 131 *Acta Psychiatrica Scandinavia* 174, 175. The meta-analysis is based on data from high-income countries because relevant data from middle- and low-income countries was not available.

degree to which it interferes with the entitlement to personal liberty. However, the ineffectiveness of the regime suggests that such a reform would, at most, constitute a 'moderate' interference with the protection of life. We would have to compare the regime with the less restrictive alternatives, including systems with stricter time limits for compulsory care, systems that allow for visits from family and friends, and fully voluntary systems, in terms of their ability to prevent suicide. The better these alternative systems performed, the weaker the reasons for maintaining the one under scrutiny would be. Depending on the results of this comparison, abolishing the system might even be classified as a 'light' interference with the protection of life.[107] If we assume that the abstract weights (of the respect for personal liberty and the protection of health) are equal and that the estimates of the degrees of interference are based on equally reliable empirical assumptions, then this means that the system is disproportionate. The amount of protection of life provided by the system does not compensate for the infringement on personal liberty it involves.

When considering systems that interfere far less with personal liberty and offer more in the way of the protection of life, classifying degrees of interference according to the triadic scale can be more difficult and are likely to generate more disagreement among those interpreting the CRPD. Think of a system of coercive care that includes a professional care apparatus. Studies suggest that these services do mitigate symptoms of depression and prevent self-destructive behaviour in the time before treatment can take effect. Inpatient suicides in these systems are relatively rare.[108] Coercive care is a measure of last resort, but, because of the difficulties involved in risk prediction, people who would not have ended their lives in any event are still hospitalised against their will and doctors fail to identify people at 'real' risk, who later end their lives by suicide. One could argue that such systems also interfere seriously with personal liberty, which constitutes a weighty reason for considering them unlawful. Against this position, it could be argued that such systems limit the use of compulsory hospitalisation as much as possible. The problems of risk prediction are epistemic problems that cannot be solved with better laws. Given that compulsory care may be the only way to prevent suicide under certain circumstances, states ought to be allowed to authorise such care in these circumstances.

Epistemic problems arise not only because our knowledge of empirical facts is incomplete. Even if we had certain knowledge of how many acts of suicide a certain system prevented, the question of how much we should *value* this fact in relation to the protection of life would remain. Article 10 of the CRPD reaffirms everyone's inherent right to life and requires states parties to ensure its effective

[107] In this case, we would have to assume that the less restrictive alternatives were not as effective as the system under review in preventing suicide and thereby protecting life. If the alternatives were equally effective and less restrictive, the system would fail to pass the necessity threshold. See section III.C.

[108] See n 106.

enjoyment by people with disabilities on an equal basis with others. However, it does not inform us about the value of preventing one or several suicides. Alexy's model of balancing requires that such uncertainties are taken into account in our decision-making.[109] The next section discusses how both empirical and normative epistemic uncertainties are taken into account at the balancing stage.

VI. DEALING WITH EPISTEMIC UNCERTAINTY

Much of the current CRPD-inspired criticism of compulsory psychiatric care concerns its alleged ineffectiveness in achieving its therapeutic and safety aims and its adverse effects on those compelled to undergo such treatment. Many commentators have highlighted the severe physical and mental suffering caused by compulsory interventions, as well as the growing body of evidence that calls into question its supposed effectiveness in preventing suicide and violence against others. Many have charged coercive care with creating more problems than it solves.[110] The critique is based on assumptions and evidence about the positive and negative effects of compulsory care of varying epistemic quality, and this fact needs to be taken into account when we assess the strength of the criticism. As noted above, in section III.D, Alexy's extended weight formula offers us a way of dealing with such empirical uncertainties by means of the variables R_i and R_j. In Alexy's original formula, R_i and R_j represented the epistemic quality not only of empirical matters ('facts') but also of normative assumptions.[111] Normative assumptions include our assumptions about the content of the law: in our case, assumptions about what the CRPD permits, commands and prohibits. Normative uncertainty arises when we are uncertain about the 'correctness' of such assumptions. Proportionality scholars have argued that, in the interests of clarity, this epistemic variable should be divided into two separate variables, one for empirical uncertainty and another for normative uncertainty.[112] In recent

[109] See section III.D.

[110] See, eg, T Minkowitz, 'The United Nations Convention on the Rights of Persons with Disabilities and the Right to Be Free from Nonconsensual Psychiatric Interventions' (2007) 34 *Syracuse Journal of International Law and Commerce* 405; P Gooding, *A New Era for Mental Health Law and Policy: Supported Decision-making and the UN Convention on the Rights of Persons with Disabilities* (Cambridge, Cambridge University Press, 2017) 70, 88–93; CRPD Committee, 'General Comment No 1 on Article 12: Equal Recognition before the Law' (19 May 2014) UN Doc CRPD/C/GC/1 para 42; Parliamentary Assembly of the Council of Europe, 'Recommendation No Rec 2158(2019)' (26 June 2019).

[111] Alexy (n 2) 414.

[112] According to Klatt, Meister and Schmidt, aggregating empirical and normative reliability as a single variable has significant disadvantages, for it may render situations involving different levels of empirical and normative reliability indistinguishable from one another. See M Klatt and J Schmidt, 'Epistemic Discretion in Constitutional Law' (2012) 10 *International Journal of Constitutional Law* 69, 91; M Klatt and M Meister, *The Constitutional Structure of Proportionality* (Oxford, Oxford University Press, 2012) 132.

writings, Alexy has adopted this view.[113] The refined weight formula reads as follows:

$$W_{i,j} = \frac{W_i \; x \; I_i \; x \; R_i^e \; x \; R_i^n}{W_j \; x \; I_j \; x \; R_j^e \; x \; R_j^n}$$

Reasoning about these two kinds of uncertainty follows the same procedure. In both cases, a triadic scale is used, and, as the weight formula indicates, empirical and normative uncertainty affects the outcome in the same way. As I mentioned above, Alexy suggests that 'certain' assumptions are assigned the number 1, 'plausible' assumptions the number 0.5, and 'not evidently false' assumptions the number 0.25.[114] This means that estimates about abstract weights and degrees of interference that are based on reliable empirical and normative premises retain their weight when balanced against the competing entities in the weight formula. Estimates that rest on uncertain knowledge, on the other hand, are undercut. Since empirical and normative premises address different matters and give rise to different questions, I will discuss them in separate subsections. The following subsection discusses the implications of empirical epistemic uncertainty for the topic of this study, and subsection B considers matters relating to normative epistemic uncertainty.

A. Empirical Uncertainty and Discretion

Estimates of 'how much' mental health laws interfere with human rights norms are based on assumptions about the concrete effects of a particular regime on those to whom it applies. How restrictive is the regime in question? For how long are people detained in closed wards? Are they granted any leaves of absence? How is the forced administration of psychiatric medication and treatment carried out? May medical staff use physical restraints on agitated patients who refuse to take medication? What kinds of care can be administered on a compulsory basis? What kinds of adverse effects are associated with compulsory hospitalisation and care? Can people with the ability to make free and informed treatment decisions be hospitalised and treated against their will? In many states parties, questions of when, how, against whom, and for how long compulsory care may be imposed are regulated in laws and policies whose practical implementation is subject to supervision. If this is the case, then such data can inform our reasoning about the degree to which such regimes interfere with personal liberty and legal capacity. Doubt over empirical facts is likely to arise in

[113] Alexy, 'Formal Principles' 514–15; R Alexy, 'The Absolute and the Relative Dimensions of Constitutional Rights' (2017) 37 *Oxford Journal of Legal Studies* 31, 38.

[114] See section III.D.

the course of reasoning about the interference with integrity implied by a system of compulsory care. Whilst the adverse effects of much psychiatric medication are well documented, there is, for example, no agreement about the long-term adverse effects of repeated sessions of electroconvulsive therapy.[115] Moreover, there is great variation in how patients experience compulsory care. Some studies have found that between 39 and 86 per cent think that their admission was right in retrospect.[116] Variations in response to this question were associated with gender, living situation and diagnosis, but there was also a connection with the legal design of the system of compulsory care. Domestic systems with stricter criteria for compulsory hospitalisation and medical treatment and systems that provided for adequate legal safeguards (such as court review, the ability to appeal and access to legal support) were associated with more positive views of compulsory care, and the most negative views came from patients subject to systems with few legal safeguards to protect their rights and interests. Other studies paint a more pessimistic picture, highlighting the distress, feelings of helplessness, and fear that people subjected to compulsory care experience.[117] Some describe their experiences of compulsory mental health care in very strong terms, for instance as 'unbelievably humiliating'.[118] Which of these pictures most accurately reflects the situation in a given state, has to be determined on a case-by-case basis.

Turning to the question of what would be lost if a particular domestic regime was repealed and replaced with a less restrictive one, any answer to this builds on assumptions about the amount of harm to health, life and safety that such a change would bring about. Ideally, such assumptions would be based on precise and reliable information about the numbers of serious health harms, suicides and violent crimes that can be averted through different regimes of coercive care and through voluntary services. However, we do not possess such information. There are few studies on the outcomes of compulsory care and the alternatives to such care, and many of the studies that have been carried out suffer from methodological weaknesses, such as small sample sizes and a high risk of selection bias. The same is true of the compulsory administration of

[115] G Kirov et al, 'Evaluation of Cumulative Cognitive Deficits from Electroconvulsive Therapy' (2016) 208 *The British Journal of Psychiatry* 266. In 2011, the Cochrane Common Mental Disorder Group initiated a systematic review to assess the benefits and harms of electroconvulsive therapy. The review was considered important for several reasons, one of which was the fact that there were discrepancies among reports of adverse effects. The final report is yet to be published. KA Leiknes et al, 'Electroconvulsive Therapy for Depression (Protocol)' (2011) 5 *Cochrane Database of Systematic Reviews*.

[116] S Priebe et al, 'Patients' Views of Involuntary Hospital Admission after 1 and 3 Months: Prospective Study in 11 European Countries' (2010) 196 *The British Journal of Psychiatry* 179.

[117] L Kuosmanen et al, 'Deprivation of Liberty in Psychiatric Hospital Care: The Patient's Perspective' (2007) 14 *Nursing Ethics* 597.

[118] O Nyttingnes, T Ruud and J Rugkåsa, '"It's Unbelievably Humiliating" – Patients' Expressions of Negative Effects of Coercion in Mental Health Care' (2016) 49 *International Journal of Law and Psychiatry* 147.

medication. This means that decision-makers will have to rely on less specific and less certain information,[119] and the level of uncertainty is likely to vary between states parties depending on their resources and on how ambitious they are about evaluating existing care systems and potential alternative services.

To determine the harm that would be caused by abolishing a particular regime of compulsory care and replacing it with a less restrictive system, we need to compare the outputs of the existing regime with the outputs of possible alternatives. As discussed above, there is evidence that voluntary care and support services are as effective as compulsory inpatient care under certain circumstances.[120] Even so, we do not know whether these alternatives would be able to cater for the needs of the entire group of people who are currently subject to compulsory care. People working in domestic psychiatric emergency care centres can provide numerous examples of situations in which they see no other way to protect the health and life of the person concerned but to commit him or her to compulsory care.[121] Situations involving people with suicidal ideation and people experiencing psychosis who do not believe they are in need of treatment would be paradigmatic examples.[122] On the other hand, there are also studies that indicate that such situations can be effectively handled with voluntary support.[123] In these circumstances, when we do not possess certain knowledge, Alexy's model provides domestic legislators with a certain amount of (epistemic) discretion. They may assume that voluntary support services will be less effective, or that they will be insufficient to protect the health and lives of the people concerned, or they may take a more optimistic view on the potential of these services. The uncertainty of these assumptions is taken into account at the balancing stage. In the weight formula this is expressed in the variable R_i^e.[124] Alexy anchors this rule (ie that domestic legislators are free to rely on uncertain assumptions) in the jurisprudence of the German Federal Constitutional Court, and he defends it with arguments about the proper separation of powers, in the German context, between the democratically elected legislature and the Court.[125] Given that certain knowledge about the effects of laws and policies

[119] On the methodological challenges involved in empirical research into the effects of compulsory care, see section II of the Introduction to this book.

[120] See section III.C.

[121] At least in Sweden, Norway and the United States, where surveys of psychiatrists' views have been carried out. See, eg, Manne Sjöstrand et al, 'Ethical Deliberations about Involuntary Treatment: Interviews with Swedish Psychiatrists' (2015) 16 *BMC Medical Ethics*. It should be noted that the United States has not yet ratified the CRPD.

[122] *Ibid*.

[123] See section III.C. See also de Jong, Schout and Abama, 'Prevention of Involuntary Admission'; J Seikkula et al, 'Five-year Experience of First-episode Nonaffective Psychosis in Open-dialogue Approach: Treatment Principles, Follow-up Outcomes, and Two Case Studies' (2006) 16 *Psychotherapy Research* 214.

[124] Alexy (n 32) 515.

[125] Alexy (n 2) 416–18. See also R Alexy, 'Comments and Responses' in M Klatt (ed), *Institutionalized Reason: The Jurisprudence of Robert Alexy* (Oxford, Oxford University Press, 2012) 331f.

is seldom available, legislators must be allowed to rely on data that cannot be established with certainty. Requiring legislators to justify their rights-restricting policies on the basis of knowledge that can be established with certainty would lead to legislative paralysis, and this cannot, Alexy asserts, be an acceptable conclusion: democratically legitimated legislatures must have the power to pursue their political goals.

B. Normative Uncertainty and Discretion

Determining the weight of arguments for and against domestic practices under human rights norms can be difficult. In part this difficulty is due to the lack of reliable empirical information, as discussed in the previous section. However, even in situations in which the empirical facts are clear, we may hesitate about how to classify an infringement of a particular CRPD norm by a particular regime of compulsory care. We may also be unsure about whether this interference is justified by positive effects the regime brings about. Consider again the example of domestic authorisations of civil detention to prevent suicide and thereby protect life. Imagine that in state party X, 1,000 people with psychosocial disabilities are hospitalised each year because they are considered to be at risk of suicide. Based on the research into risk prevention, we can assume that about 20 acts of suicide were averted by these interventions.[126] Imagine further that, on average, two persons end their lives by suicide during compulsory care each year.[127] Voluntary support services are no better at identifying those at risk, but they manage to avert approximately five acts of suicide per year. Based on this information, how weighty are the reasons in favour of keeping a regime of compulsory care to prevent suicide in state party X? Would it matter if the compulsory regime only targeted people who lacked the ability to make free and informed treatment decisions?

Doubts about how we should answer these questions arise in part from uncertainty about the normative content of the CRPD. The generally formulated rights provisions of the Convention provide no specific information about the value of preventing a certain number of suicides – or homicides for that matter. Balancing requires that we make assumptions about such matters, even if these assumptions cannot be established with certainty and may be subject to

[126] See M Large et al, 'Systematic Review and Meta-analysis of the Clinical Factors Associated with the Suicide of Psychiatric In-patients' (2011) 124 *Acta Psychiatrica Scandinavica* 18, 26–27.

[127] On the prevalence of inpatient suicide, see T Madsen, A Erlangsen and M Nordentoft, 'Risk Estimates and Risk Factors Related to Psychiatric Inpatient Suicide: An Overview' (2017) 14 *International Journal of Environmental Research and Public Health* 253, 254f. The hypothetical figure of two inpatient suicides in a population of 1,000 compulsory admissions is based on Large and colleagues' discussion of inpatient suicides in an article from 2014 in which they used one suicide per 500 admissions as the median figure for their discussion. M Large et al, 'Nosocomial Suicides' (2014) 22 *Australasian Psychiatry* 118.

(fierce) disagreement within the human rights literature. The problem with this is that false premises may enter into the balance and affect the outcome. There is thus a risk that infringements of human rights norms will be justified by arguments that rest on incorrect interpretations of what the CRPD obliges, permits and prohibits. To mitigate this problem, Alexy's model requires those applying the treaty to take the epistemic quality of normative assumptions into account during balancing (variables R_i^n and R_i^n).[128] I will return to the problematic aspects of normative epistemic discretion below when evaluating the advantages and disadvantages of drawing on Alexy's work to interpret the CRPD.[129]

VII. THE ADVANTAGES AND DISADVANTAGES OF PROPORTIONALITY REASONING

In this chapter, I have explored whether and to what extent Alexy's model of proportionality reasoning can assist us in mapping out the scope of permissible compulsory mental health interventions under the CRPD. I first asked whether Alexy's model is compatible with the objective and reasonable standard, and I concluded that the differences between Alexy's model and the objective and reasonable standard are, with one possible exception, merely matters of terminology and level of detail.[130] The possible exception concerns the amount of *discretion* each approach affords to domestic legislatures in situations of epistemic uncertainty and in so-called stalemate situations. I discuss this point further below, in subsection B. In subsection C, I suggest that Alexy's model provides answers to the questions left open by the objective and reasonable standard and thus that it offers a promising way of conducting a discrimination analysis of compulsory psychiatric care under the CRPD. Before discussing these matters, however, I will address a fundamental objection to Alexy's model of balancing, namely that the apparent level of precision provided by the weight formula is illusory because the force of legal argument cannot, in a legally sound manner, be translated into numbers.

A. The Legal Soundness of Classification Choices

In the balancing process, the combined weight of the legal reasons for and against a given law or practice are compared in accordance with the weight formula. This implies that the factors that appear in the numerator and denominator of Alexy's formula are commensurable. Any comparison between two items

[128] Alexy's talk of normative epistemic discretion presupposes that there is a distinction between what the law 'is' and our knowledge of the law.

[129] See sections VII.A and B.

[130] See section IV.

requires a shared value or quality that enables us to reason about the pros and cons of these items (*tertium comparationis*). Two items are never comparable or incomparable *simpliciter*, but only comparable with respect to something.[131] The common element with respect to which items are compared in the balancing process can be described in several ways. In his law of balancing, Alexy calls it the 'degree of satisfaction/non-satisfaction' of the relevant constitutional norm. In his (subsequently developed) weight formula, degrees of satisfaction/non-satisfaction are the sums of the weights of the arguments concerning abstract weights, degrees of interference and the reliability of the underlying premises.[132] A number of authors have taken issue with the very idea of balancing, arguing that it attempts to compare the incommensurable. In the balancing process, the degree of interference with one norm (I_i) is compared with the degree of interference with another norm (I_j), but, in truth, these two factors cannot be compared with one another, these critics allege.[133] Degrees of interference cannot be assessed using a common metric, because there is simply no one measure that captures what is important about all the individual entitlements and public interests protected under constitutional or human rights law. Thus, there is nothing that could facilitate comparison between them. The absence of a common metric seriously threatens (some would say precludes)[134] the possibility of rational argumentation about cases involving conflicts between norms, and thus seems to turn balancing into a subjective and opaque exercise.[135] While the doctrine of balancing may help us to assign the burden of proof and to formulate more precisely the questions that need to be answered, it is of 'no help at all' when we actually come to attempt to answer these questions.[136]

There is no doubt that this objection has some merit. It draws our attention to the fact that, when we seek to determine how much a domestic regime interferes with protected entitlements and interests, the degree of interference is determined in relation to each individual entitlement or interest separately. The facts and norms underpinning these classifications are different. As I explained above, arguments about the degree to which a domestic regime of compulsory mental health care interferes with the entitlements to liberty, integrity and legal capacity

[131] VA da Silva, 'Comparing the Incommensurable: Constitutional Principles, Balancing, and Rational Decision' (2011) 31 *Oxford Journal of Legal Studies* 273, 294.

[132] See section III.D.

[133] Tsakyrakis, 'Proportionality' 471f; GCN Webber, *The Negotiable Constitution: On the Limitation of Constitutional Rights* (Cambridge, Cambridge University Press, 2009) 91ff; T Endicott, 'Proportionality and Incommensurability' in G Huscroft, BW Miller, and G Webber (eds), *Proportionality and the Rule of Law: Rights, Justification, Reasoning* (Cambridge, Cambridge University Press, 2014); Aleinikoff, 'Constitutional Law' 972; J Alder, 'The Sublime and the Beautiful: Incommensurability and Human Rights' (2006) *Public Law* 697.

[134] See, eg, Tsakyrakis (n 24) 471f.

[135] See, eg, Endicott, 'Proportionality and Incommensurability' 328; Webber, 'Proportionality, Balancing' 194–98.

[136] M Jestaedt, 'The Doctrine of Balancing: Its Strengths and Weaknesses' in M Klatt (ed), *Institutionalized Reason: The Jurisprudence of Robert Alexy* (Oxford, Oxford University Press, 2012) 165.

are based on considerations about the negative implications of that regime for these entitlements. Reasoning about the extent to which modifications of the regime (making it less restrictive of personal liberty, integrity and legal capacity) would interfere with the protection of health and life, in turn, revolves around arguments about the potential increase in poor health outcomes, suicides and violent crimes that would result from such reforms. Thus, it is not clear whether 'serious' interferences with the protection of health and life should justify 'serious' interferences with personal liberty, integrity and legal capacity. Alexy has responded to these objections by asserting that two factors facilitate the comparisons between different items in his model: a common legal framework (in his case the German Constitution, in this study the CRPD) and a common scale that allows degrees of interference with different norms protected under that legal framework to be graded (the triadic scale).[137] Alexy acknowledges that the German Constitution provides little guidance about how to classify abstract weights and degrees of interference and says nothing about how to handle epistemic uncertainty.[138] Classifying degrees of interference according to the triadic scale will often be difficult and controversial, but this does not imply that the degrees of interference are incommensurable or that classifications are arbitrary as long as there are criteria for determining (or justifying) the correctness and strength of the arguments for and against a particular classification. According to Alexy, such criteria exist: they are the established rules of legal argumentation in general.[139]

In this way, Alexy links proportionality reasoning to his discourse-theoretic position on legal argumentation in general; he asserts that classification choices are rational if they can be justified.[140] According to Alexy, legal argumentation is rational if it adheres to basic rules of logic and established rules for legal argumentation, and if the end result can be justified on the basis of these rules.[141] This means that a classification can be justified in situations where the relevant common legal framework (here, the CRPD) and the triadic scale do not produce a single correct classification that defeats other alternatives. As noted above, Alexy claims that legal argumentation starts from the assumption that the interpretation and application of legal norms involves more than the subsumption of concrete circumstances ('facts') under abstractly formulated norms. It also involves judgement and discretion.[142] In situations in which the reasons in favour of two different classifications are equally weighty, the decision-maker has discretion. Thus, classification choices can be justified with legal arguments even

[137] Alexy, The Weight Formula' (n 52) 18.

[138] Alexy (n 10).

[139] R Alexy, 'Proportionality and Rationality' in VC Jackson and M Tushnet (eds), *Proportionality: New Frontiers, New Challenges* (Cambridge, Cambridge University Press, 2017) 24–25.

[140] *Ibid* 22–23.

[141] R Alexy, 'The Absolute and the Relative' 39–40. See also section II.

[142] See section II.

if they are underdetermined by those arguments.[143] The final choice between two possible classifications backed up by equally weighty legal arguments will have to be based on some other reason. But this does not necessarily make these choices legally unsound. Whether these choices are legally sound will hinge, I contend, on the amount of discretion involved in classification choices and balancing. The question of whether Alexy's model accords decision-makers too much moral and political discretion is addressed in the following subsection.

B. Too Much Discretion?

Alexy's model of proportionality reasoning grants domestic legislatures a considerable amount of discretion. First of all, legislators are free to justify rights-restricting policies and practices with reference to any aim that does not conflict with the aims, objectives and provisions of the relevant legal framework.[144] Since the objective and reasonable standard grants states a similar margin of discretion, I will not discuss this matter further. Second, legislatures are free to decide on the extent to which they wish to pursue a legitimate aim, unless the relevant legal framework says otherwise.[145] Applied to the topic of this study, this means that states parties are free to decide on the extent to which they want to protect the health and lives of people with psychosocial disabilities and to prevent violent crimes among this group, as long as the protection provided is on par with that provided to people without disabilities. Third, Alexy's model gives legislators discretion in all situations in which balancing produces a stalemate.[146] As I explained above, allowing for discretion in situations where equally strong (legal) reasons support two different interpretations of what the law demands is relatively uncontroversial.[147] In such a situation neither interpretation is better than the other, and the loss that would result from choosing one over the other is equally serious regardless of which interpretation one chooses. However, affording legislators discretion in stalemate situations becomes problematic if stalemates are the typical outcome of balancing in discrimination cases. If the outcome of the balancing process in most discrimination cases were a stalemate, then this would seriously undercut the CRPD's – and other human rights treaties' – ability to protect individuals against discrimination.

Finally, in Alexy's model legislators are free to rely on uncertain, but not evidently false, empirical or normative premises in situations in which certain knowledge cannot be obtained.[148] This raises the following question: does the

[143] Webber (n 4) 197.
[144] See section III.A.
[145] See section III.B.
[146] See section III.D.
[147] See section IV.
[148] See section VI.

CRPD's prohibition of discrimination afford this same discretion to states parties, or does it lay down additional conditions for states parties to adhere to in stalemate situations and in situations in which certain empirical and normative knowledge is lacking? As I said in section IV, the jurisprudence of the UN treaty bodies provides no conclusive answer to this question, nor do the CRPD text, the preparatory works or the states parties' communications with the CRPD Committee. In earlier jurisprudence, the UN treaty bodies explicitly rejected the doctrine of margin of appreciation applied by the ECtHR in assessing the proportionality of domestic policies and practices.[149] This has been interpreted as the UN treaty bodies taking a stand against 'cultural relativism' in human rights law.[150] Human rights are universal in the sense that they impose minimum standards that apply to all states. Whilst this is correct, it is a rather simplistic understanding of universality in this field. Human rights standards apply to countries with different legal traditions, constitutional values, economies and histories, and these differences affect how the rights are protected and, arguably, the ways in which the enjoyment of these rights may be restricted. Moreover, even if the Human Rights Committee and other UN treaty bodies have expressly rejected the margin of appreciation doctrine, their reasoning on the merits in some discrimination cases suggests that states are in fact granted a certain amount of discretion. The *Wackenheim v France* case is illustrative of this point. The claimant in the case, who suffered from human growth hormone deficiency, claimed that the prohibition of 'dwarf tossing' events, in which he would allow himself to be thrown on to an air bed for the purposes of entertainment, was discriminatory. The state defended its prohibition by claiming that it was necessary to protect public order, and the Human Rights Committee accepted this justification without much scrutiny of the empirical and normative assumptions upon which the justification was based.[151] Unlike the Human Rights Committee, the CRPD Committee has expressly recognised that states do enjoy a margin of discretion with regard to certain matters.[152] In addition, the Committee has held that 'it is generally for the courts of States parties to the Convention to evaluate facts and evidence in a particular case, unless it is found that the evaluation was clearly arbitrary or amounted to a denial of justice'.[153] This suggests that states parties to the CRPD enjoy discretion with regard to empirical questions that may influence

[149] See, eg, Human Rights Committee, 'Communication No 511/1992' *Länsman et al v Finland* (1994) CCPR/C/52/D/511/1992 para 9.4; Committee on the Elimination of Racial Discrimination, 'Communication No 30/2003' *The Jewish Community of Oslo et al v Norway* (2005) CERD/C/67/D/30/2003 para 10.3.

[150] D McGoldrick, 'A Defence of the Margin of Appreciation and an Argument for its Application by the Human Rights Committee' (2016) 65 *International and Comparative Law Quarterly* 21, 53.

[151] Human Rights Committee, 'Communication No 854/1999' *Wackenheim v France* (2002) UN Doc CCPR/C/75/D/854/1999 para 7.4.

[152] See section IV.

[153] *Jungelin v Sweden* (n 83) para 10.5; *Bacher v Austria* (n 83) para 9.7.

the balancing process. The room for political choice is not unlimited; domestic authorities must not act in an arbitrary manner or in a way that result in gross miscarriages of justice. The Committee has not commented on this matter at any length, so we are not able to draw any definite conclusions about its view. Still, the constraints on state discretion mentioned by the Committee do not appear to be significantly more stringent than Alexy's rule that domestic legislators cannot rely on empirical assumptions that are evidently false.

I turn now to the discretion granted by Alexy's model in stalemate situations and to the factors that facilitate and constrain discretion in such situations. There are several factors that affect the scope of the stalemate situation. First of all, the use of a coarse-grained scale (the triadic scale) in balancing means stalemate situations will include not only cases in which the reasons for and against a given law or practice are of exactly the same strength but also cases in which the reasons and counter-reasons are of only roughly equal strength.[154] Two mental health statutes may both be proportional (and lawful) even if one of them interferes slightly more than the other with entitlements protected under the CRPD and does not compensate for this greater degree of interference with an enhanced level of contribution to its aims. Similarly, even if one of these statutes produces a slightly higher level of health benefits than the other, this does not necessarily mean that the less efficient regime is disproportionate. Coarse-grained scales do not capture small improvements.[155] A more precise scale involving more than the three possible classifications ('serious', 'moderate' and 'light') could capture smaller improvements, but it would be difficult to apply in practice. Our capacity for normative differentiation is limited.[156]

In addition, when relevant knowledge about what the law (or the CRPD) permits, commands and prohibits is uncertain, Alexy's model provides for normative epistemic discretion in classifying abstract weights and degrees of infringement.[157] Because human rights norms are typically phrased in abstract and ideologically loaded language, providing limited information about their relative normative importance and about how to assess and rank degrees of interference, normative epistemic uncertainty is common. In contrast to Alexy and other constitutional rights scholars, interpreters of the CRPD cannot turn to a rich body of jurisprudence from a constitutional court (or similar) for guidance. In cases of normative epistemic uncertainty, Alexy's model grants decision-makers discretion to choose what assumptions to rely on as long as they adhere to established rules of legal argumentation.[158] This implies that states have a rather wide margin of discretion when seeking to comply with

[154] For a discussion of this point, see da Silva, 'Comparing the Incommensurable' 294.
[155] Alexy (n 2) 412–13.
[156] Alexy (n 2) 412–13. See also Alexy, 'On Balancing and Subsumption' (n 19) 443.
[157] See section VI.B.
[158] *Ibid.*

their legal obligations under the CRPD. On the face of it, this is puzzling. The basic idea behind human rights treaties is to ensure that fundamental rights and freedoms are protected within the states parties to these treaties. A wide margin of discretion undermines this protection, and creates a risk that classification choices will be informed by stereotypical views about people with psychosocial disabilities and biased interpretations of medical facts. Certainly, if the margin of discretion provided to decision-makers under Alexy's model gave them carte blanche, so that *every* proposition about the weight of the arguments in favour of a particular interpretation of a CRPD norm were as good as any other, then that would be wholly unsatisfactory. The boundary between the lawful and the unlawful would evaporate, and balancing would cease to be a useful tool for the purposes of this study. Alexy's model of proportionality reasoning would generate outcomes, but these outcomes would be no more predictable than those produced by the UN treaty bodies' objective and reasonable standard. The examples provided in this chapter, however, demonstrate that, while reasoning about the weight of legal arguments for and against the lawfulness of domestic regimes of compulsory mental health care under the CRPD involves a certain amount of uncertainty, this is not sufficient to justify unlimited discretion on the part of legislators. For example, few would dispute that the compulsory administration of intrusive clinical treatment is a 'serious' infringement of the entitlement to respect for integrity, and most would agree that there would have to be very weighty reasons for this practice to be justified. We can argue about whether the lack of decision-making ability on the part of those subject to this treatment would render it a 'moderate' infringement rather than a 'serious' one, but it is simply wrong to claim that domestic laws permitting the forced administration of antipsychotic medication constitute a minor interference with the entitlement to respect for integrity under the CRPD. Even if the treaty text does not explicitly reject this claim, there is no support for it in subsequent practice or the preparatory works of the CRPD, and it conflicts with positions taken by other human rights bodies on this issue.[159]

Any residual unease we may have about normative discretion seems to be linked to the fact that it entails that states parties to the CRPD are the ultimate judges of their own practices. There is indeed an important difference between (German) constitutional law and international human rights law. In Alexy's system, the German constitutional court is competent to review the legislature's interpretations of basic rights. Under the CRPD, there is no such control body. Whilst the CRPD Committee has a mandate to monitor the domestic implementation of the treaty and to consider individual complaints, its concluding observations and decisions in individual cases are not legally binding. This is a broader issue about the structure of international law: states occupy the roles of duty-bearers and interpreters at the same time. Abandoning proportionality

[159] See ch 1, section IV and ch 2, section V.

argumentation and adopting the objective and reasonable standard would not put individuals in a better position, as the latter is at least as malleable as the former.

C. Structure and Precision

What Alexy's work provides us with is a structure for solving conflicts between human rights norms. It breaks down proportionality argumentation into a step-by-step process and sets out clear criteria to be fulfilled at each step. Policies and practices that fail to meet one of these criteria are rejected as disproportionate and unlawful on that basis. If, for example, it can be established that a policy does not contribute to the achievement of its aim, then it can be deemed unlawful on that basis alone. Decision-makers do not have to proceed to the next steps and consider whether the policy in question complies with the necessity criterion or balance the reasons for and against it. Compared to the objective and reasonable standard, Alexy's framework has the advantage of being more detailed, and because of this it generates more predictable outcomes. As I said in section I, the objective and reasonable standard leaves important questions unanswered. How much must compulsory interventions contribute to their aims? How reliable must the evidence in their favour be? Which reasons are relevant to determining the reasonableness of a particular domestic regime? By what rule(s) do we determine whether that system places reasonable or undue burdens on the individuals concerned? Alexy's model provides answers to these questions, and it thereby delivers more predictable outcomes. The first three steps of Alexy's model (legitimate aim, suitability and necessity) provide clear thresholds that all laws and practices must meet to be proportionate. In the last step of the proportionality assessment, all relevant reasons are taken into account and balanced against each other. Alexy offers us a formula (the weight formula) that we can use to determine the outcome of such balancing. It identifies the factors to be taken into consideration and makes clear their relation to each other. The objective and reasonable standard lacks this level of precision and detail.[160]

Alexy's model is not without methodological weaknesses. Because his model is more precise, it is also more complex. The procedural criterion to be met at the balancing stage is intricate and demanding. Alexy does not place a limit on the reasons that are to be considered at the balancing stage; on the contrary, he asserts that *all* legally relevant reasons must be taken into account. This is an important point as, according to Alexy, the legitimacy of balancing as a form of argument for reasoning about reasonableness presupposes that all relevant

[160] Needless to say, this is only to be expected given that the objective and reasonable standard was developed by the UN treaty bodies and Alexy's model by a legal philosopher.

reasons can be taken into account.[161] Their weights are then to be assessed, taking the reliability of underlying assumptions into consideration. These assessments form the basis for the comparison of the collective weights of the arguments on either side, and thus essentially determine the outcome of balancing. As I noted several times above, apart from the instruction to adhere to the established rules of legal argumentation, the formula itself provides no guidance on how the collective weight is to be determined. What the weight formula demonstrates is that the presence of judgement and discretion in legal argumentation does not render such argumentation irrational. The formula shows that the balancing process that has to take place when constitutional rights norms collide with other constitutional norms or legitimate interests can take the form of a rational legal argument. Alexy's formula can be used to reach decisions on proportionality, as well as to make explicit the considerations and choices behind a given decision on proportionality in the narrow sense. To fully justify the result of a balancing process, we need to examine whether the normative assumptions that feed into the process cohere with the general rules of legal argumentation, such as the canons of interpretation, doctrinal analysis, the use of case law and other legal decisions, and, in this case, the outputs of the UN treaty bodies.[162] If the classification choices are legally sound and no calculation errors are made, then the result produced by the weight formula is also legally sound. This chapter has illustrated that, despite its various weaknesses, proportionality argumentation offers us a way forward by providing a more detailed framework for understanding the scope of lawful compulsory mental health interventions under the CRPD. However, to explore the potential of the proportionality test in more depth, we need to situate it in the context of non-discrimination reasoning. This is the task of the next chapter.

[161] R Alexy, 'The Reasonableness of Law' in G Bongiovanni, G Sartor, and C Valentini (eds), *Reasonableness and Law* (Dordrecht, Springer, 2009) 8.

[162] Alexy (n 13) 230ff. See also section II in this chapter.

4

Proportionality and Non-discrimination

I. THE FOCUS ON DISTRIBUTIVE JUSTICE

HUMAN RIGHTS NORMS typically oblige states to provide a minimum level of protection for certain freedoms or a minimum level of the provision of certain social goods. These levels are often determined, in particular cases, through proportionality reasoning, which seeks to establish the correct balance between two competing individual entitlements to freedoms or social goods, or between one such entitlement and a collective or public interest. Equality provisions have a different focus. They oblige states to ensure that the level of enjoyment of these freedoms and social goods is equally distributed. If people with disabilities enjoy a lower level of liberty or integrity than people without disabilities in similar situations, then there must be a justification for the disparity, or equalising action must be carried out to ensure that people with disabilities enjoy the same level of respect for liberty and integrity as others. When considering the adequacy of any proposed justification of disparities between groups in levels of human rights protection, the mere fact that the members of one group have a disability or impairment (or are characterised by any of the other recognised discrimination grounds) can never justify a lower level of protection. If a group-related difference in the level of human rights protection cannot be justified, then states have, in principle, two options. They can achieve an equal distribution either by action that increases the level of rights protection for the disadvantaged group or by action that decreases the level for everyone else.[1] Pursuing the latter course of action is only permissible if the state does not thereby reduce the level of protection below the minimum standard required under human rights law. In this way, proportionality reasoning within discrimination analysis is not focused on ensuring that people with disabilities (and other protected groups) enjoy a

[1] Some commentators dispute the idea that states are, or ought to be, entitled to decrease the level of enjoyment of personal freedom and social goods to achieve an even distribution. See, eg, S Fredman, 'Emerging from the Shadows: Substantive Equality and Article 14 of the European Convention on Human Rights' (2016) 16 *Human Rights Law Review* 273, 282.

minimum level of, for instance, personal freedom or health and safety. Rather, such reasoning is focused on ensuring that people with disabilities enjoy a level of personal freedom, health and safety *equal* to that enjoyed by people without disabilities in relevantly similar situations. The focus is thus the comparative group disadvantage experienced by (in our case) people with psychosocial disabilities. What is more, proportionality argumentation under equality norms arguably ought to pay particular attention to the specific harms caused by laws and state practices that fall within the ambit of the prohibition of discrimination. These harms have been described in different ways: as forms of socioeconomic disadvantage, powerlessness, marginalisation, exclusion, prejudice, stigma and violence.[2] These harms are not randomly distributed among individuals in a given society but are typically suffered by individuals who are subject to discriminatory policies or practices for reasons that are linked to their membership of a social group.

This chapter develops a framework for reasoning about the lawfulness of domestic regimes that fall within the definition of disability-based discrimination set out in the UN Convention on the Rights of Persons with Disabilities (CRPD). States parties to the CRPD have a general obligation to ensure that the individual entitlements set out in the Convention are implemented in the domestic context. This includes an obligation to modify or abolish existing laws that discriminate on the basis of disability.[3] My framework can assist states parties in evaluating the lawfulness of their mental health regimes, and it can provide useful information about how domestic authorisations of compulsory intervention may be adjusted so as to better comply with the Convention. This framework can be described as a more structured and detailed version of the objective and reasonable standard. Its general rules – that compulsory care regimes must serve legitimate aims, contribute to their aims, and be reasonable – are derived from the objective and reasonable standard. Alexy's work and the work of other scholars fill the gaps, in the sense that I draw on these sources to answer the questions that the objective and reasonable standard leaves unanswered.

II. PROPORTIONALITY ASSESSMENTS TAILORED TO NON-DISCRIMINATION NORMS

The framework reproduces the structure of Alexy's proportionality assessment model. As I explained in the previous chapter, Alexy divides proportionality

[2] See further, below, sections II.D and IV.

[3] Convention on the Rights of Persons with Disabilities (adopted 13 December 2006, entered into force 3 May 2008) 2515 UNTS 3 (CRPD) Arts 4(1)(a) and (b).

assessments into four stages, with a criterion to be fulfilled at each stage: the law or practice under review must have legitimate aims, be suitable, be necessary, and be proportional in the narrow sense.[4] The starting point is thus an examination of the aims behind the domestic regime under scrutiny and of the relationship between the practices of compulsory mental health care – in this book, civil detention and compulsory clinical treatment – and the aims. To be justified, the practices must contribute to the aims of protecting health and life and preventing violence, and must not interfere with the enjoyment of liberty, integrity and legal capacity any more than is necessary to achieve these aims. This initial three-step examination can be viewed as a shortcut to rejecting mental health regimes that are clearly unjustified.[5] The last stage of the framework, proportionality in the narrow sense, involves balancing the reasons for and against the mental health system under review. A number of factors are relevant to this balancing process, including the values attached to the interests at stake, the costs and benefits of permitting compulsory care (given these values), and the reliability of the undergirding assumptions about the relevant facts and norms.[6]

The fact that this is a framework for discrimination analysis means that particular attention is paid to ideas of formal and substantive equality and to the comparative group disadvantage experienced by people with psychosocial disabilities as a result of the domestic mental health regime under review. This focus has led me to include three rules in my framework that are not found in standard accounts of proportionality assessment. The first rule belongs to the suitability stage of the framework and applies to domestic mental health laws that satisfy the definition of direct discrimination. For such laws to count as suitable, the means–end relevance of targeting people with psychosocial disabilities and not others for compulsory health interventions must be demonstrated. The legal basis and precise implications of this rule are discussed in section II.B. The second is a consistency requirement. This applies at the balancing stage, and seeks to ensure that the proportionality assessment adheres to the idea of formal equality, that is, to the idea that relevantly similar cases must be treated alike. This rule is discussed further in section II.D and applied to the topic of this study in section III. Third, my framework incorporates a rule that, in the balancing process, the negative effects of a particular system of coercive psychiatry on the values and interests protected by the idea of substantive equality must be considered. These negative effects include the harms of social exclusion, public prejudice and stigma. How this rule affects the balancing process is described below in sections II.D and IV.

[4] See ch 3, section III.

[5] These rules are shortcuts in the sense that a fully-fledged balancing exercise would produce the same outcomes.

[6] See ch 3, in particular sections III.D, V and VI.

A. Legitimate Aim: Excluding Offensive Policies

To comply with the CRPD, domestic mental health laws must pursue aims that are compatible with the Convention in the sense that they do not conflict with the object, purpose or provisions of this treaty. This follows from the objective and reasonable standard and accords with Alexy's conceptualisation of what counts as a legitimate aim.[7] This requirement excludes offensive aims, such as the segregation or social exclusion of people with disabilities, and aims that are inappropriate in this specific context even if they are not inappropriate in all contexts. Punishment, for example, is a perfectly legitimate aim in the context of criminal law but not in the context of law relating to health care. Administration of medication in order to punish the person concerned constitutes abuse, if not inhuman or degrading treatment.[8] As I have already explained, all of the typical aims behind legal authorisations of compulsory mental health intervention (the protection of health and life and the prevention of violence) are compatible with the CRPD.[9]

B. Suitability: Excluding Ineffective Policies

Domestic regimes of compulsory mental health care must be designed so that they contribute to their aim(s). This follows from the objective and reasonable standard, and it is the criterion that laws and practices must meet at the suitability stage of Alexy's proportionality assessment model.[10] Compliance with the suitability criterion requires there to be a match between the prerequisites that make an individual a potential subject of compulsory care and the purposes of this care. The prerequisites for civil detention and compulsory clinical treatment must be formulated such that decision-makers may resort to compulsion in situations where it is needed and can contribute to the protection of the health and life of the person concerned and/or the prevention of violence. The suitability criterion also implies that health care services must be capable of delivering the care that contributes to these aims. As I have mentioned, the objective and reasonable standard provides no fixed thresholds for how much a domestic regime must contribute to its aim(s), nor does it specify how reliable the empirical data demonstrating such a contribution must be.[11] For this reason, I draw on Alexy's work to set a clear threshold at this stage. According to the framework outlined here, the regime under consideration meets this threshold if it makes some contribution to its aim(s) and if there is empirical evidence of this

[7] See ch 1, section VI.B and ch 3, section III.A.
[8] CRPD Arts 15 and 16; ch 1, section IV.
[9] See ch 2, section III.
[10] See ch 1, section VI.B and ch 3, section III.B.
[11] See ch 2, section VI.

contribution that is not evidently false.[12] This weeds out mental health policies that are wholly ineffective in achieving their aims – that make no contribution at all to the protection of health and life or the prevention of violence.

As this proportionality assessment framework is intended to operate within the area of non-discrimination jurisprudence, I propose to complement the suitability criterion with a requirement that the (means–ends) relevance of targeting people with psychosocial disabilities for compulsion also be demonstrated at this stage. This requirement may be inferred from the jurisprudence of the UN treaty bodies. It pertains to domestic mental health laws that apply exclusively to people with psychosocial disabilities on the grounds of their disability. Such mental health laws are typically accompanied by rules that protect people without psychosocial disabilities from coercive care. They thereby satisfy the definition of direct discrimination. The UN treaty bodies have held that states must 'explain' such differential treatment, suggesting that part of what needs to be explained is the relevance of differential treatment in achieving the aim.[13] Beyond this, however, these committees have not laid down any clear criteria or procedures for determining when a case of differentiation has been sufficiently explained. For this reason, I have chosen to include a requirement to explain the means–ends relevance of policies that directly discriminate against people with psychosocial disabilities at the suitability stage of proportionality assessment, deferring the final evaluation of the state's defences of such differential treatment to the balancing stage (see below, section II.D). The requirement to explain the means–ends relevance of a particular system of compulsory care means that any justifications that rest on evidently false or offensive claims will be rejected at this stage. For example, the claim that people with psychosocial disabilities have a skewed perception of reality and therefore do not suffer, as people without such disabilities do, when they are deprived of their liberty and the claim that people with psychosocial disabilities are dangerous because they are 'beset with evil spirits' are clearly false, and hence they could never justify the disadvantageous differential treatment of people with psychosocial disabilities. By contrast, explanations of differential treatment that are anchored in statistical data will meet the requirement.[14] Thus, the claim that people with psychosocial disabilities are more likely to lack decision-making ability and to engage in violent behaviour than people without such disabilities, will, according to this framework, suffice to establish the means–ends relevance of differential disadvantageous treatment at this stage of the assessment.

[12] See ch 3, sections III.B and VI.A.

[13] See ch 1, section VI.B.

[14] Some authors refer to such practices as 'rational discrimination'. See, eg, S Bagenstos, '"Rational Discrimination", Accommodation, and the Politics of (Disability) Civil Rights' (2003) 89 *Virginia Law Review* 825; D Hellman, *When is Discrimination Wrong?* (Cambridge, Massachusetts, Harvard University Press, 2008) 117ff; P Shin, 'Is There a Unitary Concept of Discrimination?' in D Hellman and S Moreau (eds), *Philosophical Foundations of Discrimination Law* (Oxford, Oxford University Press, 2013) 175f.

C. Necessity: Excluding Excessive Policies

In Alexy's model, the necessity criterion has a very specific meaning. It expresses the idea of Pareto optimality, and it thus serves to weed out restrictions of constitutional norms that go *beyond* what is required to achieve the aim behind the law.[15] In the context of human rights and mental health, this criterion has an intuitive appeal. Interferences with international human rights norms require justification, and the use of coercion in situations in which the same result could have been achieved by voluntary means is surely unjust. As I have said, the non-discrimination jurisprudence of the UN treaty bodies seems to express this principle.[16] I therefore include an Alexy-style necessity criterion within my framework. This criterion excludes excessive domestic regimes, such as mental health laws that provide for civil detention for longer periods than is necessary to achieve the aims of the hospitalisation. It also outlaws authorisations of forced medication in situations in which similar results could be obtained with another type of treatment that places an equal demand on public resources and that the individual accepts voluntarily.

When we apply this criterion to domestic systems of compulsory care, one question immediately arises: do we really need coercive means to attain the rather modest levels of health protection and harm prevention that coercive care systems achieve? As I have explained, there seems to be ample evidence that voluntary care and support can be just as effective as compulsory care in many cases, including in some complex ones. Where this is the case, states parties to the CRPD must refrain from coercion. This implies that states parties should shift their focus away from coercive care and towards funding and developing high-quality health care services and support systems that operate on a voluntary basis. Compulsion cannot be the standard response to people experiencing mental health problems. However, it remains uncertain whether voluntary forms of care and support can cater for the needs of all those who are currently subject to compulsory care.[17] Again, the objective and reasonable standard does not provide much guidance on how we should approach such situations of uncertainty.[18] For this reason, I draw on Alexy's model at this point. It tells us that, in situations in which knowledge of empirical facts is uncertain, legislators have (epistemic) discretion.[19] In the context of this study, this means that states parties to the CRPD may rely on the assumption that there are situations in which voluntary services will not be effective, or at least not as effective as compulsory ones. Hence they are entitled to authorise compulsion *in these situations*. There are different legal techniques for delineating the proper scope of

[15] See ch 3, section III.C.
[16] See ch 3, section IV.
[17] See ch 3, section III.C.
[18] See ch 2, section V.
[19] See ch 3, section VI.A.

compulsory care in domestic statutes. Domestic law could describe such cases in general terms, or it could simply incorporate some version of a 'least restrictive means' criterion. Many states parties have opted for the latter alternative.[20] However, in states parties where compulsory care constitutes the primary (or only) means of responding to the health care needs of people with psychosocial disabilities, the mere introduction of a 'least restrictive means' criterion would not suffice to comply with the necessity criterion described here.[21] When examining the necessity of a particular compulsory regime, *all* evidence-based alternatives suitable for the domestic context in question are to be taken into account, regardless of whether these alternatives are already provided for in that country.

It might be argued that the necessity criterion, as I have laid it out above, would not guarantee that all coercive care regimes are Pareto optimal in terms of their impact on human rights norms. Domestic regimes of coercive care could be formulated in disability-neutral terms, permitting the coercive care of *everyone* in situations in which there is a risk of harm and in which free and informed treatment decisions cannot be made. Broadening the class of people who may be subjected to coercion in this way would not obviously prevent states parties from achieving their aims of health protection and harm prevention. From an equality perspective, such laws appear as less restrictive because they do not stipulate *differential* disadvantageous treatment. The weak point of this argument is that such a policy would affect the rights of third parties, namely the entitlements to personal liberty, integrity and legal capacity of people *without* psychosocial diagnoses. According to Alexy's model, balancing is necessary whenever alternative means that are less intrusive from one perspective (here, the non-discrimination perspective) affect a third interest (here, the entitlements of people without psychosocial conditions).[22] Questions concerning the merits and demerits of maintaining separate legal regimes for people with and without psychosocial disabilities are therefore deferred to the balancing stage.

D. Proportionality: Excluding Inconsistent Policies and Policies with Unreasonable Disadvantageous Effects

Like Alexy's proportionality assessment model, the final stage in my framework consists of balancing, comparing the trade-offs involved in permitting

[20] See, eg, Initial Reports of States Parties under Article 35 of the Convention: Netherlands (submitted 13 July 2018, published 6 March 2019) CRPD/C/NLD/1 para 147; Estonia (submitted 4 December 2015, published 3 October 2017) CRPD/C/EST/1 para 91; Argentina (submitted 6 October 2010, published 28 June 2011) CRPD/C/ARG/1 paras 199–200.

[21] See P Bartlett, 'A Mental Disorder of a Kind or Degree Warranting Confinement: Examining Justifications for Psychiatric Detention' (2012) 16 *The International Journal of Human Rights* 831, 842.

[22] See ch 3, section III.C.

and prohibiting a particular domestic regime of compulsory care. If the reasons for permitting a regime are of equal weight or weightier than the reasons for prohibiting it, then the regime is proportionate and lawful under the CRPD; if, on the other hand, the reasons for prohibiting the regime are weightier than the reasons for permitting it, then the regime is disproportionate and therefore unlawful under the Convention.[23] In balancing, all relevant reasons are taken into account and weighed against each other. These include evidence about the concrete consequences of the domestic provisions under review. How many people are affected by this system? How many of them benefit from coercive care and how many do not? What other negative effects are brought about by the system? They also include arguments about the purpose and content of the legal norms at stake. How much does the system under consideration interfere with the rights to liberty, integrity and legal capacity, as protected by the CRPD? How important are the aims of protecting life and health and preventing violence, according to the Convention? Moreover, they include arguments about the reliability of the assumptions underpinning these claims about the scope and content of the CRPD norms and the effects of the domestic regimes. How reliable is the data about the positive and negative effects of compulsory care, and how certain are our normative assumptions about the CRPD's view of these positive and negative effects?

As I mentioned in the first section of this chapter, proportionality reasoning within the non-discrimination context focuses on comparative disadvantage between groups. This has implications for which legal arguments are relevant at the balancing stage, as well as for the weight we must attach to them. Möller correctly points out that the proportionality tests developed in legal practice are not well equipped for dealing with equality norms because these tests do not contain a separate 'coherence stage' in addition to the four other stages (legitimate aim, suitability, necessity and proportionality in the narrow sense).[24] A state policy may seem reasonable when seen in isolation. It may, for example, seem reasonable to sanction the compulsory treatment of people at risk of committing suicide, even if a considerable proportion of those affected by such a regime would not have gone on to commit suicide.[25] The great value we attach to life and the irreversible nature of the act could undergird such a policy. It is, however, also possible to argue that medical staff must refrain from coercion even in situations of increased risk. The difficulties involved in identifying those at 'actual' or immediate risk and the intrusive nature of compulsory hospitalisation and treatment could provide support for such a competing position. Even if both were legally tenable positions, which would imply that states had discretion and could adopt one or the other, it seems wrong to accept that compulsory

[23] See ch 3, section III.D.

[24] K Möller, *The Global Model of Constitutional Rights* (Oxford, Oxford University Press, 2012) 125–26.

[25] See ch 2, section IV.B.

interventions against people with psychosocial disabilities can be justified on the basis of the value of life and, at the same time, to accept that non-intervention against people *without* disabilities can be justified on the basis of the difficulty involved in identifying those at risk and the intrusive nature of hospitalisation. Presumably, the prohibition of discrimination requires either that all suicides may be prevented with coercive means or that none may be. The Human Rights Committee's reasoning in *Mauritian Women v Mauritius* may be interpreted as making the same claim. Discussing the relationship between Article 17 (the right to respect for privacy, family, home and correspondence) and the prohibition of discrimination laid down in the International Covenant on Civil and Political Rights (ICCPR), the Committee stated the following:

> Whenever restrictions are placed on a right guaranteed by the Covenant, this has to be done without discrimination on the ground of sex. Whether the restriction in itself would be in breach of that right *regarded in isolation*, is not decisive in this respect. It is the enjoyment of the rights which must be secured without discrimination.[26]

In another case the Committee found that the state's justification of differential treatment was not persuasive because the state had failed to explain why the reasons for letting one group enjoy a certain benefit did not apply to another group in a similar situation.[27]

To test whether legal authorisations of civil detention and compulsory clinical treatment comply with this consistency requirement, the guiding question is the following: would it have been proportionate (or reasonable) to permit such interventions against people *without* psychosocial disabilities in relevantly similar situations? The fact that a state does not permit such interventions under current law would constitute a strong indication that the answer to the question is 'no'. Under such circumstances an explanation is required, and the presence of a disability/impairment or clinical condition does not suffice as an explanation of the differential treatment of people with and without psychosocial disabilities. Article 14 of the CRPD expressly states that the presence of a disability cannot justify the deprivation of liberty, and the prohibition of discrimination embodies a similar norm.[28] Whether other explanations are acceptable will depend on their ability to make sense within the domestic legal system in question and with respect to international human rights norms. Below, in section III, I will apply this consistency requirement to the topic of this study.

Another characteristic feature of discrimination analysis is its focus on certain wrongs and harms: for instance disrespect for human dignity, stereotyping and

[26] Human Rights Committee, 'Communication No 35/1978' *Mauritian Women v Mauritius* (1981) UN Doc CCPR/C/OP/1 para 9.2(b) 2(i) 8 (emphasis added).

[27] Human Rights Committee, 'Communication No 2216/2012' *C v Australia* (2017) UN Doc CCPR/C/119/D/2216/2012 para 8.6. The case concerned access to divorce for people in unrecognised marriages. People in foreign polygamous and underage marriages had access to divorce, but people in foreign same-sex marriages did not.

[28] See ch 1, sections III and VI.B.

prejudice, socioeconomic disadvantage and social exclusion. There seems to be something particularly objectionable about infringing human rights on the basis of sex, race, disability, and so on, as opposed to restricting rights for other reasons. As Tarunabh Khaitan puts it, 'disadvantage acquires a special character when it attaches itself to groups rather than when it is distributed randomly to individuals across all groups'.[29] Having one's liberty restricted because of one's past violent behaviour is one thing; being deprived of liberty because of one's disability, sex, or skin colour is normatively different – even if the factual circumstances of detention (the location, the possibilities for leaves of absence, the quality of the food, etc) are the same. It brings about another form of harm, which needs to be taken into account in balancing. In this book, I call this equality-specific harm.

Equality scholars have made extensive efforts to describe the human interests protected by discrimination law and the harms that breaching this law entails. One influential account stresses the connection between non-discrimination and respect for dignity, identifying the harm of discrimination as a violation of human dignity. Deborah Hellman, for example, argues that wrongful discrimination is discrimination that demeans by treating a person as not fully human or as of less moral worth.[30] Similarly, Denise Réaume holds that to value human dignity means to acknowledge the inherent worth of all human beings. Consequently, violations of human dignity convey the message that some of us are worth less than others.[31] Policies that differentiate on the basis of disability, sex, race, and other such characteristics imply that these traits are (normatively) relevant to the enjoyment of human rights and that certain groups are not entitled to the same level of enjoyment of these rights. As some equality scholars would say, these groups are treated as 'second-class citizens'.[32] Discrimination theories focusing on stigma draw on similar ideas. Iyiola Solanke, for example, argues that unlawful discrimination is discrimination that stigmatises its victims.[33] Such stigmatisation occurs when people in relatively privileged positions create labels and stereotypes about members of marginalised groups in such a way as to diminish the power and social status of these marginalised individuals.

Others argue that the main problem with discrimination is that it curtails a person's freedom or autonomy. According to Sophia Moreau, the interest that is harmed by discrimination is our interest in a set of deliberative freedoms, including the freedoms to decide what we value and to live our lives in light of these values.[34] For Amartya Sen and other scholars drawing on his capability

[29] T Khaitan, *A Theory of Discrimination Law* (Oxford, Oxford University Press, 2015) 41.
[30] Hellman, *When is Discrimination Wrong?* 29–37.
[31] D Réaume, 'Dignity and Discrimination' (2002–2003) 63 *Louisiana Law Review* 1, 22.
[32] Hellman (n 14) 40ff and 48; *ibid* 29.
[33] I Solanke, *Discrimination as Stigma: A Theory of Anti-discrimination Law* (London, Hart Publishing, 2016) chs 1 and 4.
[34] S Moreau, 'What is Discrimination' (2010) 38 *Philosophy and Public Affairs* 143, 147.

approach, the key problem with inequality is that it deprives some segments of the population of their capability of pursuing a life that they consider valuable.[35] In the disability context, much attention has been devoted to the harms of inaccessibility.[36] When interacting in society, people with disabilities face not only negative attitudes but also physical obstacles and technical and language-related barriers that circumscribe their opportunities for public participation and communication with others. Removing such obstacles requires positive action and is key to combating social exclusion.

Although there are significant similarities in how these theories describe the specific harms caused by discriminatory practices, consensus on a single account of the value underpinning discrimination law remains elusive.[37] Instead, there is a growing recognition that different discriminatory practices can bring about different harms, and combinations of harms, in varying degrees.[38] As chapter one showed, the CRPD embraces this idea.[39] The preamble to the treaty explains that disability-based discrimination disrespects 'the inherent dignity and worth of the human person',[40] and it affirms the belief that the treaty, which has equality and non-discrimination as its core values, will 'make a significant contribution to redressing the profound social disadvantage' experienced by people with disabilities.[41] And just like the two previous UN treaties set up to end discrimination against a specific group, the Convention on the Elimination of Racial Discrimination (CERD) and the Convention on the Elimination of Discrimination against Women (CEDAW),[42] the CRPD includes specific obligations for states parties to combat public prejudice and discrimination from private actors.[43] Moreover, according to the CRPD Committee's conceptualisation of equality, which builds on Fredman's model of substantive equality, it

[35] Amartya Sen develops his capability approach and its relationship to (substantive) equality in a number of works, including 'Equality of What?' in S McMurrin (ed), *The Tanner Lectures on Human Values* (Cambridge, Cambridge University Press, 1980) Vol 1 and *The Idea of Justice* (Cambridge, Massachusetts, Harvard University Press, 2009) 289–97.

[36] See, eg, A Broderick, *The Long and Winding Road to Equality and Inclusion for Persons with Disabilities: The United Nations Convention on the Rights of Persons with Disabilities* (Cambridge, Intersentia, 2015); A Lawson, 'The United Nations Convention on the Rights of Persons with Disabilities: New Era or False Dawn?' (2007) 34 *Syracuse Journal of International Law and Commerce* 563; T Degener, 'Disability in a Human Rights Context' (2016) 5 *Laws* 35.

[37] Khaitan, *A Theory of Discrimination Law* 8; Shin, 'Is There a Unitary Concept of Discrimination?'.

[38] S Fredman, 'Substantive Equality Revisited' (2016) 14 *International Journal of Constitutional Law* 712. This understanding also underpins contemporary concepts of intersectional discrimination. See S Attrey, *Intersectional Discrimination* (Oxford, Oxford University Press, 2019) 162ff.

[39] See ch 1, section VI.

[40] CRPD preamble (h).

[41] CRPD preamble (y).

[42] International Convention on the Elimination of All Forms of Racial Discrimination (adopted 21 December 1965, entered into force 4 January 1969) 660 UNTS 195 (CERD) and the Convention on the Elimination of All Forms of Discrimination against Women (adopted 18 December 1979, entered into force 3 September 1981) 1249 UNTS 13 (CEDAW).

[43] CRPD Art. 4(1)(e) and 8(1)(b).

has four dimensions: a redistributive dimension, connected to socioeconomic matters; a recognition dimension, connected to respect for dignity and the aim of combating stigma and prejudice; a participatory dimension, connected to inclusion in society; and an accommodation dimension, which makes space for difference as a matter of human dignity.[44]

Systems of compulsory psychiatric care may have implications for all of these dimensions, but some are more likely to be affected than others. Targeting specific groups for civil detention risks fuelling stereotypical views and prejudice about the 'otherness' of members of these groups. Whilst many factors can contribute to public prejudice – including the way people with disabilities are portrayed in the media and the degree to which they are included in society[45] – maintaining separate regimes for the coercive care of this group sends the message that they are particularly dangerous and/or unable to take care of themselves. In addition, such regimes convey the message that any violent or destructive behaviour engaged in by members of this group stems from their medical condition, and may thus be beyond their control. Indeed, studies from Australia, New Zealand, European countries and the USA suggest that improved public awareness of the biological causes and symptoms of different psychosocial conditions has not always translated into less social stigma for people with psychosocial disabilities. Instead, such awareness may heighten the sense of the 'otherness' of this group and intensify fears about their unexpected and dangerous behaviour.[46] Stereotypical beliefs of this kind underpin social exclusion and discrimination by third parties. We tend to keep a distance from people we perceive to be violent or seriously self-destructive. We do not wish to have such people as our neighbours or colleagues, so we hesitate to develop close relationships with them.[47] In addition, stereotypical beliefs may lead employers, landlords, and others in positions of authority to make decisions that affect the ability of people with psychosocial disabilities to pursue their life projects. Indeed, there is empirical evidence to suggest that people with disabilities are over-represented among the socially excluded, the unemployed, the homeless, and the otherwise socioeconomically disadvantaged.[48]

[44] CRPD Committee, 'General Comment No 6 on Equality and Non-discrimination' (26 April 2018) UN Doc CRPD/C/GC/6 para 11.

[45] See, eg, N Raevley, A Jorm and A Morgan, 'Beliefs about Dangerousness of People with Mental Health Problems: The Role of Media Reports and Personal Exposure to Threat or Harm' (2016) 51 *Social Psychiatry Psychiatric Epidemiology* 1275.

[46] G Schomerus et al, 'Evolution of Public Attitudes about Mental Illness: A Systematic Review and Meta-analysis' (2012) 125 *Acta Psychiatrica Scandinavica* 440. See also J Phelan and B Link, 'The Growing Belief That People with Mental Illnesses Are Violent: The Role of the Dangerousness Criterion for Civil Commitment' (1998) 33 *Social Psychiatry and Psychiatric Epidemiology* 7.

[47] Schomerus et al, *ibid* 447–48.

[48] The amount of empirical evidence available concerning the relationship between disability and poverty, in its various dimensions, differs greatly between developed and developing countries, but what is available supports the general description I have provided. See World Health Organisation and World Bank, *World Report on Disability* (Malta, World Health Organisation, 2011).

Quite obviously, compulsory mental health care also limits the ability of people with psychosocial disabilities to participate in society during the time of their hospitalisation. Compulsory psychiatric care typically takes place in a closed ward, and patients have limited access to the outside world. This naturally prevents patients from participating in social activities outside the hospital setting, such as education, work, leisure, and developing relationships with partners, family members and friends – activities that are of crucial importance to most people. Although people subjected to compulsory care are not all affected in the same way or to the same extent, long-term stays in closed settings generally have negative effects on personal development.[49]

To sum up, domestic regimes of compulsory mental health care that satisfy the definition of discrimination can bring about various kinds of personal and social harm. Policies that restrict the rights of people with psychosocial disabilities on the grounds of their impairment or diagnosis arguably disrespect the dignity of the members of this group. In addition, domestic health laws typically single out people with certain conditions or impairments as particularly violent and/or vulnerable. Such laws thus confirm stereotypical beliefs about people with psychosocial disabilities as deviant, incapable, and prone to violence and self-destructive behaviour, and thereby contribute to the spread of public prejudice. This, in turn, leads private actors, such as employers and landlords, to make decisions that contribute further to the social exclusion and discrimination experienced by people with psychosocial disabilities. Finally, inpatient treatment in closed wards in psychiatric hospitals can exacerbate the socially disadvantaged position many people with psychosocial disabilities find themselves in, because it severely limits their ability to engage with the community outside the hospital and to pursue their life projects. Which of these harms a particular mental health regime causes, and 'how much' harm it causes, can only be determined on a case-by-case basis, taking into account facts about the particular regime and domestic context. The answers to these questions depend both on the legal design of the regime and on empirical matters such as the level of social inclusion and respect for difference that people with psychosocial disabilities enjoy in the country in question. I return to the question of how variations in these factors affect the outcome of balancing in section IV.

III. APPLYING THE CONSISTENCY REQUIREMENT

The consistency requirement outlined above expresses the principle of formal equality: the idea that people in relevantly similar situations should be treated alike. This idea can be traced back to Aristotle's maxim according to which like

[49] W Chow and S Priebe, 'Understanding Psychiatric Institutionalization: A Conceptual Review' (2013) 13 *BMC Psychiatry* 169, 177f.

cases must be treated alike.[50] Formal equality is one important principle underpinning the prohibition of discrimination, and in particular the prohibition of direct discrimination, in international human rights law.[51] This section discusses the implications of this requirement for the lawfulness of using compulsory clinical treatment to protect health and of using civil detention to protect life and prevent violence against others. The purpose is to illustrate how this requirement may guide decision-makers' argumentation. As this section will show, it is difficult to justify domestic regimes that allow doctors to override the free and informed treatment rejections of people with psychosocial disabilities and that sanction compulsory mental health care for public safety reasons. The value of this consistency requirement, which as we shall see puts rather few and rather mild constraints on what may count as a justification of differential treatment, is then discussed in subsection D.

A. Compulsory Intervention to Protect Health

One of the common goals of compulsory mental health care is to protect the health of the person concerned. This is often reflected in domestic mental health law, where 'risk of deterioration of health' is a common criterion that must be met to justify hospitalisation and the administration of medication against the person's will.[52] Some mental health laws restrict the use of compulsion to situations in which the risk is 'significant' or the potential deterioration of health is 'serious'.[53] It is fairly easy to imagine situations in which people without psychosocial conditions have a similar need for medical treatment and may effectively reject it. Jehovah's Witnesses refusing blood transfusions is one example; cancer patients refusing surgery or chemotherapy is another.[54] This seems contradictory. If it takes more than a risk of the patient's health seriously deteriorating to justify the compulsory care of people without psychosocial conditions, then the same ought to apply to people with such conditions. The question thus becomes whether there are other reasons that can explain the differential treatment of people who are similarly situated in this way: that is, who need treatment and reject it.

[50] Aristotle, *The Nicomachean Ethics* (translated by D Ross) (Oxford, Oxford University Press, 1980) book V, Ch 3, paras 1131a–b.

[51] J Clifford, 'Equality' in D Shelton (ed), *The Oxford Handbook of International Human Rights Law* (Oxford, Oxford University Press, 2013) 427.

[52] See ch 2, section II.

[53] EC Fistein et al, 'A Comparison of Mental Health Legislation from Diverse Commonwealth Jurisdictions' (2009) 32 *International Journal of Law and Psychiatry* 147, 150.

[54] This phenomenon has scarcely been studied. Research from the United States has shown that less than 1% of cancer patients refuse all forms of conventional treatment but that refusal rates for chemotherapy are significantly higher (3–19%). See M Frenkel, 'Refusing Treatment' (2013) 18 *The Oncologist* 634.

When evaluating the strength of such explanations, it can be useful to keep Alexy's weight formula in mind, along with its variables of abstract weight, degree of infringement, and reliability of underlying premises. Abstract weight is the weight attached to the norms at stake – here, the protection of health versus personal liberty, integrity and legal capacity – in relation to each other.[55] The degree of infringement is a measure of how much a state practice (compulsory clinical care) interferes with protected individual entitlements (integrity and legal capacity) in the concrete circumstances at hand and a corresponding estimate of how much the abolition of the practice, or a modification of the circumstances under which it is permitted, would interfere with the competing interest (the protection of health). The reliability factor relates to the empirical and normative assumptions upon which estimates about abstract weights and degrees of interference are based.[56] Take the Swedish Act on Compulsory Psychiatric Care as an example. This Act authorises the compulsory care of people with psychosocial conditions, and it operates within a legal order that, as a rule, prohibits clinical care without the consent of the person concerned, regardless of whether this results in harm to health. It is easy to establish that the discrepancy between the approach to people with psychosocial disabilities, who may, according to the Act, be treated without their consent, and the approach to people without such disabilities, who benefit from the general prohibition of compulsory care, cannot be explained using arguments about the abstract weight of the entitlements and interests at stake. It would be manifestly unjust and legally incorrect to hold that it is more important to protect the health of people with psychosocial disabilities than it is to protect the health of others, or that people with psychosocial disabilities are less entitled than people without such disabilities to respect for integrity and legal capacity.

A common argument in defence of differential treatment concerns the ability to make free and informed treatment decisions. This argument rests on the claim that certain psychosocial conditions, or the symptoms thereof, can have a detrimental impact on this ability. This claim can be backed by reliable empirical data.[57] To be convincing as an explanation of differential treatment, however, states parties must also demonstrate that decision-making ability is normatively relevant to the determination of the legitimate scope of coercive care. They could argue that the imposition of care interferes more with the integrity and legal capacity of the person concerned if he or she is able to understand the situation and the most important consequences of the decision to reject treatment. This is not to deny that the imposition of clinical care can be an equally painful and distressing experience for people who lack decision-making ability. It is to claim that the degradation of personhood or personal self-determination inherent in

[55] See ch 3, sections III.D and V.A.
[56] See ch 3, sections III.D and VI.
[57] See ch 2, section IV.A.

systems of compulsory care is most pronounced when the individual concerned is able to make free and informed treatment decisions. If we accept that decision-making ability is normatively relevant in determining whether someone may effectively reject medical treatment, however, then it ought to be relevant in any case that involves someone who lacks such ability. The argument thus implies that we should be prepared to impose treatment on people in the later stages of dementia, on people with acute head injuries, and on cancer patients who lack decision-making ability, unless other sufficiently strong reasons speak against such interventions.

The advantages and disadvantages of using decision-making ability as a criterion in this way can certainly be debated. The CRPD Committee strongly advises against doing so, as do several academic lawyers.[58] This is a much broader issue than the one dealt with in this book. For the reasons I have set out in previous chapters, I interpret international human rights law as granting states a certain margin of discretion when approaching situations in which it is not clear, despite a person's having access to support, whether free and informed decisions can be made, either because of personal factors (eg cognitive impairment) or contextual factors (eg the person being deprived of liberty or in an otherwise vulnerable situation).[59] This margin of discretion also applies to the question of what particular faculties constitute a person's 'decision-making ability'. However, if we accept that the prohibition of discrimination includes a requirement of consistency, then this requirement also applies to the use of discretionary power by states parties. This means that, whatever faculties are deemed constitutive of decision-making ability, this definition must be applied consistently: the same legal consequences ought to follow from the presence or absence of these faculties regardless of whether the situation involves a person with a psychosocial condition.

Mental health laws in many states parties to the CRPD still exhibit an anomaly in that they deprive a particular group, people with certain psychosocial disabilities, including those who are able to make free and informed treatment choices, of a right to reject treatment that is enjoyed by everyone else.[60] In defence of such mental health laws it is often argued that people with such psychosocial disabilities are (as a group) more likely than health care users in general to lack the relevant abilities. In addition, judging whether a particular

[58] CRPD Committee, 'General Comment No 1 on Article 12: Equal Recognition before the Law' (19 May 2014) UN Doc CRPD/C/GC/1 para 15. For critical academic voices, see, eg, E Flynn and A Arstein-Kerslake, 'Legislating Personhood: Realising the Right to Support in Exercising Legal Capacity' (2014) 10 *International Journal of Law in Context* 81; T Minkowitz, 'Abolishing Mental Health Laws to Comply with the CRPD' in B McSherry and P Weller (eds), *Rethinking Rights-based Mental Health Laws* (Oxford, Hart Publishing, 2010) 161; P Gooding, *A New Era for Mental Health Law and Policy: Supported Decision-making and the UN Convention on the Rights of Persons with Disabilities* (Cambridge, Cambridge University Press, 2017) 160ff.

[59] See ch 1, section V.

[60] See ch 2, section II.

treatment rejection is free and informed will in many cases be difficult and place a burden on (public) resources.[61] The complexity of the task means there is a significant risk that mistakes will be made: that medical staff will misinterpret some treatment rejections as free and informed even though they are not and therefore refrain from imposing compulsory care. On the other hand, circumscribing the right of people with psychosocial disabilities to reject treatment in this way is highly problematic. Although people with psychosocial disabilities are more likely than people without such disabilities to be in a situation in which they have a need for medical care but lack the ability (despite having support) to make a valid decision about such care, this does not necessarily mean that the majority of individuals subject to compulsory care today lack decision-making ability. Even before the CRPD entered into force and obliged states to provide access to decision-making support, studies of the decision-making abilities of psychiatric inpatients indicated that the majority of these patients possessed the ability to make free and informed treatment choices.[62] It is reasonable to expect that, if all were provided with adequate support, this proportion would be even higher. This clearly speaks in favour of requiring doctors and other decision-makers to undertake individual assessments before imposing any treatment. A failure to do so is tantamount to accepting that many free and informed treatment decisions should simply be ignored, which runs counter to human rights law. As discussed above, human rights law does not permit states to impose clinical treatment in all situations in which acting otherwise would result in harm to health.[63] The fact that a person's health would deteriorate if he or she were left untreated is not a sufficient reason to impose treatment. Only in situations in which we suspect that a treatment refusal does not reflect the person's 'true' will are states permitted to resort to coercive care. Accepting that some free and informed treatment rejections will be ignored is also problematic in view of the idea of formal equality at issue here. Consistency requires that all groups whose members lack decision-making ability be treated in a similar way. This raises difficult questions about how to define such groups. Should this list of groups include, for example, people in shock, people in severe pain, and people under the influence of medication or alcohol?

To sum up, international human rights law provides states parties with discretion in situations in which individuals are in need of medical care and free and informed treatment decisions cannot be obtained, but the requirement of consistency places some constraints on this freedom. Criteria for compulsory care must cohere with other rules and principles that govern the administration

[61] See ch 2, section IV.A.

[62] T Grisso and PS Appelbaum, 'The MacArthur Treatment Competence Study III: Abilities of Patients to Consent to Psychiatric and Medical Treatments' (1995) 19 *Law and Human Behavior* 149, 171; D Okai et al, 'Mental Capacity in Psychiatric Patients: Systematic Review' (2007) 191 *British Journal of Psychiatry* 291.

[63] See ch 1, section V.

of health care in the legal system in question. If a lack of decision-making ability is held to be a sufficient reason to justify compulsion in situations in which a failure to treat would have serious health implications, then this rule must apply regardless of whether the situation involves a person with a psychosocial condition. This makes it difficult to justify mental health laws that deprive people with certain psychosocial disabilities who are able to make free and informed treatment choices of the right to reject treatment. Even if a lack of decision-making ability, despite having access to decision-making support, may be more prevalent among people with psychosocial disabilities, it is not typical of people subject to inpatient psychiatric care. On the contrary, empirical data suggests that free and informed decisions can be facilitated with adequate support in many, if not most, cases. To be consistent, states would have to permit compulsory interventions against other groups of individuals who lack decision-making ability, which raises difficult questions about how such groups should be defined.

B. Civil Detention to Protect Life

The legal systems of states parties to the Convention approach suicide in a variety of ways. In some states, attempted suicide is still viewed as a criminal act.[64] Most states, however, view such acts as lawful but tragic events. Some states recognise a right to assistance in ending one's life under certain circumstances (so-called physician-assisted suicide). Belgium, Luxembourg, the Netherlands and Switzerland are examples of states in which physician-assisted suicide has been legal for many years.[65] Canada recently changed its legislation to provide for physician-assisted suicide following a judgment of the Supreme Court.[66] These differences apart, most states parties provide for the compulsory inpatient treatment of people with psychosocial disabilities to prevent suicide. The criteria for hospitalisation and its permitted duration vary across jurisdictions, but to my knowledge, no states provide for the compulsory care of everyone at risk of suicide. Instead, compulsory care is typically reserved for certain groups, such as people with psychosocial conditions and people with alcohol or substance abuse problems. This is the case despite the fact that (certain) psychosocial conditions and problems with alcohol and substance abuse are but two factors among many that increase the risk of suicide. Other factors associated with suicide are chronic pain, abuse, a lack of close relationships, traumatic

[64] BL Mishara and DN Weisstubb, 'The Legal Status of Suicide: A Global Review' (2016) 44 *International Journal of Law and Psychiatry* 54.

[65] L Radbruch et al, 'Euthanasia and Physician-Assisted Suicide: A White Paper from the European Association for Palliative Care' (2016) 30 *Palliative Medicine* 104, 106.

[66] *Carter v Canada (Attorney General)* 2015 SCC 5, Bill C-14.

events and financial hardship.[67] This seems inconsistent. States parties that wish to maintain this situation must therefore explain why the reasons for not intervening against other groups at increased risk of suicide do not also apply to people with psychosocial disabilities.[68]

As with compulsory intervention to protect health, it is easy to exclude the possibility that differences in abstract weight could justify the differential treatment of people with and without psychosocial disabilities in this case. It cannot be that, under human rights law, it is more important to protect the lives of people with psychosocial disabilities than it is to protect the lives of others. Furthermore, it cannot be that people with psychosocial disabilities are less entitled than people without such disabilities to respect for personal liberty, integrity and legal capacity. Other arguments in defence of differential treatment warrant more consideration. A state party could, for example, argue that certain psychosocial conditions distort one's outlook on life, creating intense psychological pain and suicidal ideation, which are symptoms of the underlying condition and do not reflect a genuine wish to end one's life. Compulsory care in these cases may therefore interfere less with the entitlement to individual self-determination that is part of the entitlement to personal liberty, integrity and legal capacity. Medical staff are not overriding the 'true' will of the person concerned but helping him or her to cope with the severe emotional stress triggered by a clinical condition. The situation of someone with chronic and severe physical pain is different, it might be argued, because the wish to end life in this case is authentic (not a symptom of a clinical condition). A related but slightly different argument starts out from the observation that the compulsory care of people with psychosocial conditions is more effective than the compulsory care of people who contemplate suicide for other reasons. Severe depression can in many cases be treated successfully.[69] In the best-case scenario, the individual leaves the hospital with a restored will to live and gets on with his or her life. If someone is suicidal because of chronic physical pain, the best-case scenario is different. A successful intervention to prevent suicide will certainly prolong the life of the person concerned, but the ailment will still cause pain and distress and may still be unbearable for the individual. Depending on how we conceptualise the value of life, one could argue that the degree of infringement of the interest in preventing suicide (and thereby protecting life) is greatest in situations in which the suicidal ideation is the result of a treatable condition.[70] As I noted

[67] World Health Organisation, *Preventing Suicide: A Global Imperative* (Luxembourg, World Health Organisation) 31.

[68] *C v Australia* (n 27) para 8.6.

[69] See ch 2, section IV.B.

[70] Needless to say, the protection of life is considered to be important under human rights law, but it is less clear *why* exactly the protection of life is considered so important. For a detailed discussion of this point, see E Wicks, *The Right to Life and Conflicting Interests* (Oxford, Oxford University Press, 2010) Ch 7, 176ff.

in chapter two, these arguments raise difficult questions about whether it is possible or desirable to distinguish personal preferences from illness-influenced changes in outlook.[71] Even if we assume that such a distinction can be made, it seems that some somatic conditions influence personal preferences in a manner that is similar to how psychosocial conditions influence such preferences. What makes the suicidal ideation of a severely depressed person who has tried a range of different treatment methods without success different from that of a person who is experiencing severe pain because of a somatic condition?

There is a third and possibly stronger argument in favour of focusing compulsory interventions on people with psychosocial disabilities. People with psychosocial disabilities are over-represented among those who commit suicide worldwide. Statistics suggest that in high-income Western countries, up to 90 per cent of people who die by suicide are people with psychosocial conditions. In low- and middle-income countries, this over-representation is less marked; in certain countries, the proportion is around 60 per cent.[72] Even if these numbers ought to be treated with caution, they clearly indicate that, if states were to refrain from compulsory intervention in situations involving an increased risk of suicide, then this change would primarily affect people with psychosocial disabilities.[73] Therefore, it could be argued that states have more reason to authorise the compulsory care of members of this group than of other groups at risk. The argument presupposes, of course, that states should be prepared to impose compulsory care on members of any group at an equally high risk of suicide, unless sufficiently strong reasons speak against such interventions.

In conclusion, it seems difficult to provide a fully consistent argument for maintaining compulsory mental health care just based on reasoning about the impact psychosocial conditions can have on our outlook on life or on arguments about the treatability of these conditions. A consistent argument for this conclusion may be possible if states parties were able to demonstrate that people subject to such a regime are at a significantly higher risk of committing suicide than people who are not subject to the regime.

C. Civil Detention to Protect Others

The risk of violence against others is a common criterion for civil detention in mental health legislation around the world, and it is seldom, if ever, matched with a similar system of detention for everyone at risk of harming others. Domestic criminal law usually provides for the pre-trial detention of suspects,

[71] See ch 2, section IV.A.

[72] See ch 2, section IV.B.

[73] Caution is warranted because of the risk of mistakes in the process of distinguishing suicide from other causes of death and in the process of establishing the underlying causes of deaths by suicide.

and those convicted of a crime may have their sentences prolonged if they are deemed dangerous. But 'pure' preventive detention is reserved for certain groups: for instance people with alcohol and substance abuse problems[74] and people with psychosocial conditions. This is the case even though these are not the only groups at an increased risk of committing violent acts. We could construct other high-risk groups based on factors that are associated with criminal violence. In the literature on risk prediction, there is broad agreement that being male, having an antisocial personality, having substance abuse problems, and having a history of violent behaviour are factors that are closely associated with the risk of violence. In fact, these factors are probably better predictors of future aggression than the presence of certain psychosocial conditions.[75] The link between violence and psychosocial conditions is thus weaker than the link between self-destructive acts and psychosocial conditions. A majority of people who commit suicide have a psychosocial condition, and there seem to be no other factors that are better predictors of future self-harm. The same cannot be said of violent crime. The fact that states authorise compulsion against people with psychosocial disabilities while refraining from such interventions against groups that present a similar level of risk of future violent behaviour reveals an inconsistency in their crime prevention policies that is difficult to justify.

Just as with interventions to protect the health and life of the person concerned, such differential treatment cannot be justified on the basis of arguments concerning the abstract weights of the values at stake. Again, it is just as important to protect the entitlements to personal liberty, integrity and legal capacity of people with psychosocial disabilities as it is to protect these entitlements for others. In addition, from the perspective of public safety, it cannot be more important to prevent violent acts committed by members of this group than it is to prevent violent acts committed by members of any other group. One could argue that perpetrators with certain psychosocial conditions are different from other perpetrators because of the influence that the symptoms of such conditions may have on our perception of and thinking about the world. People with psychotic conditions, for example, may see or hear things that do not exist, entertain false beliefs, and act violently in response to their hallucinations and delusions. Antipsychotic medication can mitigate such symptoms, and thereby reduce the risk of future violent behaviour, in some cases. Although there is no consensus in the literature, many researchers believe that the presence of clinical symptoms does not suffice as a general explanation of why some people with psychosocial disabilities (sometimes) act violently towards others.[76] Several studies indicate that many or most violent perpetrators with psychosocial diagnoses share offending patterns with perpetrators

[74] See, eg, M Israelson and A Gerdner, 'Compulsory Commitment to Care of Substance Misusers: A Worldwide Comparative Analysis of the Legislation' (2010) 3 *The Open Addiction Journal* 117.

[75] See fn 70 in ch 2.

[76] See ch 2, section IV.C.

without such diagnoses. And the effects of treatment on the risk of future violent behaviour among those without psychotic symptoms remain a matter of debate among researchers working in the area of risk prevention.[77]

Even if we were to accept that some amount of violence is preventable with psychiatric medication, the question remains: would it have been reasonable to permit the forced administration of such medication to people *without* psychosocial disabilities? Imagine that there was some medication that could make people less inclined to act violently; imagine that this medication was successful in less than half of the cases in which it was prescribed and that many of its users experienced very unpleasant side effects. Would we consider it reasonable to permit the compulsory administration of this medication to every male with an antisocial personality and a history of violent crime? I doubt it. The upshot is that, unless states parties find another reason to explain why it is reasonable to commit only people with psychosocial disabilities – and not people without such disabilities – to compulsory care to promote public safety, they fail to comply with the consistency requirement included in the proportionality assessment framework set out here. They fail to treat relevantly similar situations alike. If we accept that the prohibition of discrimination incorporates such a requirement, then states parties to the CRPD must reform their mental health laws so that compulsory hospitalisation and treatment decisions are not based on the risk of future violent behaviour.

D. The Value of a Consistency Requirement

As the preceding three sections have illustrated, a consistency requirement that reflects the idea of formal equality can help us to reason about some problematic aspects of compulsory mental health care. It shows that we should not force members of marginalised groups to undergo medical treatment under circumstances in which such intervention would have been unacceptable had it been directed towards a member of another group. All the same, the consistency requirement does not obviously direct our attention to those matters that are often considered to be of central importance when speaking about equality and non-discrimination: that is, issues of prejudice, stigma and social disadvantage. It would have been possible to consider such matters under this heading. When answering the question of whether it would have been proportionate to permit the compulsory care of people without psychosocial disabilities in relevantly similar situations, we could construct the 'relevantly similar situation' so as to include aspects of stigma, social exclusion, and so on. But since these types of harm arise only in relation to marginalised groups, or are most serious in relation to such groups, there is a risk that, in an analysis that focuses

[77] *Ibid.*

only on finding a consistent justification for compulsory care, they would not be accorded the importance they deserve. In addition, considering such factors in relation to the consistency requirement would rob the comparative reasoning carried out above of some of its intuitive appeal. It makes perfect sense to compare the situation of a person diagnosed with cancer who refuses chemotherapy with the situation of a person with a psychosocial condition who refuses psychiatric medication under circumstances in which there are reasons to doubt that the treatment refusal truly reflects a personal choice. If we add matters like public prejudice and social exclusion into the mix, the exercise becomes more speculative. In this case, our question would have had to have been: would it have been proportionate to authorise the compulsory care of cancer patients in situations in which free and informed consent cannot be obtained, bearing in mind that such authorisations contribute to stereotypical views about people with cancer among the general public, leading to social exclusion and a loss of self-respect?

In addition, the current mainstream position within the academic debate on equality and non-discrimination is that consistency cannot be the (sole) foundational value upon which equality norms rest.[78] Consistency is achieved when two people are treated equally well, but it is also achieved when two people are treated equally badly.[79] It puts few constraints on what constitutes a 'relevantly similar situation' and might therefore fail to capture some situations that violate the idea of equal treatment under human rights law.[80] A typical example is gender discrimination in the labour market against women of childbearing age. One could argue that the fact that members of this group are more likely than others to take leaves of absence to care for their children, which lead to increased costs for the employer, justifies employers in preferring male job applicants over female applicants. However, the mainstream opinion is that such disadvantageous treatment of women is not justified.[81] As the CRPD Committee notes in its general comment on equality and non-discrimination, the principle of formal equality does not embrace or accommodate differences among human beings. For this reason, legal debates about which situations constitute unlawful discrimination have moved from focusing solely on consistency of treatment to focusing on the aims of combating social disadvantage, fostering respect for difference, and promoting social inclusion.[82] The state obligation to treat people

[78] See O Mjöll Arnardóttir, 'A Future of Multidimensional Disadvantage Equality?' in O Mjöll Arnardóttir and G Quinn (eds), *The UN Convention on the Rights of Persons with Disabilities: European and Scandinavian Perspectives* (Leiden, Martinus Nijhoff, 2009) 47ff; Fredman, 'Substantive Equality Revisited' 716; Khaitan (n 29) 6.

[79] Fredman (n 38) 717.

[80] The emptiness of the idea of consistency inherent in rules of equal treatment is discussed in detail in an influential article by Peter Westen: 'The Empty Idea of Equality' (1982) 95 *Harvard Law Review* 537, 543–48.

[81] See, eg, Hellman (n 14) 120; Shin (n 14) 175f.

[82] Mjöll Arnardóttir, 'A Future of Multidimensional Disadvantage Equality?' 47ff.

with psychosocial disabilities 'on an equal basis with others' laid down in the CRPD is rooted in this development.[83] The following section discusses how social disadvantage, public prejudice, stigma and other equality-specific harms ought to affect the outcome of the balancing stage of proportionality assessments within discrimination analysis.

IV. THE ROLE OF EQUALITY-SPECIFIC HARM IN BALANCING

In the balancing process, the fact that the domestic system under review creates equality-specific harms speaks against permitting the system. The more a certain domestic mental health system demeans people with psychosocial disabilities or contributes to the public prejudice, marginalisation or socioeconomic disadvantage experienced by this group, the stronger the reasons in favour of permitting the system must be.[84] In the weight formula, equality-specific harms (represented by 'ESH') are related to I_i, that is, to the degree to which the mental health system under review interferes with the right(s) at stake.

$$W_{i,j} = \frac{W_i \, x \, I_i \, (incl.\, ESH) \, x \, R_i}{W_j \, x \, I_j \, x \, R_j}$$

Since we are operating within the realm of discrimination analysis, W_i represents the abstract weight of the entitlement to enjoy legal capacity, liberty, and/or integrity on an equal basis with others, as laid down in the CRPD, and W_j represents the abstract weight of the competing interest to ensure the equal protection of health and life.[85] For the reasons discussed above, I will proceed on the assumption that these interests are of roughly equal abstract weight and can therefore be overlooked in the following discussion.[86] I_i represents the degree to which the mental health policy or practice under consideration interferes with the entitlement to the equal enjoyment of legal capacity, liberty and integrity (under the CRPD); I_j represents the degree to which a modification of the policy or practice, so that it interferes less with the entitlement at stake (ie W_i), would harm the competing interest, the equal protection of the health and lives of people with psychosocial disabilities (Wj). R_i and R_j represent the degree of reliability of the assumptions upon which the arguments about the degrees of interference (I_i and I_j) rest.[87]

Including a direct reference to equality-specific harms in the weight formula serves as a reminder not to forget these harms in discrimination analysis. It

[83] See ch 1, section VI.
[84] See above, section II.D.
[85] See ch 3, section III.D.
[86] See ch 2, section V.A.
[87] See ch 3, sections III.D and VI.

can also help us to understand the asymmetry exhibited by discrimination analysis as it has developed within human rights jurisprudence. Not all cases of differential treatment (related to non-discrimination grounds) are equally problematic; those that reinforce public prejudice and severely limit people's abilities to pursue their life projects, thereby keeping marginalised groups at the margins, are more problematic than others and hence require weightier reasons if they are to be justified.[88] It goes without saying that the inclusion of equality-specific harms in the proportionality assessment does not imply that all cases that give rise to such harms involve a violation of the prohibition of discrimination. Equality-specific harms enter into the balancing procedure along with other factors, and in some situations they may be outweighed by these other factors. Nonetheless, their inclusion increases the likelihood that a violation will be found to have taken place. The fact that some of these harms are more likely to be present in cases involving direct discrimination explains the UN treaty bodies' (and indeed other human rights monitoring bodies' and courts') unwillingness to accept as justified policies and practices that satisfy the definition of direct discrimination.[89]

In this section, I illustrate how equality-specific harms can be balanced against the reasons in favour of permitting compulsory intervention. These reasons include the 'added value', if there is any, of maintaining domestic regimes that authorise the compulsory care of people with psychosocial disabilities but not others (directly discriminatory regimes), as well as the reasons that might compensate for the harms brought about by regimes that apply to everyone but that have a disparate impact on people with psychosocial disabilities (indirectly discriminatory regimes). The UN treaty bodies have not elaborated on how we are to identify and evaluate the weight of such reasons. Alexy's model is more instructive. It explains that the value of one particular regime over another (that interferes less with competing human rights norms) is determined by 'how much more' the former contributes to its aims than does the latter.[90] More concretely, the value of compulsory care regime X is determined by how much more it contributes to the protection of health and life than regime Y, which brings about less harm, including equality-specific harm.

I will limit my discussion to two alternative ways of regulating compulsory care for the purposes of protecting health and life. As I have demonstrated, it is difficult to find a consistent justification, under the CRPD, for the compulsory hospitalisation and treatment of people with psychosocial disabilities (and not others) for the purposes of preventing future violent behaviour.[91] Extending the authorisation of civil detention to cover other groups that pose the same level of

[88] See L Peroni and A Timmer, 'Vulnerable Groups: The Promise of an Emerging Concept in European Human Rights Convention Law' (2013) 11 *International Journal of Constitutional Law* 1056, 1075.

[89] See ch 1, section VI.B.

[90] R Alexy, 'On Constitutional Rights to Protection' (2009) 3 *Legisprudence* 1. See also ch 3, section III.D.

[91] See section III.C.

risk to others is also problematic, since it runs counter to human rights set out in other treaties. The European Convention on Human Rights (ECHR) restricts the use of civil detention to cases involving certain groups, namely juveniles, people with alcohol and substance abuse problems, migrants, and people with psychosocial conditions, and to cases where it is deemed necessary in order to prevent the spread of infectious diseases.[92] Other groups are protected against such detention. The treaty text of the ICCPR goes into less detail on this point. Article 9 states that no one shall be subjected to arbitrary arrest or detention. According to the *travaux préparatoires*, the term 'arbitrary' was inserted to provide protection against arrest and detention that was not based on law or was otherwise unjust. It was understood by the drafters that the types of detention sanctioned in Article 5 of the ECHR were not considered arbitrary under the ICCPR.[93] Indeed, the provision has been interpreted accordingly in subsequent practice. For similar reasons it is difficult to justify domestic regimes that allow doctors to override the free and informed treatment rejections of people with psychosocial disabilities.[94]

For these reasons, I will not discuss any further the possible ways that the use of compulsory care to prevent violence against others might be rendered compliant with the CRPD. Both of the domestic regimes discussed below limit the use of compulsory care to situations in which there are sound reasons to believe that a person's resistance towards medical care is not an expression of a free and informed choice and in which a failure to intervene would involve a serious risk to the individual's health and life. The main difference between the two examples I consider is that the first targets people with psychosocial disabilities only and the second regime provides for the compulsory care of everyone in these circumstances. As we will see, these two model regimes interfere with the prohibition of discrimination in different ways and to different degrees, and different arguments can be made in their defence.

A. The Compulsory Mental Health Care of Persons with Psychosocial Disabilities

The first regime permits the compulsory hospitalisation and treatment of persons with psychosocial disabilities if the following criteria are met:

- The individual is in need of care.
- The individual refuses care.

[92] Convention for the Protection of Human Rights and Fundamental Freedoms (as amended) ETS 5 Arts 5(1)(d), (e), and (f).

[93] R Sifris, 'An International Human Rights Perspective on Detention without Charge or Trial: Article 9 of the International Covenant on Civil and Political Rights' in B McSherry and P Keyzer (eds), *Dangerous People: Policy, Prediction, and Practice* (New York, Routledge, 2011) 17.

[94] See section III.A.

- The individual has access to decision-making support but fails to make a free and informed decision about the relevant care.
- There is a risk that the individual's health will deteriorate or that the individual will commit suicide if he or she does not undergo medical treatment.

This system complies with the obligation to ensure that health care users have access to decision-making support, and it complies with the consistency requirement in the sense that it ensures that people who (with or without support) are able to make free and informed health care decisions can effectively reject treatment regardless of whether they have a psychosocial disability. Moreover, we are supposing that it exists within a system that permits the compulsory care of other groups of people (eg those with cognitive and intellectual disabilities) who have similar problems with free and informed decision-making that cannot be solved through the provision of decision-making support. Nevertheless, this mental health regime explicitly refers to people with psychosocial disabilities as a group that are more likely than the average person to put their health and life at risk in a way that warrants coercive care. Empirical studies support the claim that such mental health laws are likely to fuel stereotypical views of people with psychosocial disabilities as different, as incapable of making their own decisions, and as more likely to engage in self-destructive behaviour, which, in turn, may lead to discrimination by third parties and social exclusion.[95] The precise magnitude of these harms depends on the context, in particular on the level of inclusion within society enjoyed by people with psychosocial disabilities, something that varies between states parties to the CRPD.

To assess the value of maintaining a separate system of compulsory care for people with psychosocial disabilities, we need to ask what added value such a system may produce in comparison to a system that brings about less equality-specific harm. There may be several ways to mitigate such harm, but perhaps the most obvious would be to transform the system into one that permits the compulsory care of anyone fulfilling the criteria listed above. What would be the costs of such a transformation? One reason for restricting the use of compulsory care to people with psychosocial disabilities, and some other groups, is to protect others from certain ways in which the mental health care system can be abused: for instance in order to incarcerate political dissidents or people who are merely eccentric. The case law of the European Court of Human Rights suggests that, in this area of law, the Court's primary concern has long been to avoid these sorts of abuse. In *Winterwerp v the Netherlands*, the Court established that Article 5(1)(e) of the ECHR 'obviously cannot be taken as permitting detention of a person simply because his view or behaviour

[95] See section II.D.

deviate from the norms prevailing in a particular society'.[96] The Court continues to hold that compulsory care can only be lawful under the Convention if the person concerned has a 'true mental disorder', that is, a clinical condition diagnosed on the basis of medical evidence.[97] The Court is certainly right that the use of compulsory care must be subject to safeguards in order to prevent abuse. The question is how much protection diagnostic thresholds can offer. Psychiatric diagnoses are made on the basis of the observation of combinations of symptoms, that is, descriptions of thoughts, feelings, and behaviours that deviate to a certain degree from what is considered 'normal'.[98] Social standards determine what counts as 'normal' and 'abnormal'. Whilst there is broad agreement that certain thoughts, feelings and behaviours are clinically significant, there is no clear line separating a normal presentation of distress from a symptom of certain mild clinical psychiatric conditions.[99] Hence, a more appropriate way to prevent the abuse of compulsory care systems would be to strengthen domestic monitoring and review procedures and to ensure that individuals who have been committed are protected by appropriate legal safeguards. These would include the rights to seek a second opinion, to appeal the decision to use compulsory care and to have access to legal representation during any appeal.

To conclude, the magnitude of the equality-specific harms associated with systems of compulsory care that target people with psychosocial disabilities only – public prejudice and social exclusion – will vary from state to state and may be significant. Given the importance the CRPD attaches to social inclusion and respect for difference, these effects should not be taken lightly. In addition, the chief benefit of restricting the use of compulsory care to certain groups seems to be that it protects others against some forms of abuse, but, as a reason for maintaining such a system, this is arguably not very weighty. Psychiatric diagnoses can be manipulated, meaning that any protection against abuse offered by such a system does not seem to be very robust. If this is correct, and if there are no other relevant reasons for maintaining such a system, then the reasons in favour of having separate systems for health care users with and without psychosocial disabilities will only be able to compensate for a very limited amount of equality-specific harm.

[96] *Winterwerp v the Netherlands* Series A no 33 (1979) 2 EHRR 387 para 37.

[97] *Ibid* paras 39 and 41.

[98] A Frances and R Halon, 'The Uses and Misuses of the DSM in Forensic Settings' (2013) 6 *Psychological Injury and Law* 336, 340.

[99] *Ibid*. The two major diagnostic manuals – the World Health Organisation's Classification of Behavioural and Mental Disorders and the American Psychiatric Association's Diagnostic and Statistical Manual of Mental Disorders – sound a note of caution on this matter. World Health Organisation, *The ICD-10 Classification of Mental and Behavioral Disorders: Clinical Descriptions and Diagnostic Guidelines* (Geneva, World Health Organisation, 1992) 11; American Psychiatric Association, *Diagnostic and Statistical Manual of Mental Disorders: DSM-5*, 5th edn (Arlington, American Psychiatric Association, 2013) 25.

B. The Compulsory Care of Everyone Who Lacks Decision-making Ability

The second compulsory care regime is not limited to people with psychosocial disabilities (and some other groups) but applies to everyone. It thus covers somatic as well as psychiatric care. Apart from this, however, the regime is the same: it permits compulsory care under the same circumstances as the regime in the first example. Medical staff may impose compulsory hospitalisation and treatment if the individual is in need of care, refuses treatment, fails to make a free and informed decision about the relevant care (despite having access to decision-making support), and risks the deterioration of health or suicide if medical treatment is not provided. Decision-making support is provided to those who need and want such support. The presence of a psychiatric diagnosis or disability is neither necessary nor sufficient for medical staff to conclude that a person is in need of treatment or lacks decision-making ability; it is one factor among others that staff should take into account in assessing the individual. One advantage of such a generic regime is that it would cover all situations in which compulsory care is necessary; it is not under-inclusive, as the system discussed above is. People without psychosocial conditions also commit suicide, and anyone can end up in a situation in which one is in urgent need of medical care but lacks the ability to make a free and informed treatment choice. A study from 2011 suggests that some 26 per cent of adult health care users without severe psychiatric conditions admitted for inpatient care lack the capacity to understand the relevant information about the proposed treatment, to comprehend their situation, to use reason to make a decision, and to communicate their choice.[100] Whilst many such people may not refuse treatment, it seems reasonable to assume that some of them will. A system that covers everyone enables health care staff to intervene in every situation in which such action is warranted. Given that it is just as important to protect the health and lives of people without psychosocial conditions as it is to protect the health and lives of people with them, a generic system might contribute to its aims to a greater extent.[101] Moreover, a generic system has the potential to bring about much less equality-specific harm. The legal provisions do not refer to certain psychosocial impairments or disabilities as conditions for compulsory care and hence cannot be said to reinforce stereotypical images of particular groups. On the contrary, they convey the message that anyone may be subject to compulsory care if it is necessary to protect health and life. Whether such a system *actually* produces superior outcomes in terms of less equality-specific harm and/or a greater contribution to the aims of the protection of health and life is an empirical question that cannot be resolved by abstract argumentation. The answer hinges on

[100] LL Sessums, H Zembrzuska, and JL Jackson, 'Does this Patient Have Medical Decision-Making Capacity? (2011) 306 *Journal of the American Medical Association* 420.

[101] This follows from the idea of formal equality, which is incorporated as a consistency requirement in my framework. See sections II.D and III.

the ability (and willingness) of decision-makers to correctly identify situations of risk and lack of decision-making ability.

The advantages of a generic system over one that applies solely to people with psychosocial disabilities evaporate if the generic system merely changes the wording of the relevant legal statutes (removing direct references to psychiatric diagnoses and disabilities), yet continues to apply in practice only to people with psychosocial disabilities.[102] As I have mentioned, it is difficult to assess risk and evaluate decision-making ability. As a result, such assessments will sometimes misinterpret treatment refusals, taking free and informed refusals to be unfree and uninformed, or vice versa.[103] And regimes based on such assessments will inevitably result in the compulsory care of people who would not have ended their lives in any event.[104] In a generic system overseen by knowledgeable and conscientious decision-makers, the risk posed by these epistemic problems is evenly distributed among the whole population. The situation is quite different in a system overseen by a medical profession that lacks the skills necessary to carry out such assessments or that disagrees with the system for some reason. It goes without saying that risk assessments must not become, in practice, a medical assessment of whether the person meets the criteria for a psychiatric condition, and they must not be influenced by statistically unsound beliefs about what people with psychosocial disabilities are like or how they act. The same is true of assessments of decision-making ability. Moreover, assessments of an individual's ability to understand and appreciate the nature and consequences of the treatment decision must not be made to boil down to whether the individual 'agrees with the doctor'.[105] Problems with such assessments may also arise if members of the medical profession do not agree with the criteria for the use of compulsory care. Representatives from the medical profession have, in fact, raised concerns about using decision-making ability as a criterion for the use of compulsory care within the mental health context. Tom Burns, for example, has argued that the use of this criterion puts too much emphasis on the value of autonomy.[106] According to Burns, in certain situations the interest in protecting health is more important than the obligation to respect autonomous choices, and in such situations few psychiatrists would hesitate to use compulsion.[107]

Even a generic system in which skilled decision-makers carefully identify situations in which compulsory care is warranted can be said to have a disparate impact on people with psychosocial disabilities. Because members of this group

[102] Benjamin Eidelson calls this form of indirect discrimination 'second-order discrimination'. See his *Discrimination and Disrespect* (Oxford, Oxford University Press, 2015) 40ff.

[103] See ch 2, section IV.A.

[104] *Ibid*.

[105] Bartlett, 'A Mental Disorder' 840.

[106] T Burns, 'Mental Illness Is Different and Ignoring Its Differences Profits Nobody' (2010) 20 *Journal of Mental Health Law* 34.

[107] *Ibid* 36.

are more likely to commit suicide and more likely to lack decision-making ability than people without such disabilities, they are more likely to meet the criteria for compulsory care. This means that they will also experience a larger share of the negative effects of these regimes. They will experience more frequent interferences with their rights to liberty, integrity and legal capacity than the general population, and their being subject to compulsory care will limit their opportunities for participating in society on an equal basis with others. The only way to eliminate these disproportionate effects would be to follow the CRPD Committee's recommendation to repeal all legal authorisations of compulsory care and to use voluntary care and support services instead.[108] Implementing such a change may free up resources that could be invested in support services for people experiencing crises, psychosis, suicidal ideation and other forms of emotional distress. However, this would also imply that states parties give up on the ambition of preventing the serious deterioration of health or suicide in situations in which individuals refuse to accept treatment and support on a voluntary basis. It would also prevent medical staff from stopping patients from leaving hospitals or facilities where they are being provided with crisis support. The cost of such a change of policy would be borne by those who would have benefited from these sorts of compulsory intervention. The significance of these negative effects depends, of course, on how well an entirely voluntary system performs compared to a system that sanctions compulsion as a last resort. As I explained in chapter three, there is ample evidence that voluntary care and support can be just as effective as compulsory care in many cases, including in certain complex cases.[109] Nevertheless, it is not clear that non-coercive forms of care can cater for the needs of the entire group of people who are currently subjected to compulsory care.

To sum up, several reasons speak in favour of generic regimes of compulsory care: systems that cover anyone who is unable to make a free and informed treatment choice, despite having access to support, but who needs treatment to prevent the serious deterioration of health or suicide. Such a system would enable health care staff to intervene in every situation in which intervention is warranted. In addition, the absence of explicit references to psychosocial conditions in the relevant statutes would likely mean that this regime would generate less equality-specific harm, that is, less public prejudice and social exclusion, than the alternative regime. Whether the system actually produces superior outcomes depends on the ability (and willingness) of decision-makers to correctly identify situations of risk and to evaluate decision-making ability. Even an optimal system will give rise to some harms (eg social exclusion and constraints on participation in society), and a large share of these harms will be suffered by people with psychosocial disabilities. This is not because decision-makers act

[108] CRPD Committee, 'General Comment No 1' paras 40 and 42.
[109] See ch 3, section III.C.

on the basis of biased assumptions about people with psychosocial disabilities, but because certain psychosocial conditions make it more likely the affected person will have diminished decision-making abilities and will attempt suicide. The only way to eliminate these harms is to abolish compulsory care altogether. The costs of abolition would be borne by those who would have benefited from compulsory care, and in a high-quality health care system it is reasonable to expect that many of these potential beneficiaries would also be people with psychosocial disabilities.

V. THE VALUE OF STRUCTURED PROPORTIONALITY ASSESSMENTS IN THE NON-DISCRIMINATION CONTEXT

One problem with the objective and reasonable standard developed by the UN monitoring bodies is that the criteria for determining the outcome of the test are not entirely clear.[110] This means states lack straightforward guidelines on how to balance the different factors involved in discrimination analysis. After all, it is the state that has the primary responsibility to ensure that people with disabilities enjoy their human rights on an equal basis with others at the domestic level, and to be effective in its work towards this end the state needs to know what its duties are. In this chapter, I have developed a more structured way of evaluating whether a particular regime of compulsory mental health care is justified and in compliance with the CRPD's demand that people with psychosocial disabilities enjoy legal capacity, liberty and integrity on an equal basis with others. The framework can help us to organise arguments for and against a particular system of compulsory care. It breaks down proportionality argumentation into a step-by-step process and sets out clear criteria to be fulfilled at each step. It also requires those applying it to be explicit about the weight of the arguments that support their position on the lawfulness of domestic regimes of compulsory care.

Take, for instance, the arguments put forward by the CRPD Committee in support of its position that compulsory mental health care violates the Convention. The Committee has held that empirical evidence indicates that compulsory care is ineffective and that the testimonies of people who have been committed to such care reveal the deep pain and trauma it causes.[111] It has also declared that the civil detention of people with disabilities on the basis of risk and the need for treatment constitutes an arbitrary deprivation of liberty and that forced treatment in mental health facilities on the basis that the patient has an impairment is discriminatory 'by definition'.[112] All of these arguments are

[110] *Ibid.*
[111] CRPD Committee, 'General Comment No 1' (n 58) para 42.
[112] CRPD Committee, 'General Comment No 1' (n 58) para 40; CRPD Committee, 'General Comment No 6' paras 30 and 56; CRPD Committee, 'Guidelines on Article 14 of the Convention on

certainly relevant to the process of determining the lawfulness of compulsory psychiatric care under the Convention, but they need to be further developed if we are to understand how they should influence the outcome of discrimination analysis. With regard to the claim that compulsory care is ineffective, the empirical research discussed in this book shows that our knowledge of the effectiveness of compulsory psychiatric care, as compared with that of alternative forms of care, is limited.[113] Compulsory intervention does not always result in improved well-being or more effective suicide prevention – far from it. In view of the harms brought about by such care, this fact is certainly problematic, but it is not a conclusive argument against all forms of compulsory care. Compulsory mental health care helps some and not others. The numbers of those who benefit from compulsory care vary greatly from study to study and from country to country, which means that the effectiveness of compulsory care must be assessed in relation to a particular system.[114]

The Committee is certainly right that the significant harms brought about by compulsory care are weighty reasons against such systems. Compulsory care is not only very painful for those hospitalised and treated against their will. It interferes with their rights to personal liberty, integrity and self-determination. It entails a risk that those subjected to it will have to live with irreversible health problems as a result of the adverse effects of medication or violent incidents involving staff or other patients. In addition, compulsory inpatient care prevents people from participating in social activities (education, work, cultural activities, etc) on an equal basis with others. Further, many such systems affect not only those actually subjected to coercive treatment, but also people with psychosocial disabilities more broadly, because they contribute to public prejudice and social exclusion. Just how significant these harms are in a domestic context depends on the legal design of the regime, the quality of the care provided, the capacity of the monitoring system, and the level of social inclusion enjoyed by people with psychosocial disabilities, among other factors. These are factors that vary greatly between states parties, which means that an identical legal regime may be lawful in one state but not in another, if for example the quality of care and the level of inclusion enjoyed by people with psychosocial disabilities were significantly lower in the latter state.

Regarding the claim that compulsory mental health care is discriminatory and arbitrary, I agree with the Committee that certain authorisations of compulsory intervention violate the prohibition of discrimination. These include systems that permit compulsory care in situations in which the same

the Rights of Persons with Disabilities: The Right to Liberty and Security of Persons with Disabilities Adopted during the Committee's Fourteenth Session' (17 August to 4 September 2015) paras 6 and 13.

[113] See ch 2, section IV and ch 3, section III.C.

[114] *Ibid.*

level of protection of health and life could be achieved by voluntary means, that is, with care and support provided on the basis of free and informed consent.[115] They also include systems in which the quality of the care provided is too low to compensate for the harms brought about by the system in question, equality-specific harms included. They also include domestic authorisations of civil detention and compulsory care that aim to prevent violence against others.[116] Compulsory care for the purposes of public safety may be viewed as an arbitrary deprivation of liberty in the sense that it is not based on sound reasoning. Certain other groups are equally likely to act violently against others, and it is difficult, perhaps impossible, to find a coherent explanation for why we should intervene in the case of people with certain psychosocial disabilities but not in the case of other high-risk groups.[117] On the other hand, I do not believe that civil detention to prevent suicide or to facilitate medical treatment is arbitrary or discriminatory in every case. The greater prevalence of suicidal ideation and diminished decision-making ability among people with psychosocial disabilities may explain a focus on this group. Legislation that targets people with psychosocial disabilities may not be the best way to address situations in which voluntary support is not sufficient, not least because of its stigmatising effects. However, domestic regimes of compulsory care that apply to everyone who puts their health and life at risk in circumstances in which free and informed consent cannot be obtained can be justified as proportionate, at least in a context in which the quality of care is high and those with psychosocial disabilities enjoy a relatively high level of social inclusion.

VI. A FRAMEWORK FOR EVALUATING DOMESTIC SYSTEMS OF COMPULSORY MENTAL HEALTH CARE

This section summarises the findings of this chapter as a set of criteria that domestic regimes of compulsory care must meet to comply with the CRPD. This framework is designed to help guide reasoning about the permissibility of typical domestic authorisations of compulsory mental health intervention. It may be applied both to domestic statutes that apply exclusively to people with psychosocial disabilities and to generic legislation that has a disparate impact on people with psychosocial disabilities. The assessment begins by looking at the relationship between the domestic threshold criteria for civil detention and involuntary clinical treatment and the aims that such compulsory care is supposed to achieve. This initial examination can be viewed as a simple way of

[115] See section II.C.
[116] See section III.C.
[117] *Ibid.*

rejecting, at the outset, mental health regimes that are clearly unjustified. At this stage, the following criteria must be met:

- The authorisation of compulsion must be motivated by a *legitimate aim* or *legitimate aims*.
- The authorisation of compulsion must be *suitable* and contribute to its legitimate aim(s).
- The authorisation must not go beyond what is *necessary* to achieve the aim(s).
- If the domestic health care system authorises compulsory intervention against people with psychosocial disabilities but not against others, then the state party must demonstrate the *means–ends relevance* of such differentiation.

To meet the first criterion, states parties must demonstrate that the aim(s) behind their regimes do not conflict with the object, purpose or provisions of the CRPD.[118] The protection of health and life and the promotion of public safety are legitimate aims in this sense. The second criterion is an empirical one. States must demonstrate that their regimes make a real contribution to their aims.[119] This requires that there be a match between the conditions that render a person subject to compulsory intervention and the aim(s) compulsory intervention is supposed to achieve. It also requires that the health care provided at psychiatric hospitals or other facilities is of a certain quality; these health care services must be capable of achieving their aims (eg preventing the deterioration of health and averting suicides). If there is no reliable empirical knowledge concerning the efficacy of domestic health care services, states may rely on uncertain but not evidently false data. The third criterion weeds out domestic regimes that impose restrictions that are more stringent than is necessary to contribute to the aims.[120] This criterion implies that civil detention and compulsory clinical treatment may only be authorised as measures of last resort, applicable in situations in which voluntary services are insufficient to prevent the deterioration of health and to avert suicide. This can be accomplished in various ways. Statutes could describe such situations in general terms, or they could incorporate some version of a 'necessity' or 'least restrictive means' criterion. It is important to note that, when examining the necessity of a particular compulsory regime, all evidence-based alternatives suitable for the domestic context in question are to be taken into account, regardless of whether these alternatives are already provided for in that country.[121]

The fourth criterion applies to domestic regimes that authorise the compulsory care of people with psychosocial conditions but not others. States parties

[118] See section II.A.
[119] See section II.B.
[120] See section II.C.
[121] *Ibid*.

that wish to retain such regimes must explain the means–ends relevance, given the aim(s) of coercive care, of targeting people with psychosocial disabilities for compulsion; that is, they must demonstrate that the differentiation is based on empirical data and not unsubstantiated beliefs about people with psychosocial disabilities. If a system of compulsory care fails to meet one of these requirements, it cannot be considered to be proportionate, and it therefore violates the prohibition of disability-based discrimination under the CRPD. The lawfulness of domestic regimes that satisfy the requirements listed above is determined by balancing.

To determine whether a particular regime is proportionate (in the narrow sense), decision-makers must identify the reasons that speak in favour of and against its compliance with the CRPD and balance these reasons against one another, taking the relevant rules of legal argumentation into account. For a regime to count as lawful, the following criteria must be met:

- The reasons in favour of the regime must carry equal or greater weight than the reasons against the regime.
- When assessing the reasons against the regime, the *equality-specific harms* that follow from the regime under review must be taken into account.
- If the regime authorises the compulsory treatment of people with psychosocial disabilities but not that of people without such disabilities, then the state party must demonstrate that the reasoning in favour of the regime is *consistent* with other rules and principles that govern the administration of health care vis-à-vis people without psychosocial disabilities in the legal system in question.

When determining the weights of the reasons in favour of and against a particular system, the CRPD constitutes the normative point of reference.[122] The collective weights of the reasons and counter-reasons are then balanced against each other. Balancing is a form of legal argumentation that obliges decision-makers to take all legally relevant considerations into account. This includes arguments about the scope and content of the legal norms at stake, as well as arguments about the concrete consequences of the domestic provisions under review. As the objective and reasonable standard has it, state practices that satisfy the definition of discrimination must be reasonable (not too burdensome) for those concerned.[123] This means that the reasons in favour of permitting the domestic authorisation of compulsory intervention must be (at least) as weighty as the reasons against permitting this authorisation.[124] If the reasons for and against

[122] See ch 3, section VII.A.

[123] See ch 1, section VI.B.

[124] On the question of whether the objective and reasonable standard and Alexy's proportionality assessment model treat discretion in different ways, see ch 3, section VII.B.

the regime are of equal weight, then the state party has discretion; it may either keep or abolish it.[125]

The reasons against a particular regime can be divided into two categories: reasons concerning the severity of the interference with the substantive right(s) at stake and reasons concerning equality-specific harms. The first category includes reasons relating to how much the domestic regime interferes with the entitlements to personal liberty, integrity and legal capacity set out in the CRPD. Relevant in this context are arguments about domestic thresholds for compulsory care, the time limits on care, and the conditions under which care is provided. Regimes that permit compulsory inpatient treatment for very long periods of time (eg years) and that completely cut the individual off from his or her social network arguably interfere more with liberty and self-determination than regimes that only permit short-term hospitalisation, provide for leaves of absence, and allow for visits from family and friends. Similarly, systems that only allow the compulsory administration of medication in situations in which the individual is unable to provide free and informed consent arguably interfere less with the integrity and self-determination of patients than systems that allow for compulsory administration regardless of the decision-making abilities of the patient. Systems that have specific restrictions on treatment methods that are particularly painful, intrusive or irreversible also arguably interfere less with these rights than systems that allow doctors to decide whether to use such treatment methods.

The second category covers reasoning about equality-specific harms. These include *disrespect for human dignity*, *public prejudice*, *social exclusion* and other forms of *comparative social disadvantage*.[126] As a rule, the first two kinds of harm tend to be more prominent in relation to systems that apply only to people with psychosocial disabilities. Such systems confirm and reinforce stereotypical beliefs about people with psychosocial disabilities as deviant, incapable and prone to violence and self-destructive behaviour. This, in turn, leads to discrimination by private actors, such as employers and landlords, and to the social exclusion of people with psychosocial disabilities. Generic compulsory regimes may perpetuate social exclusion and social disadvantage in other ways. Inpatient treatment in closed wards effectively prevents participation in social activities outside the hospital setting, and lengthy stays in such environments have negative effects on personal development, even if not everyone committed to compulsory care is affected in the same way or to the same extent. The magnitudes of these negative effects and their distribution among people with and without psychosocial conditions depend on several factors. These include the ability and willingness of decision-makers to correctly identify those who need compulsory care (who will benefit from treatment, and who will not?),

[125] See ch 3, section III.D.
[126] See section II.D.

the quality of the care provided, and the attitudes towards persons subjected to compulsory care (to what extent are they included and respected in the labour and housing market and in other spheres of society?).

The reasons in favour of a particular regime can also be divided into two categories. The first category includes reasons relating to how much more the system under consideration contributes to its aim(s) as compared with a system that interferes less with personal liberty, integrity and legal capacity. Again, understanding these reasons will involve an investigation of domestic thresholds for compulsory care, time limits on care and the quality of care. Obviously, the introduction of higher thresholds for compulsory intervention would prevent physicians from intervening at an earlier stage, which could ultimately increase suffering and health harms. There is still some uncertainty about whether shorter admission periods are good for patients. It may be that shorter admission periods mean that the causes and symptoms of their psychiatric conditions are not fully addressed, leading to a series of short but frequent admissions (so-called 'revolving door' admissions). A Cochrane study from 2014, however, found no link between inpatient care for short periods (below one month) and more frequent readmissions, poorer health or higher risk of death.[127] On the contrary, shorter stays were associated with better social functioning (although this is not to say that the former caused the latter). If compulsion is only used in situations in which free and informed treatment decisions cannot be obtained, then some form of individual assessment is required. This involves a risk that medical staff (or other decision-makers) will sometimes interpret unfree treatment refusals as free and informed refusals, and will thus refrain from intervention even though intervention was warranted.[128] The only way to eliminate this risk is to permit the use of compulsion even in situations where there is a doubt about whether a treatment refusal is truly free and informed, but this comes at the cost of interfering more with the right to legal capacity and self-determination.

The second category includes reasons relating to the costs of modifying the regime so that it contributes less to the spread of public prejudice, social exclusion and other forms of equality-specific harm. As I noted in section IV, regimes that restrict compulsory care to people with psychosocial disabilities protect people *without* such disabilities against some forms of abuse (eg the use of compulsory care to incarcerate political dissidents), although the level of protection such regimes offer is not very robust. A system that operates with disability-neutral criteria, in practice as well as in law, can be expected to contribute less to the negative stereotyping and social exclusion of people with disabilities. In view of the fact that people with psychosocial disabilities are more likely to commit suicide than others and more likely than members of

[127] O Babalola et al, 'Length of Hospitalisation for People with Severe Mental Illness' (2014) 1 *Cochrane Database of Systematic Reviews*.

[128] See section IV.B.

many other groups to lack decision-making ability, it is reasonable to assume that, even in a disability-neutral system, they will still be committed for compulsory care more often than others, which will, in turn, limit their opportunities for participating in society on an equal basis with others. The only way to eliminate this negative effect is to abolish compulsory care altogether. The costs of abolition would be borne by those who would have benefited from compulsory care had the system been maintained, and a large proportion of these potential beneficiaries would be people with psychosocial disabilities.

To determine whether a particular domestic regime is proportionate in the narrow sense, one must assess the strength of the reasons just discussed. If the reasons against a regime are weightier than the reasons that can be advanced in its defence, then that regime is disproportionate and in conflict with the state obligation to ensure that people with psychosocial disabilities enjoy liberty, integrity and legal capacity on an equal basis with others, as laid down in the CRPD. If, on the other hand, the reasons in favour of the regime are stronger than those against the regime, then the state party has good reason to keep it. If the reasons for and against the regime are of equal weight, then the state party has discretion; it may either keep or abolish it.[129] Needless to say, determining the outcome of the balancing exercise is a complex task.

Systems that satisfy the definition of direct discrimination are subject to a *consistency requirement*, which may serve as a shortcut to weed out systems that conflict with the idea of formal equality. Differential treatment of people with and without psychosocial disabilities in similar circumstances is disproportionate (or unreasonable) unless a consistent argument can be made to justify the difference in treatment.[130] When reasoning about whether this requirement is met in a particular case, the guiding question is: would it have been proportional to permit such intervention against people without psychosocial disabilities in relevantly similar situations? The fact that a state does not permit such intervention under current law would constitute a strong indication that the answer to the question is 'no'. The mere presence of a disability/impairment or clinical condition will, of course, not suffice as an explanation of differentiation. The acceptability of other explanations depends on whether they make sense within the domestic legal system in question and in light of international human rights norms.[131] Because of this requirement, singling out people with psychosocial disabilities for compulsory care for the purposes of preventing violence against others is difficult, perhaps impossible, to justify.

[129] See ch 3, section III.D.
[130] See sections II.D and III.
[131] *Ibid*.

Conclusion

I. TO INTERVENE OR NOT TO INTERVENE? A DIFFICULT QUESTION

LET US RETURN to the scenario I described in the Introduction. Nancy is brought to a hospital by her son, who is worried about his mother. Nancy accidently started a small fire at home because she was smoking in bed. She does not sleep at night, and she has lost interest in life and the things that used to make her happy. When offered treatment, she rejects it because she does not think that it will help her to feel better. She has tried medication before and dreads the side effects. She just wants to go home again. The doctor examining her believes that medication is absolutely necessary. Without treatment, there is a risk that her condition will deteriorate further; there is even a risk of suicide.

As this book has made clear, the decision of whether to intervene is difficult for several reasons. First of all, it is difficult because several rights and interests are at stake, including the rights to liberty, integrity and self-determination and the interest in protecting health and life. Whatever the doctor chooses to do, there will be negative consequences. Admitting Nancy for compulsory care will interfere with her right to personal liberty, and administering treatment against her wishes will interfere with her rights to self-determination and to respect for her mental and physical integrity. In addition, compulsory care involves a risk that patients will experience fear, pain, humiliation and stigma, and that they will experience other forms of harm, such as serious adverse effects from medication, which may irreversibly damage their health, and the effects of the violent behaviour of staff or other patients. Such negative experiences lead some individuals to lose faith in the capacity of the mental health care system to support them. This may lead them to avoid engaging with the health care system in future, which increases the risk of further crises.

The decision is also difficult because it has to be taken on the basis of uncertain information. Many decisions to provide psychiatric treatment depend on imperfect information about the expected effects of a certain medication or other therapy.[1] At the early stages of a treatment process, in particular, knowledge about how the individual concerned will respond to different medications is often uncertain. Finding the medication and treatment plan that will produce the best health outcomes with the fewest and mildest adverse effects often involves an amount of trial and error. On top of all this, administering

[1] See ch 2, section IV.A.

psychiatric treatment coercively often makes it less effective.[2] We also have to consider the difficulties involved in assessing suicide risk and the risk of violence in individual cases, as well as the difficulties associated with evaluating decision-making ability.[3] Finally, treatment decisions are value sensitive in the sense that the 'right' choice in a given situation (the choice that will generate the most satisfaction or well-being for the individual) depends on the patient's values and preferences. This means the right choice naturally differs between individuals, and between doctors and their patients, as the example of Nancy illustrates. Research into people's perceptions of compulsory care suggests as much. A literature review of studies of compulsory mental health care outcomes concludes that, although most inpatients show signs of clinical improvement upon discharge, the proportion of patients who consider their hospitalisation to have been helpful varies greatly, from 39 per cent to 81 per cent.[4]

This book concerns the rules that should guide doctors' decision-making given these challenges. Confronted with someone in Nancy's situation, should they respect the decision to decline medical treatment and let the patient leave the hospital? Or should the doctor first make sure that the patient has access to the support he or she wants and may need to make a free and informed decision? Is it the doctor's role to question whether treatment refusals reflect the patient's 'true' will? Are there any circumstances in which the doctor may impose treatment against the expressed will of a person with psychosocial disabilities? These questions have been at the heart of debates over the design of mental health care regimes for decades. In this book, I have discussed what the UN Convention on the Rights of Persons with Disabilities (CRPD),[5] and more specifically its obligation to ensure that people with psychosocial disabilities enjoy liberty, integrity and legal capacity 'on an equal basis with others', contributes to this discussion. Below, I summarise my findings.

II. THE LONG ANSWER TO THE QUESTION

There is no short answer to the question of whether compulsory mental health care is permissible under the CRPD. Some systems are clearly unlawful, and others can be justified. Whether a particular system can be justified depends not only on the legal design of the system but also on the realities on the ground, the quality of the care provided within the system, and the level of social inclusion enjoyed by people with psychosocial disabilities in that country. The following

[2] *Ibid.*

[3] See ch 2, sections IV.B and C.

[4] C Katsakou and S Priebe, 'Outcomes of Involuntary Hospital Admission: A Review' (2006) 114 *Acta Psychiatrica Scandinavica* 232.

[5] Convention on the Rights of Persons with Disabilities (adopted 13 December 2006, entered into force 3 May 2008) 2515 UNTS 3 (CRPD).

sections summarise the legal standards that domestic systems must abide by to comply with the CRPD. This summary, of course, also provides an overview of the many ways in which compulsory mental health care policies and practices may violate the Convention. It starts, in subsection A, with a recapitulation of the constraints on compulsory care that can be inferred from an interpretation of the treaty text according to the rules for the interpretation of international treaties. Subsection B outlines the additional constraints that we can deduce from discrimination analysis, including proportionality argumentation, and subsection C discusses CRPD-compliant practices.

A. The Limits Set by the Treaty Text

As I made clear in chapter one, the treaty text is silent on the key question discussed in this book: the treaty neither prohibits nor explicitly permits compulsory mental health care. This marks a departure from previous human rights law, which presupposed that such care was necessary under certain circumstances and granted states and the medical profession a significant amount of discretion to determine the situations that warranted intervention with compulsory means. Although the CRPD neither permits nor prohibits the compulsory care of people with psychosocial disabilities, it incorporates several provisions that have direct implications for the organisation and regulation of mental health care. The most important rules are found in Articles 12 (equal recognition before the law), 14 (liberty and security of person), 15 (freedom from torture or cruel, inhuman or degrading treatment or punishment), 17 (protecting the integrity of the person) and 25 (health). An interpretation of these rules allows us to conclude that certain mental health practices clearly violate the CRPD. These include laws and practices according to which the presence of a psychosocial condition, impairment or disability is a sufficient reason to commit someone for compulsory inpatient care at a closed ward and/or to compel someone to receive medical care. This clearly violates the right to equal enjoyment of legal capacity and liberty, as protected under Articles 12(2) and 14(1)(b) of the Convention. Article 12(3) further asserts that the primary response to situations in which someone finds it difficult to make a free and informed decision about whether to accept medical care and treatment must be to ensure that the individual has access to appropriate support. If a free and informed decision to reject a certain form of treatment can be facilitated with the assistance of such support, then that decision must be recognised as legally valid. Article 25(d) asserts that health professionals should, as a general rule, provide care to people with disabilities 'on the basis of free and informed consent'. Whether this rule allows for exceptions – and, if it does, under what circumstances – depends, in the end, on discrimination analysis.

Finally, the prohibition of torture and inhuman and degrading treatment outlaws the worst forms of malpractice that take place within the field of mental health care. Under no circumstances may domestic regimes subject people to medical or scientific experimentation without their consent.[6] Even if much psychiatric care involves a certain amount of trial and error, the aim of the treatment prescribed must be to cure, alleviate symptoms, or otherwise improve the individual's condition, and not to experiment or generate new knowledge. Moreover, the treatment must be based on scientific knowledge and prescribed on the basis of clinical expertise. The use of unscientific or outdated treatment methods is clearly unlawful. The same is true of overmedication and the use of medication to intimidate or punish the patient. This constitutes ill treatment and may amount to torture. Other forms of malpractice outlawed by Article 15 include the use of cage beds and net beds, solitary confinement for long periods of time and the excessive use of straps, belts and other restraints.[7] Article 16 complements the prohibition of inhuman and degrading treatment with a prohibition of less severe abusive practices.

B. The Limits Set by Discrimination Analysis

As I have made clear throughout this book, the prohibition of discrimination implicit in the obligation to ensure the equal enjoyment of the rights to integrity, liberty and legal capacity introduces new thresholds for domestic regimes to meet. Domestic authorisations of civil detention and compulsory clinical care typically apply only to people with psychosocial disabilities and thereby satisfy the definition of direct discrimination.[8] Further, systems that permit the compulsory care of anyone who requires inpatient treatment on health grounds but lacks the ability to make a valid decision about the relevant treatment fulfil the definition of disability-based discrimination. Such formally neutral systems have a disparate impact on people with psychosocial disabilities and therefore constitute indirect discrimination.[9] The prohibition of discrimination does not, however, prohibit all domestic laws and practices that can be subsumed under this definition. Systems that pursue *legitimate aims*, *contribute* to their aims, and are *reasonable* in light of their aims can be justified as lawful.[10]

Most, if not all, domestic mental health regimes serve legitimate aims. The protection of health and life and the promotion of public safety are aims that states parties to the CRPD are obliged to pursue, though not necessarily with compulsory means.[11] The second criterion (contribution) is more problematic.

[6] CRPD Art 15.

[7] P Fennell, 'Art.15 Protection against Torture and Cruel or Inhuman or Degrading Treatment or Punishment' in I Bantekas, MA Stein and D Anastasiou (eds), *The UN Convention on the Rights of Persons with Disabilities: A Commentary* (Oxford, Oxford University Press, 2018) 460–62.

[8] See ch 1, section VI.A.

[9] *Ibid.*

[10] See ch 1, section VI.B.

[11] See ch 2, section III.

The effects of civil detention and compulsory clinical intervention are poorly understood, and any estimate of their therapeutic effects and of how many acts of suicide and violence against others they prevent will suffer from some degree of uncertainty. Nevertheless, empirical evidence supports the position that compulsory hospitalisation and treatment do prevent the serious deterioration of health, self-destructive behaviour and violence against others in many cases – though certainly not in all.[12] What is more, the prohibition of discrimination requires some form of explanation of either the rationale behind the differential treatment of people with and people without a disability or of the disparate impact on the former. For systems that directly discriminate, there must be an explanation of why it is necessary to differentiate between health care users on the basis of disability. For systems that operate with disability-neutral criteria, there must be an explanation of why they nevertheless have a disparate impact on people with psychosocial disabilities. Is there a valid explanation for the disproportionate impact, or is the system biased and influenced by unsubstantiated beliefs (prejudices) about people with psychosocial disabilities? If a system differentiates between people with and people without psychosocial disabilities to the detriment of the former and there is no good reason for this disproportionate impact, the system is unlawful. The same is true of systems that rely on biased information about protected groups.

The third criterion of the objective and reasonable standard is that mental health systems must be reasonable in light of their aims. In order to determine whether a system is reasonable, a number of reasons are taken into account. These include the importance of the entitlements and interests at stake, the concrete effects of the regime under review, and the existence of any less restrictive ways of achieving the aims. From the jurisprudence of the UN treaty bodies alone, it is unclear how precisely these reasons are to be assessed and balanced against each other in individual cases. Alexy's proportionality assessment model equips us with a set of rules that can help us to determine the outcome of these processes. According to his model, the fact that treatment must be 'necessary' implies that compulsion may not be used if health and life can be effectively protected through voluntary care and support.[13] There are different legal techniques for ensuring that domestic statutes comply with this requirement. Domestic law could describe the types of cases in which compulsion may be used in general terms, or it could simply incorporate some version of a 'least restrictive means' criterion.[14] The variables in Alexy's weight formula identify the important factors that must be taken into account when determining the reasonableness of a particular system and illustrate how these factors relate to each other. First, we must assess how important the rights and interests at stake

[12] See ch 2, section IV.
[13] See ch 3, section III.C.
[14] See ch 4, section II.C.

are relative to each other: in the context of this study, the relative importance of, on the one side, respect for liberty, integrity and legal capacity and, on the other side, the protection of health and life. It is my conclusion that the CRPD does not establish a hierarchy between these rights and interests, and so decision-makers are not required to prefer one over the other in all circumstances.[15] Instead, their relative importance in a given case depends on a contextual assessment that takes into account the degree to which the system under review interferes with these rights and contributes to these interests, and the reliability of underlying premises.[16] The jurisprudence of the UN treaty bodies affirms that legal argumentation about reasonableness within discrimination analysis involves a contextual assessment and balancing of the rights and interests at stake; what Alexy's model contributes is an added level of detail and a structure that shows how the relevant arguments relate to each other.[17]

One important category of reasons against permitting systems of compulsory mental health care concerns the degree to which such care interferes with the rights to liberty, integrity and legal capacity. The more a system interferes with these rights, the stronger the counter-reasons must be if the system is to be justified.[18] How much a particular system interferes with the rights to liberty, integrity and legal capacity depends on questions such as the following:

- How many people are committed under the regime?
- For how long are they typically committed?
- How do they experience their treatment?
- How restrictive is the regime?
- Are inpatients allowed to take leaves of absence, and may they receive visitors?
- Are there any restrictions on the types of treatment that may be administered against a person's will?
- May people who possess decision-making abilities be forced to undergo treatment during compulsory inpatient care?

It is also important to consider the reliability of the data underpinning the answers to these questions. Finally, decision-makers must take into consideration the amount of equality-specific harm brought about by a particular system, a topic to which I return below.

The weight of the reasons in favour of maintaining a particular system of compulsory care depends on the 'added value' the system provides as compared with less restrictive regimes.[19] How much more deterioration of health is avoided,

[15] See ch 3, section V.A.
[16] See ch 3, section III.D.
[17] See ch 3, sections IV and VII.C.
[18] See ch 3, sections III.D.
[19] *Ibid.*

and how many more acts of suicide are avoided, by the regime under consideration, as compared with a less restrictive one? Less restrictive regimes include those that interfere less with personal liberty, integrity or legal capacity and those that cause less equality-specific harm. For example, one way of mitigating the infringement of liberty a system involves would be to place stricter time limits on compulsory inpatient care. One way to mitigate the infringement of integrity would be to exclude certain particularly intrusive treatment methods from the range of treatments that may be imposed against a person's expressed wishes. The downside of such modifications is that they may result in a lower quality of care. In certain cases, medical staff may be prevented from using the most suitable treatment method or may be compelled to discharge individuals who would benefit from further treatment. It should be acknowledged that Alexy's model does not help us to determine the precise weight of a given argument for or against compulsory care. Such matters are to be determined in accordance with the relevant rules of legal argumentation. Nevertheless, Alexy's model clarifies the threshold that must be met in the balancing process. A domestic system is reasonable – and thereby compatible with the CRPD – if the reasons in favour of permitting the system are at least as weighty or strong as the reasons against permitting it.[20]

In chapter four, I fine-tuned Alexy's proportionality assessment model to make it fit the non-discrimination context. In this context, we must take equality norms into consideration and focus on distributive (in)justice. The prohibition of discrimination implies that laws and practices that create or contribute to comparative disadvantage that affects members of protected groups must be justified to be lawful. This focus on distributive justice across groups (here: persons with psychosocial disabilities and persons without such disabilities) led me to add three rules to Alexy's model: (1) a requirement to demonstrate the means–ends relevance of differential treatment on the basis of psychosocial disability; (2) a requirement of consistency in reasoning about the reasonableness (or proportionality in the narrow sense) of a particular system; and (3) a requirement to take into account the specific harms caused by systems that satisfy the definition of disability-based discrimination set out in the CRPD. The first two rules apply to domestic regimes that authorise compulsory interventions against people with psychosocial disabilities, or any subgroup thereof, but not against other health care users, and thereby satisfy the definition of direct discrimination. The means–ends requirement obliges states to explain the logic behind restricting the use of compulsory care to people with psychosocial disabilities in light of the aims of this form of care.[21] Are there good grounds for the domestic legislation restricting the use of compulsory care in this way? The threshold to be met is low. The requirement

[20] *Ibid.*
[21] See ch 4, section II.B.

may be viewed as a shortcut, allowing decision-makers to weed out systems that rest on evidently false, prejudicial or offensive claims about people with psychosocial disabilities. Explanations of differential treatment of people with and people without disabilities that are anchored in statistical data will meet the requirement.[22] Thus, the claim that people with certain psychosocial disabilities are more likely to have diminished decision-making abilities, or are more likely to engage in self-destructive and violent behaviour, will suffice to establish the means–ends relevance of differential disadvantageous treatment.

The consistency requirement is more demanding. People with psychosocial disabilities must be treated in the same way as people without such disabilities, unless a consistent argument can be made to justify a difference in treatment.[23] Consistency is important for several reasons. Many would agree that it is a basic requirement in much legal and moral argumentation and it is an essential element of the idea of 'treating like cases alike' which is part and parcel of discrimination law. The very fact that someone possesses a psychosocial disability cannot justify limitations on human rights.[24] In addition, this rule ensures that we do not underestimate the harms caused by compulsory care – such as the distress of being locked up and unable to control the chemicals that are introduced into one's body – simply because these harms affect people with psychosocial conditions. It aims further to ensure that we do not overestimate the value of protecting health and life and preventing violence simply because the situation is one involving someone with a psychosocial condition. When assessing regimes of compulsory care that aim to protect health, prevent suicide and prevent violence against others to determine whether they meet this requirement, I have found that it is possible to develop a consistent argument for maintaining a separate regime for people with certain psychosocial conditions for the purposes of preventing suicide in states where the overwhelming majority of those who commit suicide are people with such conditions.[25] It is also possible to provide a consistent argument for the compulsory care of people with psychosocial disabilities in situations in which free and informed treatment decisions cannot be obtained, despite patients having access to support, as long as such care may also be imposed upon all other people with similarly diminished decision-making abilities.[26] It is, however, difficult to produce a consistent argument for the maintenance of separate regimes for the purposes of preventing violent crime.[27] The problem, from the point of view of the consistency requirement, is that it is easy to identify other groups that present a similarly increased risk of criminal violence. Within the field of risk prediction, there is

[22] *Ibid.*
[23] See ch 4, section III.
[24] CRPD Art 14(1)(b). See also ch 1, section VII.
[25] See ch 4, section III.B.
[26] See ch 4, sections III.A and B.
[27] See ch 4, sections III.C.

broad agreement that being male, having an antisocial personality, and having a history of violent behaviour are factors that are as closely associated with violence as clinical symptoms.[28] The inconsistency cannot be dealt with by simply extending authorisations of civil detention to cover these other groups, as this would contravene human rights laid down in other treaties, including Article 9 of the International Covenant on Civil and Political Rights (ICCPR) and Article 5 of the European Convention on Human Rights (ECHR).[29] My conclusion is therefore that states parties to the CRPD must reform their mental health laws so that compulsory hospitalisation and treatment may not be imposed for the purposes of preventing future violent behaviour.

The third rule requires us to take the equality-specific harms that follow from a particular system into account in the balancing process. These include disrespect for human dignity, public prejudice, social exclusion and other forms of comparative social disadvantage.[30] The rule applies to all domestic regimes of compulsory care that have a disparate impact on people with psychosocial disabilities: not only systems that apply solely to this group but also systems that apply to all but that affect this group more than others. It may be possible to explain a disparate impact in terms of the fact that suicide and certain forms of self-harm and decision-making impairment are more prevalent among people with certain psychosocial conditions. However, we must be cautious here; a disparate impact, especially a significant one, may indicate that compulsion has been 'overused' against people with psychosocial disabilities because of the biases of medical professionals.[31] It may be helpful to bear in mind that empirical evidence suggests that a majority of those committed for compulsory care possess the abilities necessary to make free and informed treatment choices, even without decision-making support.[32] What is more, the proportion of health care users *without* severe psychiatric conditions who possess these abilities may only be around 74 per cent.[33]

The magnitude of the equality-specific harm caused by a particular system depends on several factors, including the legal design of the regime, the ability (and willingness) of medical staff and other decision-makers to correctly identify situations that warrant intervention, and the level of social inclusion enjoyed by people with psychosocial disabilities in the state in question.[34] As a rule,

[28] eg JL Skeem et al, 'Offenders with Mental Illness Have Criminogenic Needs, Too: Toward Recidivism Reduction' (2014) 38 *Law and Human Behaviour* 212; A Buchanan and M Leese, 'Quantifying the Contributions of Three Types of Information to the Prediction of Criminal Conviction Using the Receiver Operating Characteristic' (2006) 188 *British Journal of Psychiatry* 472.

[29] See ch 4, section IV.

[30] See ch 4, section II.D.

[31] See ch 4, section IV.B.

[32] D Okai et al, 'Mental Capacity in Psychiatric Patients: Systematic Review' (2007) 191 *British Journal of Psychiatry* 291.

[33] LL Sessums, H Zembrzuska and JL Jackson, 'Does this Patient Have Medical Decision-Making Capacity? (2011) 306 *Journal of the American Medical Association* 420.

[34] See ch 4, section IV.B.

domestic regimes that authorise the compulsory care of people with psychosocial disabilities but not others will often generate more harm than systems that apply to everyone. This is because systems that restrict the use of compulsory care to people with certain psychosocial conditions can be said to convey a demeaning message: that members of this group are different, are incapable of making decisions about their care and are self-destructive.[35] This constitutes an affront to the dignity of members of this group, and it can reinforce negative stereotypes about people with psychosocial disabilities among the public at large. Such stereotypes underpin social exclusion and discrimination by third parties.

It follows from the above that a first step towards mitigating equality-specific harm at the domestic level is to ensure that the system applies to everyone who puts their health or life at risk under certain circumstances. Taking this step would not have any obvious negative effects on the ability of the system to achieve its aims. It may even enhance the ability of the system to achieve the aims of protecting health and life, as it would enable decision-makers to intervene in every situation in which intervention would be beneficial. Broadening systems of compulsory care so that they apply to everyone does, however, have negative implications for people without psychosocial conditions; it weakens their protection against certain forms of abuse, such as the use of coercive care to incarcerate political dissidents.[36] As I have explained, the weight of these reasons is arguably not very great.[37] Psychiatric diagnoses can be manipulated, so the protection against abuse currently enjoyed by people without psychosocial conditions does not seem to be very robust in any case. In addition, a more appropriate way to combat abuses of compulsory care systems would be to strengthen domestic monitoring and review procedures, granting individuals the right to seek a second opinion, to appeal decisions, and to have access to legal representation. The precise 'added value' offered by one system as compared with a less restrictive one can only be determined by taking into account the context in which the system operates. It will depend on the quality of domestic care services and on the capacity of medical staff to correctly identify situations in which compulsory care can make a difference by preventing the deterioration of health and/or self-destructive acts.

If we accept my claim that Alexy's rules for proportionality analysis can help us to determine the scope of lawful mental health intervention under the CRPD, then the arguments I have outlined above are those that determine the lawfulness of domestic regimes of compulsory care. The fact that a domestic regime contributes to its aims is never by itself sufficient to justify compulsory care, nor is the argument that the therapeutic benefits of compulsory care balance out the infringements of liberty and integrity brought about by these practices. To fully

[35] *Ibid.*
[36] See ch 4, section IV.A.
[37] *Ibid.*

justify compulsory care regimes that fall within the definition of disability-based discrimination, states parties must develop a consistent defence of their regimes and demonstrate that their benefits are at least on a par with the harm, *including* the equality-specific harm, caused by these regimes.

C. CRPD-compliant Compulsory Mental Health Interventions to Protect the Health and Lives of Patients

As this book has demonstrated, the CRPD does permit some forms of compulsory care for the purposes of protecting the health and life of the person concerned. States parties enjoy a margin of discretion in choosing how to approach situations in which an individual is in need of medical care and a free and informed treatment decision cannot be obtained, even though the individual has access to decision-making support. The consistency requirement places some constraints on this freedom.[38] If compulsory care is deemed reasonable in situations in which a failure to treat would have serious health implications, then this rule must apply regardless of whether the situation involves a person with a psychosocial condition. Several states parties have adopted this approach, replacing thresholds that referred to the presence of certain psychiatric conditions with thresholds referring to the lack of an ability to make free and informed decisions, despite having access to support.[39] Such a lack may be due to a psychosocial condition, but it may also be the result of other factors. With regard to compulsory interventions for the purposes of preventing suicide, it seems to be difficult to find a fully consistent argument for such interventions based on reasoning about the impact psychosocial conditions can have on our outlook on life or on reasoning about the 'treatability' of these conditions.[40] Instead, a consistent justification of compulsory care to prevent acts of suicide may be based on the fact that, in many high-income Western states parties, most people who commit suicide have a psychosocial condition. As I mentioned in chapter two, studies suggest that in such countries up to 90 per cent of people who commit suicide have a psychosocial condition, and depressive symptoms and other related symptoms are present among the remaining 10 per cent.[41] Given this empirical evidence, it is possible to produce a consistent argument for restricting the use of compulsion, for the purposes of suicide prevention, to people with certain psychosocial conditions. There is no other group of people who are at a similar risk of ending their lives by their own hands. Again, however, these numbers must be treated with caution. Several commentators

[38] See ch 4, section III.A.
[39] See ch 2, section II.
[40] See ch 4, section III.B.
[41] World Health Organisation, *Preventing Suicide: A Global Imperative* (Luxembourg, World Health Organisation) 40. See, further, ch 2, section IV.B.

have argued that there is a tendency in the West to view suicide as an expression of depression, or a similar psychosocial condition, even in cases in which no such diagnosis was recorded before the death.[42] Should new information about rates of suicide among different groups emerge, states must, of course, be prepared to alter their legislation to ensure that groups at an equally high risk are treated in an even-handed manner. Obviously, one way to ensure that medical staff and other decision-makers treat people at a similar risk of self-destructive behaviour equally is for states to opt for compulsory treatment policies that apply to everyone regardless of disability. States parties that provide for physician-assisted suicide under certain circumstances must ensure that questions about the patient's reasoning skills and authenticity are dealt with in an even-handed manner.[43] Again, the easiest way to accomplish this at the legislative level is to enact disability-neutral statutes.

Another reason to prefer disability-neutral legislation is that it does not single out people with psychosocial disabilities as deviant. On the contrary, it conveys the message that anyone may at some point require compulsory treatment to protect his or her health and life. This is an important consideration, not least given the fact that, in many domestic contexts, stereotypical beliefs about people with psychosocial disabilities are widespread and members of this group experience marginalisation, unemployment and other forms of socioeconomic disadvantage as a result. That said, generic legislation that allows for the compulsory treatment of anyone in a situation in which there is a certain level of risk to health and life and free and informed consent cannot be obtained, will not necessarily be compliant with the CRPD. Given that such legislation will have a disparate impact on people with psychosocial disabilities, it is important also to consider factors like the quality of the care provided and the capacity of health care staff to correctly identify the cases in which intervention will have therapeutic benefits or avert suicide. Simply extending the scope of a system of substandard care to everyone will never be enough to make that system justifiable and reasonable. The therapeutic benefits of a given system must be weighty enough to compensate for the infringements of liberty, integrity and legal capacity it brings about. As I explained in chapter four, equality-specific harms enter into the balancing process along with other factors. In the weight formula, these harms are included under I_i, that is, the variable representing the degree to which the mental health system under review interferes with the right(s) at stake.[44]

$$W_{i,j} = \frac{W_i \; x \; I_i \; (incl. ESH) \; x \; R_i}{W_j \; x \; I_j \; x \; R_j}$$

[42] JTO Cavanagh et al, 'Psychological Autopsy Studies of Suicide: A Systematic Review' (2003) 33 *Psychological Medicine* 395, 401.

[43] See ch 4, section III.B.

[44] See ch 4, section IV.

Furthermore, we must bear in mind that proportionality assessments of this sort are time specific in the sense that their outcome is affected by scientific developments and changing social realities. With the development of voluntary alternatives to compulsory care that prove to be as effective as compulsory means in preventing serious deterioration of health and suicide, it will become harder to justify compulsory care.[45] The compelling evidence demonstrating the detrimental effects of compulsory mental health care shows that there is a convincing case for investing time and resources in evaluating the potential of existing voluntary alternatives to compulsory care and in continuing to develop practices that will reduce the need to use compulsion within health care and perhaps even eliminate this need altogether in the longer term. Gooding and colleagues' scoping review of current efforts to reduce, prevent and end coercion provides an overview of available alternatives and discusses their limitations and the need for further research and service development.[46]

Moreover, there have been rapid technical developments in this field. It is now possible for artificial conversational agents – 'chatbots' and 'machine counsellors' – based on natural language processing to provide online or computer-based mental health services, such as cognitive behavioural therapy, trauma therapy and suicide helpline services.[47] These services are currently being developed and tested on people seeking help and undergoing treatment on a voluntary basis, and it remains unclear whether they can cater for the health care needs of those currently subject to compulsory treatment. Artificial intelligence and machine learning hold some promise, however, with regard to suicide prediction, which is one of the most challenging tasks facing mental health clinicians working within coercive psychiatry today. People who will go on to commit suicide are often reluctant to disclose suicidal ideation preceding the act, and the risk assessment tools currently available to clinicians are not particularly effective.[48] Artificial intelligence may assist clinicians in identifying, in a more time- and resource-effective way, new risk factors, and complex combinations of factors, that both increase and decrease risks.[49] It is also possible to use 'big data' techniques involving large numbers of potential risk predictors to improve our understanding in this area. Researchers have used algorithms to scan large amounts of data, including medical records, social media activity and functional neurobiological information, in order to identify those at risk of suicide, and

[45] This follows from the necessity requirement; see ch 4, section II.C.

[46] P Gooding et al, *Alternatives to Coercion in Mental Health Settings: A Literature Review* (Melbourne, Melbourne Social Equity Institute, 2018).

[47] TM Fonseka, V Bhat and SH Kennedy, 'The Utility of Artificial Intelligence in Suicide Risk Prediction and the Management of Suicidal Behaviors' (2019) 53 *Australian & New Zealand Journal of Psychiatry* 954, 957–59; P Gooding, 'Mapping the Rise of Digital Mental Health Technologies: Emerging Issues for Law and Society' (2019) 67 *International Journal of Law and Psychiatry* 1, 5.

[48] See Ch 2, section IV.B.

[49] CG Walsh, JD Ribeiro and JC Franklin, 'Predicting Risk of Suicide Attempts over Time Through Machine Learning' (2017) 5 *Clinical Psychological Science* 457, 458.

these algorithms have been shown to outperform traditional methods of suicide risk prediction.[50] Still, the clinical value of these advances should not be overestimated. No algorithm has yet been able to distinguish effectively between people who will actually end their lives within the coming days or weeks and people who will not.[51] As a result, these technologies are still primarily used in research rather than in clinical decision-making. In addition, in so far as these artificial tools rely on data that is typically unavailable to clinicians, such as information about social media activity, their use raises questions about the protection of personal privacy that require careful consideration.[52]

III. CONCLUDING REMARKS ON THE FUTURE OF MENTAL HEALTH LAW AND POLICY

As I noted in the Introduction to this book, transforming mental health legislation to make it comply with the CRPD will be no easy task.[53] It is a project beset with both legal and political difficulties. It is clear from state practice that many governments are still committed to treating mental health care as a case apart, and the Convention's reliance on an imprecise concept of equal treatment is inconvenient for those responsible for its practical implementation. However, when it comes to implementing international norms at the domestic level, the advantages of the non-discrimination perspective should not be overlooked. Its elastic contours allow for law and policy to develop in line with societal changes. Instead of providing detailed answers to multifaceted and ethically challenging questions, it allows states parties to decide how conflicting interests should be balanced – as long as the balance does not have an unjustifiable disparate impact on people with disabilities. The treaty text does not provide definitive solutions to the perennial dilemmas that arise from the often conflicting ideals of liberty and integrity, on the one hand, and the goals of health protection and risk prevention, on the other. These are vexed ethical issues that every society will have to deal with. The demand of equal treatment laid down in the CRPD adds another dimension to that debate, challenging us to find new ways of thinking about mental health law. Since the beginning of the negotiation process in the Ad Hoc Committee, the Convention on the Rights of Persons with Disabilities has spurred a debate about the legitimacy and lawfulness of compulsory care. This debate did not end with the completion of the drafting process but continues at the national level in many states parties, in the dialogue between the CRPD Committee and the states parties, and in the academic literature. As many have

[50] Fonseka, Bhat and Kennedy, 'The Utility' 955–57.

[51] See Walsh, Ribeiro, and Franklin, 'Predicting Risk' 467.

[52] For a discussion on this matter see, eg, M Marks, 'Artificial Intelligence Based Suicide Prediction' (2019) 21 *Yale Journal of Law and Technology* 98, 116.

[53] See Introduction, section IV.

stressed, it is of the utmost importance that people with psychosocial disabilities and their representative organisations are actively involved in this debate. This follows from the Convention itself, but it is just as important for another reason.[54] After all, mental health laws are supposed to protect the health and the lives of people with psychosocial disabilities, and the effects of any changes to such laws will primarily be felt by them.

At the time of writing, the debate over the future of mental health care is being conducted within the Council of Europe in a fashion that recalls the discussions that took place before the Ad Hoc Committee in New York over a decade ago. On the one side, we have influential actors advocating a ban on compulsory mental health care; on the other side, many state representatives are arguing that such care is necessary but can be improved through stricter supervision. For many years now, the Council's Committee on Bioethics has been working to develop an additional protocol to the Convention on Human Rights and Biomedicine.[55] The precise aim of the protocol has been described in different ways, but one important goal is to strengthen the legal and procedural safeguards for people who are committed for compulsory care.[56] The case law of the Strasbourg Court provides many examples of domestic mental health policy going terribly wrong, not only failing to prevent discriminatory and abusive practices from occurring, but also leaving the victims without due process and means to obtain redress.[57] In order to clarify state obligations in this area, the protocol codifies rules and principles established in the jurisprudence of the Strasbourg Court: for instance, the rule that involuntary measures may only be used as a last resort and must be proportionate to their purposes, and the rule that patients must have access to appropriate support and procedural safeguards that enable them to effectively exercise their rights. However, the protocol, or rather the draft versions of it, have met with strong opposition from the Parliamentary Assembly of the Council of Europe, the Council's Commissioner for Human Rights, non-governmental organisations representing people with psychosocial disabilities, and the CRPD Committee. Although these critics agree that the 'overuse' of compulsion is a problem within the mental health care systems of many Member States of the Council of Europe and that human rights law has an important role to play in preventing such malpractice, they do not believe that the right response to these problems is simply to refine the scope for the legitimate use of compulsion. Drawing on the CRPD

[54] CRPD preamble para (o) and Art 33(3).

[55] Convention for the Protection of the Human Rights and Dignity of the Human Being with regard to the Application of Biology and Medicine (1997) ETS 164.

[56] Council of Europe, '"Ending Coercion in Mental Health: The Need for a Human Rights-based Approach" Parliamentary Assembly Recommendation 2158 (2019)' (reply adopted by the Committee of Ministers, 12 February 2020) para 3.

[57] See, eg, *X v Finland* App no 34806/04 (ECtHR, 3 July 2012); *Plesó v Hungary* App no 41242/08 (ECtHR, 2 October 2012); *Bureš v Czech Republic* App no 37679/08 (ECtHR, 18 October 2012).

and the CRPD Committee's interpretation of the Convention, they argue that Council of Europe Member States should not permit compulsory care at all, as it conflicts with the standards laid down in the CRPD.[58] If anything, these critics believe, the protocol should provide guidance on how Member States can avoid the use of coercive care and develop voluntary care and support services instead.

It remains to be seen how this critique will ultimately influence the protocol, if indeed there is a protocol at all. Whatever path the drafters of the protocol choose to take, reforming domestic mental health care systems to make them less dependent on the use of compulsion, or even to eliminate the use of compulsion altogether, will take time. In many countries, this will amount to a fundamental shift in psychiatric services, which cannot happen overnight. Learning how to approach ethically challenging situations within clinical practice, such as what to do when someone in need of care refuses treatment, often happens 'on the job', with clinicians learning from colleagues and other staff. Studies indicate that organisational culture has a great influence over how frequently and in what situations hospital staff resort to compulsory means.[59] Where coercive care is used too frequently, poor legislation is seldom the only problem. To reduce the use of compulsion in a particular hospital or ward, it takes a change of culture; the perceptions staff have of when compulsion is warranted and legitimate, and how it ought to be imposed, need to change. However, the question of how to bring about such a change of culture is not one that has received much attention in the literature, and more research is needed in this area in the future.

For policy-makers who wish to take the first steps towards a more equal health care system, this book has provided some concrete guidance. It has laid out a framework that can assist them in evaluating their mental health legislation and has provided recommendations on how laws can be reformed – without simply abolishing coercive care altogether – to make them better comply with the Convention. It is my hope that this book will have thus contributed to the development of more just mental health care regimes in the CRPD era.

[58] Parliamentary Assembly of the Council of Europe, 'Recommendation No Rec 2158(2019)' (26 June 2019); Council of Europe, 'Comments by Dunja Mijatović, Council of Europe Commissioner for Human Rights on the Draft Additional Protocol to the Convention on Human Rights and Biomedicine concerning the Protection of Human Rights and Dignity of Persons with Mental Disorder with regard to Involuntary Placement and Involuntary Treatment' (8 November 2018); Council of Europe Committee on Bioethics, 'Additional Protocol on the Protection of the Human Rights and Dignity of Persons with Mental Disorders with regard to Involuntary Placement and Involuntary Treatment: Compilation of Comments Received during the Public Consultation' (9 December 2015) DH-BIO/INF(2015)20 6, 18, 93 and 99.

[59] M Zinkler, 'Germany without Coercive Treatment in Psychiatry: A 15 Month Real World Experience' (2016) 5 *Laws* 15; P Gooding, B McSherry and C Roper, 'Preventing and Reducing "Coercion" in Mental Health Services: An International Scoping Review of English-language Studies' (2020) *Acta Psychiatrica Scandinavica* 1.

Appendix: Convention on the Rights of Persons with Disabilities (Extract)

ARTICLE 2 – DEFINITIONS

For the purposes of the present Convention: [...]

'Discrimination on the basis of disability' means any distinction, exclusion or restriction on the basis of disability which has the purpose or effect of impairing or nullifying the recognition, enjoyment or exercise, on an equal basis with others, of all human rights and fundamental freedoms in the political, economic, social, cultural, civil or any other field. It includes all forms of discrimination, including denial of reasonable accommodation; [...]

ARTICLE 12 – EQUAL RECOGNITION BEFORE THE LAW

1. States Parties reaffirm that persons with disabilities have the right to recognition everywhere as persons before the law.
2. States Parties shall recognize that persons with disabilities enjoy legal capacity on an equal basis with others in all aspects of life.
3. States Parties shall take appropriate measures to provide access by persons with disabilities to the support they may require in exercising their legal capacity.
4. States Parties shall ensure that all measures that relate to the exercise of legal capacity provide for appropriate and effective safeguards to prevent abuse in accordance with international human rights law. Such safeguards shall ensure that measures relating to the exercise of legal capacity respect the rights, will and preferences of the person, are free of conflict of interest and undue influence, are proportional and tailored to the person's circumstances, apply for the shortest time possible and are subject to regular review by a competent, independent and impartial authority or judicial body. The safeguards shall be proportional to the degree to which such measures affect the person's rights and interests.
5. Subject to the provisions of this article, States Parties shall take all appropriate and effective measures to ensure the equal right of persons with disabilities to own or inherit property, to control their own financial affairs and to have equal access to bank loans, mortgages and other forms of financial credit, and shall ensure that persons with disabilities are not arbitrarily deprived of their property.

ARTICLE 14 – LIBERTY AND SECURITY OF PERSON

1. States Parties shall ensure that persons with disabilities, on an equal basis with others:
   a) Enjoy the right to liberty and security of person;
   b) Are not deprived of their liberty unlawfully or arbitrarily, and that any deprivation of liberty is in conformity with the law, and that the existence of a disability shall in no case justify a deprivation of liberty.
2. States Parties shall ensure that if persons with disabilities are deprived of their liberty through any process, they are, on an equal basis with others, entitled to guarantees in accordance with international human rights law and shall be treated in compliance with the objectives and principles of the present Convention, including by provision of reasonable accommodation.

ARTICLE 17 – PROTECTING THE INTEGRITY OF THE PERSON

Every person with disabilities has a right to respect for his or her physical and mental integrity on an equal basis with others.

ARTICLE 25 – HEALTH

States Parties recognize that persons with disabilities have the right to the enjoyment of the highest attainable standard of health without discrimination on the basis of disability. States Parties shall take all appropriate measures to ensure access for persons with disabilities to health services that are gender-sensitive, including health-related rehabilitation. In particular, States Parties shall:

a) Provide persons with disabilities with the same range, quality and standard of free or affordable health care and programmes as provided to other persons, including in the area of sexual and reproductive health and population-based public health programmes;
b) Provide those health services needed by persons with disabilities specifically because of their disabilities, including early identification and intervention as appropriate, and services designed to minimize and prevent further disabilities, including among children and older persons;
c) Provide these health services as close as possible to people's own communities, including in rural areas;
d) Require health professionals to provide care of the same quality to persons with disabilities as to others, including on the basis of free and informed consent by, inter alia, raising awareness of the human rights, dignity,

autonomy and needs of persons with disabilities through training and the promulgation of ethical standards for public and private health care;

e) Prohibit discrimination against persons with disabilities in the provision of health insurance, and life insurance where such insurance is permitted by national law, which shall be provided in a fair and reasonable manner;

f) Prevent discriminatory denial of health care or health services or food and fluids on the basis of disability.

Bibliography

Alder, J, 'The Sublime and the Beautiful: Incommensurability and Human Rights' (2006) *Public Law* 697.

Aleinikoff, TA, 'Constitutional Law in the Age of Balancing' (1987) 96 *The Yale Law Journal* 943.

Alexy, R, *Theorie der Juristischen Argumentation: Die Theorie des Rationalen Diskurses als Theorie der Juristischen Begründung* (Frankfurt am Main, Suhrkamp, 1978).

—— *Theorie der Grundrechte* (Frankfurt am Main, Suhrkamp, 1986).

—— 'On the Structure of Legal Principles' (2000) 13 *Ratio Juris* 294.

—— 'On Balancing and Subsumption' (2003) 16 *Ratio Juris* 433.

—— 'Constitutional Rights, Balancing, and Rationality' (2003) 16 *Ratio Juris* 131–40.

—— 'The Weight Formula' in J Stelmach, B Brożek and W Załuski (eds), *Studies in the Philosophy of Law: Frontiers of the Economic Analysis of Law* (Cracow, Jagiellonian University Press, 2007) 9–27.

—— 'On Constitutional Rights to Protection' (2009) 3 *Legisprudence* 1.

—— 'The Reasonableness of Law' in G Bongiovanni, G Sartor and C Valentini (eds), *Reasonableness and Law* (Dordrecht, Springer Netherlands, 2009) 3–15.

—— *A Theory of Constitutional Rights* (translated by J Rivers) (New York, Oxford University Press, 2010).

—— *A Theory of Legal Argumentation* (translated by R Adler and N MacCormick) (Oxford, Oxford University Press, 2010).

—— 'Comments and Responses' in M Klatt (ed), *Institutionalized Reason: The Jurisprudence of Robert Alexy* (Oxford, Oxford University Press, 2012) 319–56.

—— 'Constitutional Rights and Proportionality' (2014) 22 *Revus* 51.

—— 'Formal Principles: Some Replies to Critics' (2014) 12 *International Journal of Constitutional Law* 511.

—— 'The Absolute and the Relative Dimensions of Constitutional Rights' (2017) 37 *Oxford Journal of Legal Studies* 31.

—— 'Proportionality and Rationality' in VC Jackson and M Tushnet (eds), *Proportionality: New Frontiers, New Challenges* (Cambridge, Cambridge University Press, 2017).

American Psychiatric Association, *Diagnostic and Statistical Manual of Mental Disorders: DSM-5*, 5th edn (Arlington, American Psychiatric Association, 2013).

Andrews, DA and Bonta, J, *The Psychology of Criminal Conduct*, 5th edn (New Providence, Matthew Bender & Company, 2010).

Aristotle, *The Nicomachean Ethics* (D Ross trans, Oxford, Oxford University Press, 1980).

Arstein-Kerslake, A and Flynn, E, 'The General Comment on Article 12 of the Convention on the Rights of Persons with Disabilities: A Roadmap for Equality before the Law' (2016) 20 *The International Journal of Human Rights* 471.

Attrey, S, *Intersectional Discrimination* (Oxford, Oxford University Press, 2019).

Babalola, O, Gormez, V, Alwan, NA, Johnstone, P and Sampson, S, 'Length of Hospitalisation for People with Severe Mental Illness' (2014) 1 *Cochrane Database of Systematic Reviews*.

Bach, M and Kerzner, L, *A New Paradigm for Protecting Autonomy and the Right to Legal Capacity* (Law Commission of Ontario, 2010).

Bagenstos, S, '"Rational Discrimination", Accommodation, and the Politics of (Disability) Civil Rights' (2003) 89 *Virginia Law Review* 825.

Barak, A, *Proportionality: Constitutional Rights and Their Limitations* (translated by D Kalir) (Cambridge, Cambridge University Press, 2012).

Bartlett, P, 'A Mental Disorder of a Kind or Degree Warranting Confinement: Examining Justifications for Psychiatric Detention' (2012) 16 *The International Journal of Human Rights* 831.

Bayefsky, Am, 'The Principle of Equality or Non-Discrimination in International Law' (1990) 11 *Human Rights Law Journal* 1.

Bird, V, Miglietta, E, Giacco, D and Bauer, M, 'Factors Associated with Satisfaction of Inpatient Psychiatric Care: A Cross Country Comparison' (2020) 50 *Psychological Medicine* 284.

Bonta, J, Law, M and Hanson, K, 'The Prediction of Criminal and Violent Recidivism among Mentally Disordered Offenders: A Meta-Analysis' (1998) 123 *Psychological Bulletin* 123.

Boyle, S, 'How Should the Law Determine Capacity to Refuse Treatment for Anorexia?' (2019) 64 *International Journal of Law and Psychiatry* 250.

Broderick, A, *The Long and Winding Road to Equality and Inclusion for Persons with Disabilities: The United Nations Convention on the Rights of Persons with Disabilities* (Cambridge, Intersentia, 2015).

Bruce, A, *Which Entitlements and for Whom? The Convention on the Rights of Persons with Disabilities and Its Ideological Antecedents* (Lund, Mediatryck, 2014).

Buchanan, A and Brock, D, *Deciding for Others: The Ethics of Surrogate Decision-making* (Cambridge, Cambridge University Press, 1990).

Buchanan, A and Leese, M, 'Detention of People with Dangerous Severe Personality Disorders: A Systematic Review' (2001) 358 *The Lancet* 1955.

—— 'Quantifying the Contributions of Three Types of Information to the Prediction of Criminal Conviction Using the Receiver Operating Characteristic' (2006) 188 *British Journal of Psychiatry* 472.

Burns, T, 'Mental Illness Is Different and Ignoring Its Differences Profits Nobody' (2010) 20 *Journal of Mental Health Law* 34.

Calton, T, Ferriter, M, Huband, N and Spandler, H, 'A Systematic Review of the Soteria Paradigm for the Treatment of People Diagnosed with Schizophrenia' (2008) 34 *Schizophrenia Bulletin* 181.

Cavanagh, JTO, Carson, AJ, Sharpe, N and Lawrie, SM, 'Psychological Autopsy Studies of Suicide: A Systematic Review' (2003) 33 *Psychological Medicine* 395.

Chang, Z, Lichtenstein, P and Långström, N, 'Association between Prescription of Major Psychotropic Medications and Violent Reoffending After Prison Release' (2016) 316 *Journal of the American Medical Association* 1798.

Choudhury, T, 'Interpreting the Right to Equality under Article 26 of the International Covenant on Civil and Political Rights' (2003) 1 *European Human Rights Law Review* 24.

Chow, W and Priebe, S, 'Understanding Psychiatric Institutionalization: A Conceptual Review' (2013) 13 *BMC Psychiatry* 169.

Clifford, J, 'Equality' in D Shelton (ed), *The Oxford Handbook of International Human Rights Law* (Oxford, Oxford University Press, 2013).

Coid, J, Ullrich, S, Callis, K, Kerrs, R, Barker, D, Cowden, F and Stamps, R, 'The Relationship between Delusions and Violence: Findings from the East London First Episode Psychosis Study' (2013) 70 *Journal of the American Medical Association Psychiatry* 465.

Corsi, JL, 'Article 5 Equality and Non-Discrimination' in I Bantekas, MA Stein, and D Anastasiou (eds), *The UN Convention on the Rights of Persons with Disabilities: A Commentary* (Oxford, Oxford University Press, 2018) 140–71.

Craigie, J, and Bortolotti, L, 'Rationality, Diagnosis, and Patient Autonomy in Psychiatry' in JZ Sadler, KWM Fulford, and C Werendly van Staden (eds), *The Oxford Handbook of Psychiatric Ethics* (Oxford, Oxford University Press, 2015).

Dawson, J, 'A Realistic Approach to Assessing Mental Health Laws' Compliance with the UNCRPD' (2015) 40 *International Journal of Law and Psychiatry* 70.

Degener, T, 'Disability in a Human Rights Context' (2016) 5 *Laws* 35.

Dhanda, A, 'Legal Capacity in the Disability Rights Convention: Stranglehold of the Past or Lodestar for the Future?' (2007) 34 *Syracuse Journal of International Law and Commerce* 429.

Diseth, R and Høglend, P, 'Compulsory Mental Health Care in Norway: The Treatment Criterion' (2014) 37 *International Journal of Law and Psychiatry* 168.

Donnelly, M, *Healthcare Decision-making and the Law: Autonomy, Capacity, and the Limits of Liberalism* (Cambridge, Cambridge University Press, 2010).

Douglas, K, Guy, L and Hart, S, 'Psychosis as a Risk Factor for Violence to Others: A Meta-Analysis' (2009) 137 *Psychological Bulletin* 679.

Drew, N, Funk, M, Tang, S, Lamichhane, J, Chávez, E, Katontoka, S, Pathare, S, Lewis, O, Gostin, L and Saraceno, B, 'Human Rights Violations of People with Mental and Psychosocial Disabilities: An Unresolved Global Crisis' (2011) 378 *The Lancet* 1664.

Dute, J, 'Should Substituted Decision-making Be Abolished?' (2015) 22 *European Journal of Health Law* 315.

Dworkin, R, *Taking Rights Seriously* (Cambridge, Massachusetts, Harvard University Press, 1977).

Eidelson, B, *Discrimination and Disrespect* (Oxford, Oxford University Press, 2015).

Elbogen, E and Johansson, S, 'The Intricate Link between Violence and Mental Disorder: Results from the National Epidemiologic Survey on Alcohol and Related Conditions' (2009) 66 *Archives of General Psychiatry* 152.

Endicott, T, 'Proportionality and Incommensurability' in G Huscroft, BW Miller and G Webber (eds), *Proportionality and the Rule of Law: Rights, Justification, Reasoning* (Cambridge, Cambridge University Press, 2014) 311–42.

European Union Agency for Fundamental Rights, *Involuntary Placement and Involuntary Treatment of Persons with Mental Health Problems* (Luxembourg, Publications Office of the European Union, 2012).

Fazel, S and Grann, M, 'The Population Impact of Severe Mental Illness on Violent Crime' (2006) 163 *American Journal of Psychiatry* 1397.

Fazel, S, Singh, JP, Doll, H and Grann, M, 'Use of Risk Assessment Instruments to Predict Violence and Antisocial Behaviour in 73 Samples Involving 24 827 People: Systematic Review and Meta-Analysis' (2012) 345:e4692 *British Medical Journal*.

Fazel, S, Zetterqvist, J, Larsson, H, Långström, N and Lichtenstein, P, 'Antipsychotics, Mood Stabilisers, and Risk of Violent Crime' (2014) 384 *The Lancet* 1206.

Feltz-Cornelis, CM van der, Sarchiapone, M, Postuvan, V, Volker, D, Roskar, S, Tančič Grum, A, Carli, V, McDaid, D, O'Connor, R, Maxwell, M, Ibelshäuser, A, Van Audenhove, C, Scheerder, G, Sisask, M, Gusmão, R and Hegerl, U, 'Best Practice Elements of Multilevel Suicide Prevention Strategies: A Review of Systematic Reviews' (2011) 26 *Crisis* 327.

Fennell, P, 'Art.15 Protection against Torture and Cruel or Inhuman or Degrading Treatment or Punishment' in I Bantekas, MA Stein and D Anastasiou (eds), *The UN Convention on the Rights of Persons with Disabilities: A Commentary* (Oxford, Oxford University Press, 2018).

Fennell, P and Khaliq, U, 'Conflicting or Complementary Obligations? The UN Disability Rights Convention, the European Convention on Human Rights, and English Law' (2011) 6 *European Human Rights Law Review* 662.

Fistein, EC, Holland, AJ, Claire, ICH and Gunn, MJ, 'A Comparison of Mental Health Legislation from Diverse Commonwealth Jurisdictions' (2009) 32 *International Journal of Law and Psychiatry* 147.

Flammer, E and Steinert, T, 'Association between Restriction of Involuntary Medication and Frequency of Coercive Measures and Violent Incidents' (2016) 67 *Psychiatric Services* 1315.

Flynn, E, 'Mental (In)Capacity or Legal Capacity? A Human Rights Analysis of the Proposed Fusion of Mental Health and Mental Capacity Law in Northern Ireland' (2013) 64 *Northern Ireland Legal Quarterly* 485.

—— 'Disability, Deprivation of Liberty, and Human Rights Norms: Reconciling European and International Approaches' (2016) 22 *International Journal of Mental Health and Capacity Law* 75.

—— 'State Intervention in the Lives of People with Disabilities: The Case for a Disability-neutral Framework' (2017) 13 *International Journal of Law in Context* 39.

Flynn, E and Arstein-Kerslake, A, 'Legislating Personhood: Realising the Right to Support in Exercising Legal Capacity' (2014) 10 *International Journal of Law in Context* 81.

Fonseka, T, Bhat, V and Kennedy, SH, 'The Utility of Artificial Intelligence in Suicide Risk Prediction and the Management of Suicidal Behaviors' (2019) 53 *Australian & New Zealand Journal of Psychiatry* 954.

Frances, A and Halon, R, 'The Uses and Misuses of the DSM in Forensic Settings' (2013) 6 *Psychological Injury and Law* 336.

Fredman, S, 'Emerging from the Shadows: Substantive Equality and Article 14 of the European Convention on Human Rights' (2016) 16 *Human Rights Law Review* 282.

—— 'Substantive Equality Revisited' (2016) 14 *International Journal of Constitutional Law* 712.

Freeman, MC, Kolappa, K, Almeida, MC de, Kleinman, A, Makhashvili, N, Pakathi, S, Saraceno, B and Thornicroft, G, 'Reversing Hard Won Victories in the Name of Human Rights: A Critique of the General Comment on Article 12 of the UN Convention on the Rights of Persons with Disabilities' (2015) 2 *Lancet Psychiatry* 844.

Frenkel, M, 'Refusing Treatment' (2013) 18 *The Oncologist* 634.

Georges, J-J, Onwuteaka-Philipsen, BD, Heide, A van der, Wal, G van der and Maas, PJ van der, 'Requests to Forgo Potentially Life-Prolonging Treatment and to Hasten Death in Terminally Ill Cancer Patients: A Prospective Study' (2006) 31 *Journal of Pain and Symptom Management* 100.

Gooding, P, 'Supported Decision-Making: A Rights-Based Disability Concept and Its Implications for Mental Health Law' (2013) 20 *Psychiatry, Psychology and Law* 431.

—— *A New Era for Mental Health Law and Policy: Supported Decision-making and the UN Convention on the Rights of Persons with Disabilities* (Cambridge, Cambridge University Press, 2017).

—— 'Mapping the Rise of Digital Mental Health Technologies: Emerging Issues for Law and Society' (2019) 67 *International Journal of Law and Psychiatry* 1.

Gooding, P and Flynn, E, 'Querying the Call to Introduce Mental Capacity Testing to Mental Health Law: Does the Doctrine of Necessity Provide an Alternative?' (2015) 4 *Laws* 245.

Gooding, P, McSherry, B and Roper, C, 'Preventing and Reducing "Coercion" in Mental Health Services: An International Scoping Review of English-language Studies' (2020) *Acta Psychiatrica Scandinavica* 1.

Gooding, P, McSherry, B, Roper, C and Grey, F, *Alternatives to Coercion in Mental Health Settings: A Literature Review* (Melbourne, Melbourne Social Equity Institute, 2018).

Gosney P and Bartlett, P, 'The UK Government Should Withdraw from the Convention on the Rights of Persons with Disabilities' (2019) 14 *The British Journal of Psychiatry* 1.

Grisso, T and Appelbaum, PS, 'The MacArthur Treatment Competence Study III: Abilities of Patients to Consent to Psychiatric and Medical Treatments' (1995) 19 *Law and Human Behavior* 149.

Harris, EC and Barraclough, B, 'Suicide as an Outcome for Mental Disorders: A Meta-Analysis' (1997) 170 *British Journal of Psychiatry* 205.

Hawton, K, Witt, K, Salisbury, TT, Arensman, E, Gunnell, D, Hazell, P, Townsend, E and Heeringen, K van, 'Psychosocial Interventions for Self-harm in Adults (Review)' (2016) 5 *Cochrane Database of Systematic Review*.

Hellman, D, *When is Discrimination Wrong?* (Cambridge, Massachusetts, Harvard University Press, 2008).

Hennekens, C and Buring, J, *Epidemiology in Medicine* (Philadelphia, Lippincot Williams and Wilkins, 1987).

Hindmarch, T, Hotopf, M and Owen, G, 'Depression and Decision-making Capacity for Treatment or Research: A Systematic Review' (2013) 14 *BMC Medical Ethics* 54.

Israelson, M and Gerdner, A, 'Compulsory Commitment to Care of Substance Misusers: A Worldwide Comparative Analysis of the Legislation' (2010) 3 *The Open Addiction Journal* 117.

Jaworska, A, 'Respecting the Margins of Agency: Alzheimer's Patients and the Capacity to Value' (1999) 28 *Philosophy and Public Affairs* 105.

Jespersson, M, 'Personal Ombudsman in Skåne: A User-controlled Service with Personal Agents' in P Stastny and P Lehmann (eds), *Alternatives Beyond Psychiatry* (Berlin, Peter Lehmann Publishing, 2007) 299–303.

Jestaedt, M, 'The Doctrine of Balancing: Its Strengths and Weaknesses' in M Klatt (ed), *Institutionalized Reason: The Jurisprudence of Robert Alexy* (Oxford, Oxford University Press, 2012) 152–73.

Jong, G de, Schout, G and Abama, T, 'Prevention of Involuntary Admission through Family Group Conferencing: A Qualitative Case Study in Community Mental Health Nursing' (2014) 70 *Journal of Advanced Nursing* 2651.

Kaltiala-Heino, R, Laippala, P and Salokangas, R, 'Impact of Coercion on Treatment Outcome' (1997) 20 *International Journal of Law and Psychiatry* 311.

Katsakou, C and Priebe, S, 'Outcomes of Involuntary Hospital Admission: A Review' (2006) 114 *Acta Psychiatrica Scandinavica* 232.

—— 'Patients' Experiences of Involuntary Hospital Admission and Treatment: A Review of Qualitative Studies' (2007) 16 *Epidemiologia e Psichiatria Sociale* 172.

Keers, R, Ullrich, S, Destavola, B and Coid, J, 'Association of Violence with Emergence of Persecutory Delusions in Untreated Schizophrenia' (2014) 171 *American Journal of Psychiatry* 332.

Kelly, B, Burnett, P, Pelusi, D, Badger, S, Varghese, F and Robertson, M, 'Terminally Ill Cancer Patients' Wish to Hasten Death' (2002) 16 *Palliative Medicine* 339.

Khaitan, T, *A Theory of Discrimination Law* (Oxford, Oxford University Press, 2015).

Kirov, G, Owen, L, Ballard, H, Leighton, A, Hannigan, K, Llewellyn, D, Escott-Price, V and Atkins, M, 'Evaluation of Cumulative Cognitive Deficits from Electroconvulsive Therapy' (2016) 208 *The British Journal of Psychiatry* 266.

Kisely, S and Campbell, L, 'Compulsory Community and Involuntary Outpatient Treatment for People with Severe Mental Disorders (Review)' (2014) 12 *Cochrane Database of Systematic Reviews*.

Klatt, M and Meister, M, *The Constitutional Structure of Proportionality* (Oxford, Oxford University Press, 2012).

Klatt, M and Schmidt, J, 'Epistemic Discretion in Constitutional Law' (2012) 10 *International Journal of Constitutional Law* 69.

Kuosmanen, L, Hätönen, H, Malkavaara, H, Kylmä, J and Välimäki, M, 'Deprivation of Liberty in Psychiatric Hospital Care: The Patient's Perspective' (2007) 14 *Nursing Ethics* 597.

Large, M, Ryan, C, Walsh, G, Stein-Parbury, J and Patfield, M, 'Nosocomial Suicides' (2014) *Australasian Psychiatry* 22, 118–21.

Large, M, Ryan, C, Singh, S, Paton, M and Nielssen, O, 'The Predictive Value of Risk Categorization in Schizophrenia' (2011) 19 *Harvard Review of Psychiatry* 25.

Large, M, Smith, G, Sharma, S, Nielssen, O and Singh, SP, 'Systematic Review and Meta-analysis of the Clinical Factors Associated with the Suicide of Psychiatric In-patients' (2011) 124 *Acta Psychiatrica Scandinavica* 18.

Lawson, A, 'The United Nations Convention on the Rights of Persons with Disabilities: New Era or False Dawn?' (2007) 34 *Syracuse Journal of International Law and Commerce* 563.

Legg, A, *The Margin of Appreciation in International Human Rights Law: Deference and Proportionality* (Oxford, Oxford University Press, 2012).

Leiknes, K, Berg, R, Smedslund, G, Jarosch-von Schweder, L, Øverland, S, Hammerstrøm, K and Høie, B, 'Electroconvulsive Therapy for Depression (Protocol)' (2011) 5 *Cochrane Database of Systematic Reviews*.

Lestas, G, *A Theory of Interpretation of the European Convention on Human Rights* (Oxford, Oxford University Press, 2007).

Lewis, O, 'Legal Capacity in International Human Rights Law' (PhD thesis, Leiden University, 2015).

Lindahl, L, 'On Robert Alexy's Weight Formula for Weighing and Balancing' in AS Dias, JA Raposo, JL Alves, LD d'Almeida, and P de Sousa Mendes (eds), *Liber Amicorum de José de Sousa e Brito em Comemoração do 70.° Aniversário: Estudos de Direito e Filosofia* (Coimbra, Almedina, 2009) 355–75.

Macpherson, R, Edwards, T, Chilvers, R, David, C and Elliott, H, 'Twenty-four Hour Care for Schizophrenia (Review)' (2009) 2 *Cochrane Database of Systematic Reviews*.

Madsen, T, Erlangsen, A and Nordentoft, M, 'Risk Estimates and Risk Factors Related to Psychiatric Inpatient Suicide: An Overview' (2017) 14 *International Journal of Environmental Research and Public Health* 253.

Mann, JJ, Apter, A, Bertolote, J, Beautrais, A, Currier, D, Haas, A, Hegerl, U, Lonnqvist, J, Malone, K, Marusic, A, Mehlum, L, Patton, G, Phillips, M, Rutz, W, Rihmer, Z, Schmidtke, A, Shaffer, D, Silverman, M, Takahashi, Y and Varnik, A, 'Suicide Prevention Strategies: A Systematic Review' (2005) 294 *Journal of the American Medical Association* 2064.

Manoranjitham, SD, Rajkumar, AP, Thangadurai, P, Prasad, J, Jayakaran, R and Jacob, KS, 'Risk Factors for Suicide in Rural South India' (2009) 196 *British Journal of Psychiatry* 26.

Marks, M, 'Artificial Intelligence Based Suicide Prediction' (2019) 21 *Yale Journal of Law and Technology* 98.

McGoldrick, D, 'A Defence of the Margin of Appreciation and an Argument for its Application by the Human Rights Committee' (2016) 65 *International and Comparative Law Quarterly* 21.

McSherry, B, 'Protecting the Integrity of the Person: Developing Limitations on Involuntary Treatment' in B McSherry (ed), *International Trends in Mental Health Laws* (Leichhardt, The Federation Press, 2008) 111–15.

Meynen, G and Swaab, D, 'Why Medication in Involuntary Treatment May Be Less Effective: The Placebo/Nocebo Effect' (2011) 77 *Medical Hypotheses* 993–95.

Millner, A, Sveticic, J and De Leo, D, 'Suicide in the Absence of Mental Disorder? A Review of Psychological Autopsy Studies Across Countries' (2013) 59 *International Journal of Social Psychiatry* 545.

Minkowitz, T, 'The United Nations Convention on the Rights of Persons with Disabilities and the Right to Be Free from Nonconsensual Psychiatric Interventions' (2007) 34 *Syracuse Journal of International Law and Commerce* 405.

—— 'Abolishing Mental Health Laws to Comply with the CRPD' in B McSherry and P Weller (eds), *Rethinking Rights-based Mental Health Laws* (Oxford, Hart Publishing, 2010) 151–77.

Mishara, BL and Weisstubb, DN, 'The Legal Status of Suicide: A Global Review' (2016) 44 *International Journal of Law and Psychiatry* 54.

Mjöll Arnardóttir, O, 'A Future of Multidimensional Disadvantage Equality?' in O Mjöll Arnardóttir and G Quinn (eds), *The UN Convention on the Rights of Persons with Disabilities: European and Scandinavian Perspectives* (Leiden, Martinus Nijhoff, 2009) 41–66.

Möller, K, 'Balancing and the Structure of Constitutional Rights' (2007) 5 *International Journal of Constitutional Law* 453.

—— *The Global Model of Constitutional Rights* (Oxford, Oxford University Press, 2012).

Moreau, S, 'What is Discrimination' (2010) 38 *Philosophy and Public Affairs* 143.

Murphy, S, Irving, C, Adams, C and Waqar, M, 'Crisis Intervention for People with Severe Mental Illnesses (Review)' (2015) 12 *Cochrane Database of Systematic Reviews*.

Newton-Howes, G and Mullen, R, 'Coercion in Psychiatry Care: Systematic Review of Correlates and Themes' (2011) 62 *Psychiatric Services* 465.

Nilsson, A, 'Objective and Reasonable? Scrutinising Compulsory Mental Health Interventions from a Non-discrimination Perspective' (2014) 14 *Human Rights Law Review* 459.

Nilsson, T, Wallinius, M, Gustavson, C, Anckarsäter, H and Kerekes, N, 'Violent Recidivism: A Long-Time Follow-Up Study of Mentally Disordered Offenders' (2011) 6:e25768 *PLoS One*.

Nyttingnes, O, Ruud, T and Rugkåsa, J, '"It's Unbelievably Humiliating' – Patients' Expressions of Negative Effects of Coercion in Mental Health Care' (2016) 49 *International Journal of Law and Psychiatry* 147.

Okai, D, Owen, G, McGuire, H, Singh, S, Churchill, R and Hotopf, M, 'Mental Capacity in Psychiatric Patients: Systematic Review' (2007) 191 *British Journal of Psychiatry* 291.

Owen, GS, Szmukler, G, Richardson, G, David, AS, Raymont, V, Freyenhagen, F, Martin, W and Hotopf, M, 'Decision-making Capacity for Treatment in Psychiatric and Medical In-Patients: Cross-Sectional, Comparative Study' (2013) 203 *The British Journal of Psychiatry* 461.

Pavlovic, R, Pavlovic, A and Donaldson, S, 'Open Dialogue for Psychosis or Severe Mental Illness (Protocol)' (2016) 10 *Cochrane Database of Systematic Reviews*.

Perlin, M and Szeli, E, 'Art.14 Liberty and Security of the Person' in I Bantekas, MA Stein, and D Anastasiou (eds), *The UN Convention on the Rights of Persons with Disabilities: A Commentary* (Oxford, Oxford University Press, 2018) 402–25.

Peroni, L and Timmer, A, 'Vulnerable Groups: The Promise of an Emerging Concept in European Human Rights Convention Law' (2013) 11 *International Journal of Constitutional Law* 1056.

Peterson, J, Skeem, JL, Hart, E, Keith, F and Vidal, S, 'Analyzing Offense Patterns as a Function of Mental Illness to Test the Criminalization Hypothesis' (2010) 61 *Psychiatric Services* 1217.

Phelan, J and Link, B, 'The Growing Belief That People with Mental Illnesses Are Violent: The Role of the Dangerousness Criterion for Civil Commitment' (1998) 33 *Social Psychiatry and Psychiatric Epidemiology* 7.

Phillips, M, Yang, G, Zhang, Y, Wang, L, Ji, H and Zhou, M, 'Risk Factors for Suicide in China: A National Case-control Psychological Autopsy Study' (2002) 360 *The Lancet* 1728.

Pokorny, AD, 'Prediction of Suicide in Psychiatric Patients: Report of a Prospective Study' (1983) 40 *Archives of General Psychiatry* 249.

Poscher, R, 'The Principles Theory: How Many Theories and What Is Their Merit?' in M Klatt (ed), *Institutionalized Reason: The Jurisprudence of Robert Alexy* (Oxford, Oxford University Press, 2012) 218–47.

Powell, J, Geddes, J, Deeks, J, Goldacre, M and Hawton, K, 'Suicide in Psychiatric Hospital In-patients: Risk Factors and their Predictive Power' (2000) 176 *British Journal of Psychiatry* 266.

Priebe, S, Katsakou, C, Glöckner, M, Dembinskas, A, Fiorillo, A, Karastergiou, A, Kiejna, A, Kjellin, L, Nawka, P, Onchev, G, Raboch, J, Schuetzwohl, M, Solomon, Z, Torres-González, F, Wang, D and Kallert, T, 'Patients' Views of Involuntary Hospital Admission after 1 and 3 Months: Prospective Study in 11 European Countries' (2010) 196 *The British Journal of Psychiatry* 179.

Priebe, S, Katsakou, C, Yeeles, K, Amos, T, Morriss, R, Wang, D and Wykes, T, 'Predictors of Clinical and Social Outcomes Following Involuntary Hospital Admission: A Prospective Observational Study' (2011) 261 *European Archives of Psychiatry and Clinical Neuroscience* 377.

Quinn, G and Arstein-Kerslake, A, 'Restoring the "Human" in "Human Rights": Personhood and Doctrinal Innovation in the UN Disability Convention' in C Gearty and C Douzinas (eds), *The Cambridge Companion to Human Rights Law* (Cambridge, Cambridge University Press, 2012) 36–55.

Rachlinsk, JJ, 'Evidence-based Law' (2011) 96 *Cornell Law Review* 901.

Radbruch, L, Leget, C, Bahr, P, Müller-Busch, C, Ellershaw, J, Conno, F de and Vanden Berghe, P, 'Euthanasia and Physician-assisted Suicide: A White Paper from the European Association for Palliative Care' (2016) 30 *Palliative Medicine* 104.

Radhakrishnan, R and Andrade, C, 'Suicide: An Indian Perspective' (2012) 54 *Indian Journal of Psychiatry* 304.

Raevley, N, Jorm, A and Morgan, A, 'Beliefs about Dangerousness of People with Mental Health Problems: The Role of Media Reports and Personal Exposure to Threat or Harm' (2016) 51 *Social Psychiatry Psychiatric Epidemiology* 1275.

Raymont, V, Bingley, W, Buchanan, A, David, AS, Hayward, P, Wessely, S and Hotopf, M, 'Prevalence of Mental Incapacity in Medical Inpatients and Associated Risk Factors: Cross-Sectional Study' (2004) 364 *The Lancet* 1421.

Réaume, D, 'Dignity and Discrimination' (2002–2003) 63 *Louisiana Law Review* 1.

Rosen, M, *Dignity: Its History and Meaning* (Cambridge, Massachusetts, Harvard University Press, 2012).

Russien, AM, Widdershoven, GAM, Meynen, G, Abma, TA, and Balkom, AJLM van, 'A Systematic Review of the Literature about Competence and Poor Insight' (2012) 125 *Acta Psychiatrica Scandinavica* 103.

Schauer, F, 'Balancing, Subsumption and the Constraining Role of Legal Text' in M Klatt (ed), *Institutionalized Reason: The Jurisprudence of Robert Alexy* (Oxford, Oxford University Press, 2012) 307–16.

Schomerus, G, Schwahn, A, Holzinger, A, Corrigan, P, Grabe, HJ, Carta, M and Angermeyer, M, 'Evolution of Public Attitudes about Mental Illness: A Systematic Review and Meta-analysis' (2012) 125 *Acta Psychiatrica Scandinavica* 440.

Schutter, O De and Ringelheim, J, 'Ethnic Profiling: A Rising Challenge for European Human Rights Law' (2008) 71 *The Modern Law Review* 358.

Seatzu, F, 'Art.17 Protecting the Integrity of the Person' in I Bantekas, MA Stein, and D Anastasiou (eds), *The UN Convention on the Rights of Persons with Disabilities: A Commentary* (Oxford, Oxford University Press, 2018).

Seed, T, Fox, J and Berry, K, 'The Experience of Involuntary Detention in Acute Psychiatric Care: A Review and Synthesis of Qualitative Studies' (2016) 61 *International Journal of Nursing Studies* 82.

Seikkula, J, Aaltonen, J, Alakare, B, Haarakangas, K, Keranen, J and Lehtinen, K, 'Five-year Experience of First-episode Nonaffective Psychosis in Open-dialogue Approach: Treatment Principles, Follow-up Outcomes, and Two Case Studies' (2006) 16 *Psychotherapy Research* 214.

Seikkula, J and Olson, M, 'The Open Dialogue Approach to Acute Psychosis: Its Poetics and Micropolitics' (2003) 42 *Family Process* 403.

Sen, A, 'Equality of What?' in S McMurrin (ed), *The Tanner Lectures on Human Values* (Cambridge, Cambridge University Press, 1980) Vol 1.

—— *The Idea of Justice* (Cambridge, Massachusetts, Harvard University Press, 2009).

Series, L, 'Article 12 CRPD Equal Recognition Before the Law' in I Bantekas, MA Stein and D Anastasiou (eds), *The UN Convention on the Rights of Persons with Disabilities: A Commentary* (Oxford, Oxford University Press, 2018).

Sessums, LL, Zembrzuska, H and Jackson, JL, 'Does This Patient Have Medical Decision-making Capacity? (2011) 306 *Journal of the American Medical Association* 420.

Shin, P, 'Is There a Unitary Concept of Discrimination?' in D Hellman and S Moreau (eds), *Philosophical Foundations of Discrimination Law* (Oxford, Oxford University Press, 2013) 163–81.

Sifris, R, 'An International Human Rights Perspective on Detention without Charge or Trial: Article 9 of the International Covenant on Civil and Political Rights' in B McSherry and P Keyzer (eds), *Dangerous People: Policy, Prediction, and Practice* (New York, Routledge, 2011) 13–23.

Silva, VA da, 'Comparing the Incommensurable: Constitutional Principles, Balancing and Rational Decision' (2011) 31 *Oxford Journal of Legal Studies* 273.

Silver, E, 'Understanding the Relationship Between Mental Disorder and Violence: The Need for a Criminological Perspective' (2006) 30 *Law and Human Behaviour* 685.

Sjöstrand, M, Sandman, L, Karlsson, P, Helgesson, G, Eriksson, S and Juth, N, 'Ethical Deliberations about Involuntary Treatment: Interviews with Swedish Psychiatrists' (2015) 16 *BMC Medical Ethics*.

Skeem, JL, Manchak, S and Peterson, JK, 'Correctional Policy for Offenders with Mental Illness: Creating a New Paradigm for Recidivism Reduction' (2011) 35 *Law and Human Behaviour* 110.

Skeem, JL, Winter, E, Kennealy, PJ, Louden, JE and Tatar, JR II, 'Offenders with Mental Illness Have Criminogenic Needs, Too: Toward Recidivism Reduction' (2014) 38 *Law and Human Behaviour* 212.

Skodlar, B, Tomori, M and Parnas, J, 'Subjective Experience and Suicidal Ideation in Schizophrenia' (2008) 49 *Comprehensive Psychiatry* 482.

Solanke, I, *Discrimination as Stigma: A Theory of Anti-discrimination Law* (London, Hart Publishing, 2016).

Steinert, T, Noorthoorn, EO and Mulder, CL, 'The Use of Coercive Interventions in Mental Health Care in Germany and the Netherlands: A Comparison of the Developments in Two Neighboring Countries' (2014) 2 *Frontiers in Public Health* 141.

Stone Sweet, A and Mathews, J, 'Proportionality Balancing and Global Constitutionalism' (2008) 47 *Columbia Journal of Transnational Law* 72.

Szmukler, G and Dawson, J, 'Reducing Discrimination in Mental Health Law: The "Fusion" of Incapacity and Mental Health Legislation' in T Kallert, J Mezzich, and J Monahan (eds), *Coercive Treatment in Psychiatry* (Chichester, Wiley-Blackwell, 2011) 97–119.

Szmukler, G and Rose, N, 'Risk Assessment in Mental Health Care: Values and Costs' (2013) 31 *Behavioral Sciences and the Law* 125.

Theodoridou, A, Schlatter, F, Ajdacic, V, Rössler, W and Jäger, M, 'Therapeutic Relationship in the Context of Perceived Coercion in a Psychiatric Population' (2012) 200 *Psychiatry Research* 939.

Tsakyrakis, S, 'Proportionality: An Assault on Human Rights?' (2009) 7 *International Journal of Constitutional Law* 468.

Tversky, A and Kahneman, D, 'Judgment Under Uncertainty: Heuristics and Biases' (1974) 185 *Science* 1124.

Vijayakumar, L and Rajkumar, S, 'Are Risk Factors for Suicide Universal? A Case-control Study in India' (1999) 99 *Acta Psychiatrica Scandinavica* 407.

Viljoen, JL, Cochrane, DM and Johnson, MR, 'Do Risk Assessment Tools Help Manage and Reduce Risk of Violence and Reoffending? A Systematic Review' (2018) 42 *Law and Human Behaviour* 181.

Waddington, L and McSherry, B, 'Exceptions and Exclusions: The Right to Informed Consent for Medical Treatment of People with Psychosocial Disabilities in Europe' (2016) 23 *European Journal of Health Law* 279.

Waldron, J, 'Is Dignity the Foundation of Human Rights?' in R Cruft, SM Liao, and M Renzo (eds), *Philosophical Foundations of Human Rights* (Oxford, Oxford University Press, 2015) 117–37.

Walsh, CG, Ribeiro, JD and Franklin, JC, 'Predicting Risk of Suicide Attempts over Time Through Machine Learning' (2017) 5 *Clinical Psychological Science* 457.

Walsh, G, Sara, G, Ryan, CJ and Large, M, 'Meta-analysis of Suicide Rates among Psychiatric In-patients' (2015) 131 *Acta Psychiatrica Scandinavia* 174.

Webber, GCN, *The Negotiable Constitution: On the Limitation of Constitutional Rights* (Cambridge, Cambridge University Press, 2009).

—— 'Proportionality, Balancing, and the Cult of Constitutional Rights Scholarship' (2010) 23 *Canadian Journal of Law and Jurisprudence* 179.

Weller, P, *New Law and Ethics in Mental Health Advance Directives: The Convention on the Rights of Persons with Disabilities and the Right to Choose* (Hove, Routledge, 2015).

Westen, P, 'The Empty Idea of Equality' (1982) 95 *Harvard Law Review* 537.

Wicks, E, *The Right to Life and Conflicting Interests* (Oxford, Oxford University Press, 2010).

World Health Organisation (WHO), *The ICD-10 Classification of Mental and Behavioral Disorders: Clinical Descriptions and Diagnostic Guidelines* (Geneva, WHO, 1992).

—— *Towards a Common Language for Functioning, Disability and Health* (Geneva, WHO, 2002).

—— *Preventing Suicide: A Global Imperative* (Luxembourg, WHO, 2014).

—— 'Suicide in the World: Global Health Estimates' (WHO, 2019).

WHO and World Bank, *World Report on Disability* (Malta, WHO, 2011).

Zinkler, M, 'Germany without Coercive Treatment in Psychiatry: A 15 Month Real World Experience' (2016) 5 *Laws* 15.

Zinkler, M and Peter, S von, 'End Coercion in Mental Health Services: Toward a System Based on Support Only' (2019) 8 *Laws* 19.

Index

www.ingramcontent.com/pod-product-compliance
Ingram Content Group UK Ltd.
Pitfield, Milton Keynes, MK11 3LW, UK
UKHW020818290926
15470UKWH00003B/1235

9 781509 931576